Pra
Conspirac

"*Abuza has long been one of America's leading experts on terrorism and insurgency in Southeast Asia. Conspiracy of Silence is easily the most informative book on the nature of the conflict in southern Thailand and the weakness of the Thai government's response so far.*"
—**Daniel Byman**, Georgetown University

"*The book brings to the fore several issues that have been ignored in the discussion on the southern Thai violence thus far, focusing on the possible links between some of the southern Thai Muslim militants and other militant Muslim groups in Southeast Asia and the Muslim and Arab world. It alerts us to the dangers of groups like the Jema'ah Islamiyah becoming strongly involved with the southern Thai militants in the event of greater repression by the Thai state. It provides useful material to Thai security and state forces planning solutions to the current violence in the south.*"
—**Saroja Dorairajoo**, National University of Singapore

"*This authoritative book enumerates the lethality of Thailand's Malay-Muslim insurgency in unrivaled detail. It brings much of the burgeoning output on Thailand's southern violence into coherence and perspective. Abuza's focus on the external terrorist germination in the spiraling insurgent violence will discourage complacency and goad the Thai authorities to get their act together. The strands of inquiry and argument in this book will not satisfy all, but none will want to miss its density of facts, force of presentation, and admonition of workable solutions. This fine book adds immense value and balance to the consequential literature on Thailand's deadly southern insurgency.*"

—**Thitinan Pongsudhirak**, Chulalongkorn University

Conspiracy of Silence

The Insurgency in Southern Thailand

Conspiracy of Silence

The Insurgency in Southern Thailand

Zachary Abuza

UNITED STATES INSTITUTE OF PEACE PRESS
Washington, DC

UNITED STATES INSTITUTE OF PEACE
1200 17th Street NW, Suite 200
Washington, DC 20036-3011
www.usip.org

First published 2009

Printed in the United States of America

The paper used in this publication meets the minimum requirements of American National Standards for Information Science—Permanence of Paper for Printed Library Materials, ANSI Z39.48-1984.

Library of Congress Cataloging-in-Publication Data
Abuza, Zachary.
Conspiracy of silence : the insurgency in Southern Thailand/Zachary Abuza.—1st ed.
    p. cm.
    Includes bibliographical references and index.
    ISBN 978-1-60127-002-3 (pbk. : alk. paper)
1. Political violence—Thailand, Southern. 2. Insurgency—Thailand, Southern. 3. Thailand, Southern—History—Autonomy and independence movements. I. Title.
    HN700.55.Z9V533 2009
    303.6'409593—dc22
                    2008056084

Contents

Illustrations

Figures

Tables

Foreword

Although the militant Islamist insurgency in Thailand is now well into its fifth year and has led to the deaths of thousands, it has been little studied in the West and is even less well understood. While there are two obvious reasons for the general lack of attention—the world's focus has been on other conflict zones, such as Iraq and Afghanistan, and the violence has been confined to southern Thailand—the volume's title suggests a third reason. Unlike media-savvy separatist movements in other parts of the globe, the militants in southern Thailand have spoken almost exclusively through violence and have largely refrained from stating a political platform or even taking credit for their actions. Without a known who or why, efforts to report on or study the conflict have been difficult.

Relying principally on his own on-the-ground research, interviews, and press reports, Zachary Abuza—a senior fellow at the United States Institute of Peace in 2004–05—attempts to answer these two unknowns by examining the historical roots of the insurgency and providing a detailed assessment of the present crisis. While the reader will discover Abuza's detailed findings on who is behind the insurgency and why, it is no secret that the insurgency has a decidedly Islamist character and has been responsible for horrific acts of violence. He finds no credible evidence that external actors are presently involved in the violence, but he does warn that international jihadist groups may ultimately involve themselves in the conflict and escalate both its intensity and lethality. In this sense, the manuscript reminds readers that in today's world it is difficult for ethnic and religious conflicts to remain local. Indeed, as Abuza documents, the insurgents in southern Thailand have already begun to employ strategies and techniques first mastered by insurgents in Iraq. He further documents that they have provided assistance to—if not actively partnered with—al Qaeda and Jemaah Islamiyah.

As a case study, the manuscript underscores another characteristic of such conflicts: This era's principal struggle is not one between Islam and the Judeo-Christian West. Although this belief is actively advanced and promoted in certain quarters, the reality is that the motivation behind ethnic and religious conflicts is far more complex. In southern Thailand, insurgent violence has struck not only the south's Buddhist community—many having fled en masse from the region —but also the Muslim community at large. Local Muslims have clearly suffered as a result of being caught in the crossfire between the insurgents and sometimes oppressive Thai government actions, but they also have been directly targeted by militants for any number of perceived offenses—such as not sharing extremist beliefs, or for daring to work at state-funded jobs. As this particular conflict demonstrates, the battle is dynamic and highly ideological—between a perversion of Islam and the civilizational values of the modern state system.

Symptomatic of the militants' extreme tactics are their likely links to the region's illicit drug trade. Although such an unholy marriage has yet to be categorically confirmed in southern Thailand, the association of drug trafficking with terrorism is increasingly encountered in disparate regions of the globe, from Afghanistan to Colombia. Such a relationship is not always a marriage of convenience—of terrorist and insurgent groups searching for a steady and reliable source of funding. Indeed, in the southern Thai case, insurgent groups are known to prey on the most vulnerable members of society—particularly those who have a history of drug use—by offering them a newer, "purer" identity. While such a recruitment strategy is not surprising, the revelation that insurgent groups have likely used drugs to motivate new members to commit violent acts is more so, particularly given the belief system they espouse. As Abuza notes, evidence suggests that methamphetamines have been given to young southern Thai militants to give them a "sense of invulnerability." He further notes that such a pattern has been witnessed elsewhere in Southeast Asia, which speaks to the insidious and multidimensional nature of the drug trade in the context of extremist violence.

Conspiracy of Silence is only the most recent in a long line of important, timely United States Institute of Peace Press volumes on these and other salient issues. Past volumes that highlight the need for the international community to pay attention to seemingly local conflicts include *How We Missed the Story: Osama bin Laden, the Taliban, and the Hijacking of Afghanistan*, by Roy Gutman; *Preventing Violent Conflict* and *Twenty-First-Century Peace Operations*, edited by William J. Durch. Volumes that address the complex causes of terrorism and sectarian violence include *My Kashmir: Conflict and the Prospects for an Enduring Peace*, by Wajahat Habibullah; and *Suicide Bombers in Iraq: The Strategy and Ideology of Martyrdom*, by Mohammed Hafez. Volumes that touch briefly on the nexus between the drug trade and terrorism include *Colombia: Building Peace in a Time of War*, edited by Virginia M. Bouvier.

Conspiracy of Silence is the latest volume in the Perspective series, a product of the United States Institute of Peace Press. Each book in this series explores, in a concise format, a particular conflict that may not currently be at the center of U.S. policy debates or a focused aspect of conflict management, prevention, or transition from war. The series is designed to help the international community form appropriate responses and to contribute to building peace around the world.

RICHARD H. SOLOMON, PRESIDENT
UNITED STATES INSTITUTE OF PEACE

Acknowledgments

This book would not have been possible without the assistance of many people in the United States, Thailand, Singapore, and Malaysia; and I am indebted to them. John Dacey reviewed the manuscript at two different stages with an intense and helpful eye. His comments and insights were invaluable. Prof. Panitan Wattanyagorn of Chulalongkorn University spent far too much of his time sharing knowledge and opening doors for me. I am truly grateful for his kind assistance and friendship. Sunai Phasuk of Human Rights Watch also gave me a lot of insight. Col. Atthaporn Bosuwan was generous in his time and insights. I also would like to thank Dr. Bridget Welsh of Johns Hopkins Paul H. Nitze School of Advanced International Studies (SAIS), Dr. Joseph Liow of the Institute of Defense and Security Studies, Dr. Ian Storey of the Institute of Southeast Asian Studies, and Francesca Lawe-Davies of the International Crisis Group for their comments, criticisms, and suggestions. I would also like to thank Catharin Dalpino of Georgetown University, Dr. Paul Stares formerly of the United States Institute of Peace, Colin Rubenstein of the Australia/ Israel and Jewish Affairs Council, and Julia Philipp for their support and guidance.

A number of friends in the fourth estate gave me guidance and shared their thoughts, often late into the night. They include Anthony Davis of *Jane's Defense Weekly*; Denis Gray and Rungrawee Chalermsripinyorat of the Associated Press; Simon Elegant and Andrew Marshall of *Time* magazine; Kavi Chongkittavorn of the *Nation* (Bangkok); Mageswary Ramakrishna and Andrew Perrin, both formerly of *Time*; Michael Sullivan of the *Sunday Times* (London); Eliza Griswold; and Simon Montlake of the *Christian Science Monitor*, who graciously invited me to speak at the Foreign Correspondents' Club of Thailand on two occasions. I owe a particular debt of gratitude to Don Pathan of the *Nation*, who shared his deep knowledge of southern Thailand and was always generous with his time and documents. I would also like to thank Natalie O'Brien, Cameron Stewart, and Simon Kearney of the *Australian* for their support and assistance.

I am grateful to Khun Joe Anuporn, Tej Bunnag, General Surapong, and Colonel Weerachon for their time, insights, and support. I would also like to thank my former classmate Kathy Rusakiati at Thailand's

xiv   **Acknowledgments**

Ministry of Foreign Affairs and dozens of Thai and Malaysian government and security officials who have asked to remain anonymous for their comments, suggestions, and willingness to be interviewed. I would also like to thank U.S. and other Western diplomats and law enforcement officials in Bangkok for their time and comments. C. Christine Fair of the Rand Corporation and Husain Haqqani of Boston University and the Hudson Institute helped steer me through the South Asian sections. Eric Brown, also of the Hudson Institute, supported the work on religious ideology, which was published in the fall 2006 edition of *Current Trends in Islamist Ideology*. I would also like to thank Erich Marquardt, formerly of the Jamestown Foundation, who helped publicize my research in shorter articles for the journal *Terrorism Monitor*.

I could not have completed this project without the very able assistance of my research assistant, Win Ma Ma Aye of SAIS, who tracked down data and articles and provided significant assistance in compiling and maintaining the database. Her hard work, good cheer, and resourcefulness made this book possible. I would also like to thank my friend Sirilak Khetsoongnoen, who assisted with the translation of all documents.

Gen. Russell Howard and Stacy Neal at the Jebsen Center at Tufts University's Fletcher School of Law and Diplomacy were supportive of the project.

I would like to thank Alan Song of the Smith Richardson Foundation, which awarded me a small grant to bring the manuscript to conclusion. I would also like to thank Kenneth Weinstein, president of the Hudson Institute, for his support and administration of the grant.

At Simmons College, I would like to thank my department chair, Cheryl Welch, for her patience and encouragement; Dean Diane Raymond and Jon Kimball for their support; and Ruth Fasoldt for everything.

Finally, this book could not have been accomplished without the support of my family. My children, Taeko and Charley, endured long absences and learned to count backward in the process. I will always be grateful to them for their love, patience, and hospitality at the "blue house."

Although many people helped, this work reflects the views of the author alone.

Abbreviations

ASEAN	Association of Southeast Asian Nations
BBMP	Barisan Bersatu Mujahideen Pattani (United Mujahideen Front of Pattani)
BIPP	Barisan Islam Pembebasan Pattani (Islamic Liberation Front of Pattani)
BNPP	Barisan Nasional Pembebasan Pattani (Pattani National Liberation Front)
BRN	Barisan Revolusi Nasional (National Revolution Front)
BRN-C	Barisan Revolusi Nasional–Coordinate (National Revolution Front–Coordinate)
CDR	Council for Democratic Reform
CPM	Communist Party of Malaya
CPM-43	Civilian-Police-Military Joint Unit No. 43
CPT	Pak Komunist Haeng Prathet Thai (Communist Party of Thailand)
DSI	Department of Special Investigations
GAMPAR	Gabungan Melayu Pattani Raya (the Association of Malays of Greater Pattani)
GMIP	Gerakan Mujahideen Islamiya Pattani (Pattani Islamic Mujahideen Movement)
HUJI	Harakat ul Jamaah Islami
HUJI-B	Harakat ul Jamaah Islami-Bangladesh
IED	Improvised explosive device
IIRO	International Islamic Relief Organization (Saudi Arabia)
IRCC	Islamic Religious Committee Council
ISA	Internal Security Act (Malaysia)
JI	Jemaah Islamiyah
JS	Jemaah Salafi
KMM	Kumpulan Mujahideen Malaysia
MERC	Medical Emergency Relief Charity (Indonesia)
MILF	Moro Islamic Liberation Front
MNLF	Moro National Liberation Front
MWL	Rabitat al-Alam al-Islami (Muslim World League) (Saudi Arabia)
NIA	National Intelligence Agency

NRC	National Reconciliation Commission
NSC	National Security Council
OAQ	Om al-Qura Foundation (Cambodia and Thailand)
OIC	Organization of the Islamic Conference
PAS	Parti Islam Se-Malaysia (Islamic Party of Malaysia)
PERKIM	Malaysian Islamic Welfare Organization
PPM	Pattani People's Movement
PULO	Bertubuhan Pembebasan Pattani Bersatu (Pattani United Liberation Organization)
RKK	Runda Kumpulan Kecil
RM	Rabitatul Mujahideen
RSO	Rohinga Solidarity Organization
RTA	Royal Thai Army
RTP	Royal Thai Police
SBPAC	Southern Border Provincial Administrative Committee
SBPPC	Southern Border Provinces Peace Building Command
TRT	Thai Rak Thai
UMNO	United Malays National Organization
UNHCR	UN High Commissioner for Refugees

Map of Thailand

Source: Map produced by the CIA, 2005. Courtesy of the University of Texas Libraries, University of Texas at Austin.

Introduction

In the five years since January 2004, sectarian violence has flared in the three southern Thai provinces of Pattani, Narathiwat, and Yala, leaving 3,000 people dead, roughly 8,000 wounded, and more than 100 people missing. Attacks have led to counterattacks, with each, in turn, escalating the lethality and mutual recriminations and mistrust between the Buddhist Thais and the majority ethnic Malay Muslims. Many Thai security officials are bracing for a broader sectarian conflict. As of January 2008, there had been some 8,500 violent incidents. The conflict in southern Thailand dwarfs any other conflict in East or Southeast Asia in its level of violence and has only gained momentum as efforts to quell the violence, now under two governments, have repeatedly failed.

The violence has taken many by surprise, as the insurgency in southern Thailand generally died out in the early to mid-1990s. In November 2001, Thailand's then prime minister, Thaksin Shinawatra, triumphantly declared that the conflict had been resolved and by 2002 had dismantled many of the organs established to quell the insurgency. The south has never been without violence, but after a lull and a shift to more economically motivated violence came this shocking resurgence. One group of Thai researchers using police data found that 1,975 "violent incidents" had occurred since 1993, but they were alarmed to find that only 21 percent of the incidents occurred before 2001 (an average of 66 incidents per year).[1] In 2004, 1,253 violent acts were recorded. Over half (496) of the more than 914 violent crimes reported in the south in 2004 were linked to the insurgency.[2] The number of recorded

---

1. Violent incidents include bombings; arson attacks; assaults; raids on police or army convoys, police stations, and army camps; assassinations and attempted assassinations; and sabotage. One Thai scholar recorded 2,500 violent incidents from 1994 through 2003. (See Chaiwat Satha-Anand, presentation at the Asia Foundation, Washington, D.C., April 7, 2005.)

2. This study was conducted by Prof. Srisompop Jitprimosi of Prince of Songkhla University in a report titled "One Decade and a Year of Violence in the Southern Border: Mysteries of the Problem and a Solution." For details, see Noppadol Phetcharat, "Major Spike in Violence Under This Government—Study," *Nation*, December 20, 2004.

incidents—everything from arson attacks to bombs to drive-by shootings of both Muslims and Buddhists—was more than 2,000 in 2006.

Although there was hope that the ouster of Prime Minister Thaksin in a bloodless coup on September 19, 2006, would lead to a resolution of the conflict, the rate of violence spiked dramatically. According to Prince of Songkhla University's Intellectual Deep South Watch (IDSW), the average number of violent incidents in the five months before the coup was 146 per month; in the five months after the military takeover, it rose to 169.4 per month.[3] By June 2007 more than 130 people were being killed each month.

By the close of 2008, there had been almost 900 successful bombings, causing more than 2,523 casualties, and many more attempted bombings. Additionally, there have been more than 700 arson attacks, and militants have assassinated nearly 1,400 people. In all, the nearly 3,000 deaths at the hands of Thai Islamic militants include 133 soldiers, more than 150 police, nearly 1,300 civilians, roughly 70 teachers, 5 monks, 210 headmen/local officials, and more than 40 government officials and civil servants. Militants have beheaded more than 35 people, and there have been almost twice that number of attempted or botched decapitations.

The violence has become horrific, with insurgents increasingly hacking apart their victims, setting their corpses—and in a few instances, living people—afire. Victims who were almost never targeted in previous iterations of the Malay insurgency, such as women, children, and monks, are now routinely killed. The social fabric of the south has been destroyed. Arson attacks on schools and murders of teachers, often in front of their students, have shuttered schools for months on end. Ethnic cleansing has led to the wholesale emigration by Buddhists from the region—roughly 50,000 people (15 percent of the 360,000 Buddhist community). Once mixed communities are now exclusively Muslim. Although Buddhists still live in the south, most live in the cities and towns. Those who do remain in villages live in heavily armed Buddhist enclaves. It is hard to imagine that society will return to normal—and that the Buddhist minority will return to their homes—even if the insurgency is put down.

---

3. Supalak Ganjanakhundee, "Soft Approach in South Failing," *Nation*, March 19, 2007.

Ten of the thirty-three districts (*tambon*) in the southern border provinces are "plagued by violence," according to the Ministry of the Interior, and the number is increasing.[4] The situation is growing out of control; the caretaker prime minister and former military chief Gen. Surayud Chulanont has said that the insurgency has crossed a threshold: "This long-standing and bitter problem has become chronic. If this wound is not treated properly, it will grow to become a malignant tumor that cannot be cured."[5] Already, there is concern that the insurgency has taken on a life of its own. By the end of 2007, the number of people supporting the insurgents—thought to be none in 2004—was estimated to be more than 10,000. This support for the insurgents has grown for no other reason than that the Thai government has proved to be incapable of ensuring their security and they believe they'll be targeted if they do not support the insurgents.

Secessionist insurgency is not new to southern Thailand; there is more than a century's worth of militant nationalist aspiration. The south has also always been plagued by violence and criminality, and smuggling and the underground economy have always dominated the local economy, which is controlled by "godfathers" and gangs. Many argue that this violence is simply tied in with control over cross-border trade. Yet the sheer degree of violence and the type of victims really renders that conclusion unfit. Officials have detected no more criminal activity or smuggling than in the past.[6] And the victim type begs the question of economic motivation in all the killings and bombings. What is the profit motive to beheading more than thirty people?

While Thailand's history has been dominated by periods of insurgency from both minorities and communists, this insurgency is different in many ways. First, the degree and scope of violence has never been greater. More people have been killed in the past four years than in the previous decade of the insurgency that ended in the mid-1990s. The victims are also discernibly different. The mode of killings has also changed. While the previous insurgency in the 1970s–90s was a rural-

---

4. "Army to Take Control of 10 Districts," *Nation*, June 28, 2005.
5. "Surayud Warns of Full-Scale Rebel Uprising," *Nation*, February 22, 2005; "BK Senators Condemn State of Emergency Decree," *Nation*, August 27, 2005.
6. Author interview, Bangkok, July 17, 2006.

based phenomenon and one fought with small arms, today's insurgents use improvised explosive devices (IEDs) to cause indiscriminant violence. Killings are far more brutal: beheadings, machete attacks, and desecration of corpses are routine occurrences. It has led to ethnic cleansing, and insurgents routinely leave leaflets threatening to engage in more ethnic cleansing.

Second, the insurgency is not about controlling physical space but about controlling mental space. Many analysts, both Thai and foreign, continue to label it as a domestic insurgency and to use outdated and ill-suited anticommunist terminology, refusing to use the word "jihad."[7] However, this insurgency has fundamental religious overtones and a degree of radical jihadist violence that have not been seen before. Currently the insurgency is as much a battle within the Muslim community as it is an overt sectarian conflict, with the insurgents trying to impose very hard-line Salafism on the population. Few analysts have noted that 55 percent of the victims of the insurgents have been fellow Muslims— mostly local village chiefs, collaborators, and those who espouse working with the Thai state. Without regard for public opinion and unconcerned about a popular backlash, militants are now regularly issuing decrees that compel the population to adopt Wahhabite norms and customs, and engaging in the Wahhabite practice of *takfir* (condemning fellow Muslims as apostates), which is fundamentally changing the culture of the south. They have established a parallel state structure, including de facto sharia courts to keep people out of the legal dispute-resolution mechanisms, networks of midwives to prevent women from giving birth in state-run hospitals, and private Islamic schools to keep people from the secular school system. It is a cultural insurgency, not simply a secessionist rebellion. This has important ramifications for counterinsurgency efforts; mere decapitation of the organization's leadership will not suffice.

Finally, there is a historically unprecedented degree of cooperation among the insurgents today, the earlier utter lack of which splintered the insurgents in the 1970s to early 1990s and limited their effectiveness. In the 1970s to 1990s, the groups were woefully divided in terms

---

7. International Crisis Group (ICG), *Southern Thailand: Insurgency, Not Jihad*, Asia Report No. 98 (Singapore/Brussels: ICG, May 18, 2005), 5–6.

of both ideology and goals. Some were Salafi, some ethnonationalist, and others were allied with the Malayan Communist Party. Some wanted an independent state, some an independent Islamic state, some union with Malaysia, and others simply greater autonomy in Thailand. Without any cooperation, they lacked the critical mass to take on the Thai government, which was able to pick the insurgency apart one faction at a time. This is no longer the case. Today's insurgents are unified in terms of ideology and goals, both of which are rooted in a more hard-line and less tolerant interpretation of Islam. The Thai National Security Council acknowledged that there is "a new Islamic group" that "through increasing contacts with extremists and fundamentalists in Middle Eastern countries, Indonesia, Malaysia, and the Philippines, [has] metamorphosed into a political entity of significance."[8]

To date, there has still been neither a claim of responsibility nor any stated goals from the insurgents. Many commentators dismiss the insurgents for that very reason, arguing that they are a bunch of nihilist teenagers, bent on creating havoc. But their silence is intentional. For one thing, it is what the military calls a force multiplier; their silence makes them appear larger. It is also a remarkable demonstration of internal cohesion—and command and control. No one is breaking ranks. It has also been beneficial in terms of internal security; it has left Thai security forces flummoxed and unable to determine even the organizations' hierarchies. But their aims are clear: they are engaged in ethnic cleansing, driving the Buddhist population out, and implementing their own Islamist shadow government and social institutions. Just because they have not publicly stated what it is they want does not mean that they don't have an agenda and political program. Indeed, they do communicate their demands at the local level through leaflets.

The Thai government—under the Thaksin Shinawatra administration; Gen. Sonthi Boonyaratglin's junta, known as the Council for National Security; and the democratic government restored in February 2008—has demonstrated an appalling lack of understanding of the insurgents' goals and ideology. "We cannot compromise," a militant told *Time* magazine. "The Thai government is not interested in talking to us. The fight will go on. We want independence. Nothing less than

---

8. National Security Council member quoted in Shawn Crispin, "Strife Down South," *Far Eastern Economic Review*, January 22, 2004.

that."[9] Yet despite such proclamations, the Thai government is in denial. More than four years into the insurgency, General Sonthi still refused to see any Islamist component to it and argued that they are fighting for autonomy, not secessionism. Unable to ask even the right questions about the nature of the insurgency, the government has formulated disastrous and ineffective policies. And it is not just the government. The National Reconciliation Council asserted in its final report that the insurgents are not secessionists, but every indication is that is exactly what they are. The long-term goal is clearly to establish an independent state, governed to a degree with sharia law and other Islamic institutions. There is also clearly a goal to rid the region of what they consider to be corrupting Thai culture.

The short- and medium-term goals of the insurgents are threefold: to make the region ungovernable, to provoke heavy-handed government responses that will further alienate the Muslim community, and to impose their values and authority on the local community. Regarding the first, they not only seek to make the region ungovernable but they also want people to lose all faith in civic institutions and the ability of the Thai state to offer them a degree of protection. They clearly would like to provoke more crackdowns that would convince the local population of their rhetoric that the Thai state is abusive and patently anti-Muslim. Additionally, they are establishing a parallel set of institutions in which they can exert their authority while eliminating other contenders for power. In short, there is not a conflict in Southeast Asia that has the potential to escalate or have such a negative impact on regional security than the one in southern Thailand. And yet, we know very little about the insurgency.

This violence raises five important and interrelated sets of questions:

1. What has caused this sudden upsurge? Are international factors at work, or is this merely a domestically driven phenomenon, the result of decades of local and bureaucratic politics, ineffectual policies and poor governance, crime, corruption, unequal resource allocation, and ethnic tension deriving from social and economic inequity?

---

9. Simon Elegant and Andrew Perrin, "The Road to Jihad?" *Time–Asian Edition*, May 10, 2004.

2. Who is behind the unrest? It is unprecedented in degree and coordination, leading many to wonder whether international elements are involved. Are the various groups coordinating their activities? Why has there been a conspiracy of silence, with no single group taking responsibility for the unrest?

3. What do the militants want? Why has there been no articulation of demands? Is it possible they simply want violence for its own sake, to create the conditions for their movement to grow? Or does the silence indicate a lack of centralized control and cohesion, and differing goals? Are the militants absolutist, unwilling to accept any form of compromise?

4. Are Thai government efforts and policies exacerbating the situation? What are the right/effective and wrong/provocative approaches?

5. What are the ramifications for Thailand and the region?

In setting out to answer these questions, this book's first chapter seeks to briefly explain the historical roots of the southern Thai conflict and the failure of the secessionist insurgency from the 1970s to the 1990s and the government's success in quelling the insurgency by the early 1990s. The second chapter analyzes the outbreak of the conflict in 2004 and the government's immediate handling of the situation, as well as the post-9/11 context that framed the violence. The third chapter examines the insurgency's development, documenting the waves of violence and the change in tactics by the insurgents. The fourth chapter provides a detailed analysis of the groups and organizations behind the violence, while the fifth chapter looks at known connections between them and external actors and transnational terrorist groups. The sixth chapter seeks to explain the failure of the government's various counterinsurgency programs, and the seventh chapter looks at the implications of the conflict on both Thailand and the region. Each chapter touches on the book's three central hypotheses.

First, the Thai government of Thaksin Shinawatra exacerbated the problem at every point through its policies and misplayed its hand woefully since the global war on terror began in September 2001. As a result, the large number of deaths at the hands of Thai security forces has created a culture of impunity and injustice that further alienates the population.

Second, while the roots of the conflict are domestic, other groups— such as Harakat-ul-Jihad al-Islami of Bangladesh (HUJI-B), the (Burmese) Rohinga Solidarity Organization (RSO), and the Southeast Asian regional terrorist group Jemaah Islamiyah (JI)—have involved themselves in the conflict to a very limited extent; such involvement has the potential to escalate both the intensity and the lethality of the insurgency. As Joseph C. Liow of the Institute of Defence and Security Studies notes, "It is the very existence of residual grievances within the Malay-Muslim community that will determine whether or not international Islamic terrorist networks can establish a foothold in Thailand."[10] Already, Muslim moderates have been forced to flee or have been cowed into silence (many of the militants' victims are Muslims whom the militants believe to be collaborators), creating space for Salafis and jihadists and, thus, exacerbating the problem.[11] Groups such as JI have proved in the Maluku Islands (Indonesia), Sulawesi (Indonesia), and Mindanao (Philippines) that they do not wait until they are invited; they inject themselves into conflicts where they believe gains can be made from supporting their persecuted coreligionists.

Third, the actors behind the unrest have not articulated demands, goals, or a platform. There is a conspiracy of conspicuous silence. This silence indicates two things. First, there is an unprecedented degree of command and control among the historically fractious Thai groups; they are working together and coordinating their actions. Second, the militants have little interest in negotiating with either the Thai government or local moderate Muslim leaders. They are trying to provoke a heavy-handed government response in the belief that it will drive more people into their arms and create an environment conducive to their organizational development and objectives.

---

10. Joseph Chinyong Liow, "The Security Situation in Southern Thailand: Toward an Understanding of Domestic and International Dimensions," *Studies in Conflict and Terrorism* 27 (2004): 532.

11. Salafis are committed to establishing an Islamic state governed by sharia but pursue their goals only through *da'wah*—proselytizing alone; jihadists espouse violence in pursuit of an Islamic state.

Definitional Note

In this book, Thailand's "south" refers to the three provinces of Narathiwat, Yala, and Pattani, an area of 9,036 square kilometers historically known as Pattani Raya (Greater Pattani), and not to the Southern Region (Pak Tai), an official group of fourteen provinces. When noted in the text, references to Thailand's "south" may also include the province of Satun and three abutting districts in the province of Songkhla. Songkhla's three Muslim-dominated districts, where attacks have been spreading, were put under martial law in 2005. Songkhla's largest city, Hat Yai, the major trading and financial center for the south, has also been the target of recent attacks. Unlike the other three provinces and Songkhla, however, Satun—a Muslim-majority province—has witnessed no attacks.[12] There are three explanations for the lack of violence there: (1) the population of Satun speaks Thai, not Bahasa Malayu, and is better integrated into the greater Thai culture and society—as Robert Albritton of the University of Mississippi concluded, there are vast differences in attitudes, values, loyalty to the Thai state, and degrees of assimilation between Thai and Malayu-speaking Muslims of the south;[13] (2) the ports along the province's western coast are too important for the infiltration and exfiltration of militants—any attacks would bring the region under greater scrutiny; and (3) the two bordering Malaysian states, Perlis and Kedah, were until March 2008 under firm United Malays National Organization/Barisan Nasional (UMNO/BN) control and, thus, policing efforts along the border have been more effective than elsewhere.[14] Regardless, the Thai military has stepped up its patrols of the Satun

---

12. Martin Petty, "The Muslim Province Where Peace Reigns," *Thai Day*, February 15, 2006. For an excellent analysis of Satun, see Thomas I. Parks, "Maintaining Peace in a Neighborhood Torn by Separatism: The Case of Satun Province in Southern Thailand" (unpublished manuscript, November 11, 2005).

13. Robert B. Albritton, "The Muslim South in the Context of the Thai Nation" (unpublished manuscript, November 2007), 13.

14. The United Malays National Organization (UMNO) is the dominant political party in Malaysia, having ruled since the country's founding in 1957. The Barisan Nasional (BN), the ruling political party coalition of which UMNO is the primary member and controlling force, also includes the Malaysian Chinese Association (MCA) and the Malaysian Indian Congress (MIC).

coast.[15] As one military official explained, "Satun is a safe haven for insurgent leaders because there is no violence raging around them. The government should not take it for granted that the situation is normal. It is only giving a false sense of security. We should send the military in there as well."[16]

There are roughly 5 million Muslims in Thailand (7 percent of the total population), 99 percent of whom are Sunni and most of whom speak Bahasa Malayu, which is written in Yawi, an Arabic script, with roughly four million living in the south. Muslims comprise about 80 percent of the population of the four southern provinces—Narathiwat (80–85 percent), Pattani (80–85 percent), Yala (65 percent), and Satun (65 percent)—and account for 1.3 million of the 1.8 million people in those provinces. Approximately 360,000 Buddhists live in the three provinces (28 percent of the total population), the majority of whom live in urban areas. This population spread gives these provinces more of a Malay character than a Thai one. Additionally, there are pockets of Muslims in Bangkok, Ayuddahya, and Fang, in the far north.

---

15. The Thai chief of navy, Adm. Sathirapan Keyanont, ordered security to be stepped up off the coast of Satun Province and dispatched three more vessels to patrol the waters off the coast as a result of growing concern about the relationship between the south and Aceh (Indonesia). Lt. Gen. Nipat Thonglek, head of a Thai delegation sent to monitor the Aceh cease-fire, asserted that connections between the Thai militants and the Free Aceh Movement (GAM) rebels in Aceh still existed. See Wassana Nanuam, "Army Camp on Alert for Fresh Raid," *Bangkok Post*, January 5, 2006.

16. Wassana Nanuam Anucha Charoenpo, "Insurgents 'Use Satun to Plan Attacks,'" *Bangkok Post*, May 2, 2006.

1

Historical Roots of
the Conflict

The Colonial Era

The Buddhist Kingdom of Pattani, which was "once the largest and most populous of the Malay states on the peninsula,"[1] predated the arrival of Islam to the region by several hundred years. Its court ultimately converted to Islam in 1457, giving rise to the Muslim Kingdom of Pattani (Pattani Darussalam), the area of which included the present-day Thai provinces of Narathiwat, Pattani, and Yala and the Malaysian states of Kelantan, Terengganu, Perlis, and Kedah. In the fifteenth century under the Ayutthaya kingdom (1350–1767), the Thais began to exert strong influence over the Malay Peninsula, although this influence was periodically interrupted by the state's frequent wars with Burma, most notably following the Burmese invasion of Ayuddahya in 1767.[2] The Thai state was strengthened following the founding of the Chakri Dynasty in 1782, and by 1789 it had conquered the Kingdom of Pattani, imposing a tributary system over what are now the northern Malay states of Kedah, Pattani, Kelantan, and Terengganu. Although Thai officials worked to bring Thai culture and language to the southern region, Thai rule was fairly benign as long as the Malay rulers accepted Thai suzerainty and traveled to Bangkok every three years to make obeisance (*tawai bangkom*).[3] Sharia courts, for example, remained in operation under the Pattani sul-

---

This chapter is adapted from Zachary Abuza, *Militant Islam in Southeast Asia: Crucible of Terror* (Boulder, Colo.: Lynne Rienner Publisher, 2003).

1. Wan Kadir Che Man, *Muslim Separatism: The Moros of the Southern Philippines and the Malays of Southern Thailand* (Singapore: Oxford University Press, 1990), 34.

2. For more, see Thongchai Winichakul, *Siam Mapped* (Bangkok: Silkworm Books, 1997).

3. Barbara Watson Andaya and Leonard Y. Andaya, *A History of Malaysia*, 2nd ed. (Honolulu: University of Hawaii Press, 2001), 110–12.

tan.[4] Starting in 1816, however, the Thai government began to decrease local autonomy by dividing the region into seven provinces to facilitate tax collection, leading to large-scale revolts in 1832.[5]

Although concurrent British colonization during the nineteenth century slowed Thai attempts to move further into the Malay Peninsula, the British initially accepted a degree of Thai control over the region. The British East India Company went so far as to lease Penang from the Thai court.[6] The development of modern states, which accentuated the need for clearer demarcations of territory, also served to deepen Thai control over the region, as did King Chulalongkorn's government reforms in the 1890s, which led to the establishment of a strong centralized bureaucracy with central control over the provinces. The Malay *prathesaraj* (semi-independent vassals), for instance, were put under the direct control of the Ministry of the Interior. In fact, the central government was strong enough that it did not have to cut autonomy deals with the local Muslim sultans and began to directly appoint and dispatch governors and administrators from Bangkok.[7] And in British Malaya, the British appointed district officers, ensuring that the region had extensive central oversight. Unlike the situation in the Philippines, where local-level government officials tacitly supported the Muslim separatists, an elite class of Muslims who controlled revenues and patronage networks never emerged in Thailand. As a result, Muslim separatists who resisted centralized political control on the peninsula found no politically powerful allies.

In 1897, the British and Thais signed a secret agreement that recognized Thai suzerainty over the regions of Kelantan and Terengganu as long as the Thais denied commercial access to the region to third parties—that is, to Britain's European competitors. But following a series of commercial deals between British businessmen and the Kelantan gov-

---

4. Sulaiman Doroh, "Enforcement of Shar'iah in Thailand: Islamic Family and Inheritance Laws in the Southern Provinces," in *Islam and Democracy: The Southeast Asian Experience*, ed. Hussin Mutalib (Singapore: Konrad Adenauer Foundation, 2004), 55.

5. Wan Kadir, *Muslim Separatism*, 35.

6. Andaya and Andaya, *A History of Malaysia*, 111.

7. Ibid., 194–196.

ernment and an appeal by the raja of Pattani to the British to help put a stop Thai aggression, the Thai kingdom became increasingly concerned about losing control and angered at independent Malay governors. This ultimately led the Thais to harshly put down a rebellion in Kelantan in February 1902 and to arrest the raja of Pattani the following year. Shortly thereafter, fearful of Thai aggression, the Malay governor requested "British protection and a British Resident."[8]

In October 1902, there was another Anglo-Thai agreement, but this one saw the departure of the Thai garrison from Malaysia; that year also saw the formal incorporation of the Kingdom of Pattani into the Thai kingdom. Under the agreement, Thailand was able to increase central-government control over the remainder of its Malay-dominated territory. Under duress, in 1909, the Thais turned over all Malay states to the British. However, the current border between the two states, delineated in their 1909 treaty, left three provinces in Thailand with a majority Muslim-Malay population. The implementation of the 1909 treaty and the imposition of Thai political and legal institutions ended the authority of the sharia courts, although they were gradually reintroduced and integrated into the Thai legal system after 1917.[9] By that time, the three provinces were treated like any other Thai province.

Although Malay ethnic, social, and cultural identities initially remained largely unaffected by the treaty, as residents on both sides regularly crossed the border, the Thai state gradually began to push the development of a Thai national identity in the southern provinces. In 1921, for example, Thailand imposed a national curriculum in the Thai language and more controls and restrictions on Islamic schools.[10] Thai authorities also crushed a Muslim tax rebellion in 1922 and 1923, although King Vajiravudh, increasingly fearful of British aggression, did lessen the tax burden to win popular support among Muslims.[11] After the fall of the absolute monarchy in the 1932 Revolution, the Sapiban

---

8. Ibid., 199.

9. Doroh, "Enforcement of Shar'iah in Thailand," 57–60.

10. The 1921 Compulsory Primary Education Act. See Wan Kadir, *Muslim Separatism*, 64; *Liow*, "The Security Situation in Southern Thailand," 533.

11. Wan Kadir, *Muslim Separatism*, 64.

system that had given the Malay aristocracy a degree of local political and religious control was scrapped and replaced by a more restrictive provincial system. The highly centralized nature of the Phibul regime degraded local autonomy further by pressuring Malays to assimilate and by abolishing all Islamic laws.[12] The Thai Customs Decree (Thai Ratthaniyom) in 1939, meanwhile, banned the use of the Malay language and the wearing of Malay dress and forced all Thai citizens, regardless of ethnicity or religion, to adopt common Thai customs.[13] With Buddhism becoming the state religion and the symbol of the nation, this ethnic Thai chauvinism—and the irredentist nature of the new regime—was reflected in the new name of the state itself, which changed from Siam to Thailand in 1939.

Until the 1940s, the south remained primarily in the hands of the hereditary elite. During World War II, the Thais, who were aligned with the Japanese, retook the northern Malay British colonial provinces of Kelantan, Terengganu, Kedah, and Perlis. Although they were forced to return them at war's end, they successfully imposed central-government control on them for a few years.[14] After the war, both the British and the Americans supported the territorial integrity of Thailand and would not countenance either Pattani independence or its union with the new Federation of Malaya.[15] In 1945, for instance, the British rejected the demands of the newly created Gabungan Melayu Pattani Raya (GAMPAR, or the Association of Malays of Greater Pattani), which lobbied for union with Malaya,[16] and hence improved relations with the government in Bangkok, including on issues of border security.

In a move to placate the Muslim community, the government reintroduced Islamic family law in the four southern provinces in

---

12. Doroh, "Enforcement of Shar'iah in Thailand," 58.

13. Nantawan Haemindra, "The Problem of Muslims in the Four Southern Provinces of Thailand," *Journal of Southeast Asian Studies* 7, no. 2 (1976): 208–225; Pasuk Phongpaichit and Chris Baker, *Thailand: Economy and Politics* (New York: Oxford University Press, 1995), 270.

14. Wan Kadir, *Muslim Separatism*, 65; Duncan McCargo, "Southern Thai Politics: A Preliminary Overview" (Working Paper No. 3, Parliamentary Online Information Service [POLIS], February 2004), 3.

15. See Duncan McCargo, "Southern Thai Politics," 6.

16. Wan Kadir, *Muslim Separatism*, 65–66.

1946,17 but this did little to quell Muslim demands. That same year, for example, Haji Sulong Tomina led the Dusun Nyur Rebellion, in which Muslim villagers fought state police and soldiers.[18] Then, in early 1947, Sulong established the Pattani People's Movement (PPM), calling for self-rule, language and cultural rights, and sharia law. Arrested by Thai authorities on January 16, 1948, he was acquitted of treason but still served seven years on lesser charges. Revolts became commonplace, including one in 1948 that left 400 people dead and some 2,000 to 6,000 refugees in Malaysia. That same year a quarter-million Thai Malays petitioned the United Nations for accession to the new Federation of Malaya.

The Advent of Muslim Secessionism

Political power in Thailand in most of the post-WWII era was dominated by anticommunist and development-oriented military officers who were determined to maintain centralized control over the country. As part of the state's counterinsurgency campaign in the 1950s, the Nikhom program saw the resettlement of 102,000 Buddhists from the northeastern part of the country into the Malay south.[19] The military never countenanced autonomy for any ethnic or regional group, much less the Malay Muslims, and the military had near-total political control from the 1950s through the 1980s. Only when Thailand experienced brief nonmilitary-dominated democratic interludes (1945–47 and 1973–76) were demands for autonomy or independence "voiced with any vigor."[20]

Scholars Pasuk Phongpaichit and Chris Baker argue that the harsh policies of Field Marshals Phibul Songkhram and Sarit Thanarat in the 1950s and 1960s may have "crushed the moderate leadership of the

---

17. Doroh, "Enforcement of Shar'iah in Thailand," 58.

18. For more, see ICG, *Southern Thailand: Insurgency, Not Jihad*, 5–6; Thanet Aphornsuwan, "Origins of Malay-Muslim 'Separatism' in Southern Thailand" (Working Paper Series No. 32, Asia Research Institute, Singapore, 2004).

19. Chaiwat Satha-Anand, *Islam and Violence: A Case Study of Violent Events in the Four Southern Provinces, Thailand, 1976–1981*, USF Monographs in Religion and Public Policy No. 2 (Tampa, Fla.: University of South Florida, 1987), 13.

20 Eva-Lotta E. Hedman and John T. Sidel, *Philippine Politics and Society in the Twentieth Century* (New York: Routledge, 2000), 176.

Malay Muslims in the southern border region," but they created space for more radical leaders to rise to prominence.[21] For example, Haji Sulong Tomina, who demanded autonomy but never led an armed rebellion, was "disappeared" while in government custody in 1952. And his son, who successfully ran as a member of parliament, was jailed for three years in 1957 for raising Muslim demands in parliament. Accused by Prime Minister Sarit of plotting a separatist revolt, he ultimately fled to Malaysia.[22] Political scientists Astri Suhrke and Surin Pitsuwan concur with the analysis of Pasuk Phongpaichit and Chris Baker, suggesting that, in the early 1970s, a "counter-elite" to the traditional aristocracy emerged from the ranks of Islamic clerics trained in the Middle East (mainly Egypt and Pakistan).[23]

Initially, there were three principal Muslim separatist groups in Thailand: the Barisan Nasional Pembebasan Pattani (Pattani National Liberation Front, or BNPP), founded by Malay aristocrats; the Bertubuhan Pembebasan Pattani Bersatu (Pattani United Liberation Organization, or PULO), led by Haji Hadi Mindosali and Haji Sama-ae Thanam (Haji Ismail Ghaddafi); and the Barisan Revolusi Nasional (National Revolution Front, or BRN).[24] All were founded to establish an independent homeland in southern Thailand. Although Islam was part of the groups' identity, it was not the central factor in their political struggle. As Joseph C. Liow has written, "It is not Islam per se that has politicized the Muslims in the south, but the fact that these Muslims identify themselves as Malay and relate to the Thai state and the Thai nationalist project as Malays that is of utmost importance."[25]

The BNPP was established in 1959–60 by Tengku Abdul Jalal, the former deputy of GAMPAR who was jailed following World War II for

21. Phongpaichit and Baker, *Thailand: Economy and Politics*, 292.

22. Chaiwat, *Islam and Violence*, 14.

23. Astri Suhrke, "Irredentism Contained: The Thai Muslim Case," *Comparative Politics* 7, no. 2 (1975): 187–203; Suhrke, "Loyalists and Separatists: The Muslims in Southern Thailand," *Asian Survey* 57 (1977): 237–250; Surin Pitsuwan, "Elites, Conflicts and Violence: Conditions in the Southern Border Provinces," *Asian Review* 1 (1987): 83–96.

24. See Wan Kadir, *Muslim Separatism*; Syed Serajul Islam, "The Islamic Independence Movements in Pattani in Thailand and Mindanao of the Philippines," *Asian Survey* 38, no. 5 (May 1998): 441–456.

25. Liow, "The Security Situation in Southern Thailand," 534.

his activism in demanding regional autonomy and the son of Sultan Tunku Abdul Kader, who fled to Malaya in 1932. With its links to the Kelantan-based GAMPAR, the BNPP was divided among those factions that either favored independence, integration with Malaysia, or autonomy within Thailand, and by debates over the implementation of sharia. Although the organization was much less willing to countenance armed struggle than other separatist groups, it did resist Buddhist settlements. The BNPP had two important overseas offices, Rumah Pattani (Pattani House) at Egypt's Al-Azhar University and Akhon (Brother) in Mecca, Saudi Arabia. It sent a couple hundred members for training in Libya and Syria, and had some ties to the Palestine Liberation Organization (PLO). The BNPP was the most religiously motivated of the Thai organizations and, by 1986, ten of thirteen central committee members were Middle East–trained *ustadz* (Islamic teachers).[26] Accordingly, the BNPP used Islamic schools as the centerpiece of its recruitment and indoctrination efforts, and the group received support from Saudi Arabian charities such as the Muslim World League and the Kuwaiti Islamic Call Society. As Wan Kadir Che Man has written, "The BNPP is a conservative group committed to orthodox Islam. As stated in its constitution, the basic political ideology of the BNPP is based on the Al Quran, Al Hadith and other sources of Islamic law."[27]

Tengku Abdul Jalal, who presided over a fifteen-person committee, led the BNPP for most of the period from 1959 to 1977. At his death, Azuddin Abdul Salleh and Muhammad Harris Hadaji succeeded him,[28] but by 1982, with most of its leaders in exile, the BNPP functionally ceased to exist as an insurgent group in southern Thailand.[29] In fact, as Chaiwat Satha-Anand states, the BNPP was never effective because it was "too closely linked towards the former elites and religious leaders."[30] In 1985, radical elements of the BNPP, under the leadership of Wahyuddin Muhammad, broke away and formed the Barisan Bersatu Mujahideen Pattani (United Mujahideen Front of Pattani, BBMP).

26. Wan Kadir, *Muslim Separatism*, 103.

27. Ibid., 105.

28. Ibid., 11.

29. Peter Chalk, "Separatism and Southeast Asia: The Islamic Factor in Southern Thailand, Mindanao, and Aceh," *Studies in Conflict and Terrorism* 24 (2001): 260.

30. Chaiwat, *Islam and Violence*, 15.

This group renamed itself Barisan Islam Pembebasan Pattani (Islamic Liberation Front of Pattani, BIPP) in 1986.[31] Defunct by the mid-1980s, the BBMP/BIPP was primarily a *da'wah* (proselytizing) and propaganda body and had no armed wing.

Founded in India in 1968 by Kabir Abdul Rahman, a Pattani aristo-crat and Islamic scholar educated in the Middle East, PULO was seen as more pragmatic, less religious, and more broad-based than the BNPP. The founding ideology was "religion, race, homeland, humanitarian-ism." His goal was to establish an independent Muslim state through armed struggle (conducted by the armed wing, the Pattani United Lib-eration Army, or PULA). Based in Kelantan, Malaysia, and Mecca, Saudi Arabia, PULO also had an important office in Damascus. The organization eventually splintered, yielding New PULO, led by Hayi Abdul Rohman Bazo,[32] and Barisan Nasional Baru (New National Front, or BNB), both founded in 1995 by disaffected members.[33]

The BRN, meanwhile, was opposed to the nationalist agenda of PULO and mistrusted the BNPP's goal of restoring the feudal Pattani sultanate. Founded in March 1963 by Ustadz Haji Abdul Karim Hassan,[34] the BRN was created in part as a result of popular unrest over an attempt by Prime Minister Field Marshal Sarit Thanarat to place all *pondoks* (Thai Islamic schools, also referred to as madrassas) under the purview of the Ministry of Education.[35] With close ties to the Com-

---

31. Sabrina Chua, "Political Islam in Southern Thailand—A Radicalisation?" (paper presented at the Conference on the Dynamics and Structure of Terrorist Threats in Southeast Asia, Kuala Lumpur, April 18–20, 2005), 5; ICG, *Southern Thailand: Insurgency, Not Jihad*, 10.

32. Bazo and his deputy, Hadji Mae Yala, were two of four Thai Muslim leaders arrested by Malaysian authorities in 1998. After the arrests, Saarli Taloh-Meyaw headed New PULO until his death in February 2000. Shamsudin Khan, an exiled leader of PULO, now lives with other aging exiles in Sweden.

33. The BNB was more of a socioeconomic development movement, concerned with economic disparities between the south and the rest of Thailand. See Chalk, "Separatism and Southeast Asia," 244, 260.

34. A native of Narathiwat, Ruso District.

35. Prime Minister Thanarat launched a new round of assimilation policies, including the 1961 Education Improvement Program, which imposed a secular curriculum on pondoks to be taught along with the traditional Islamic curriculum; schools that refused to comply were shut down.

Figure 1.1 Genealogy of Major Thai Separatist Organizations (1940–present)

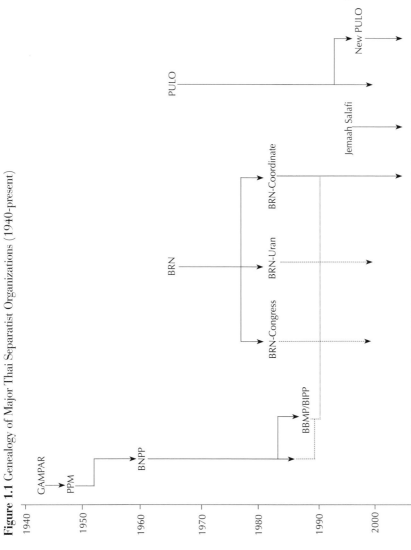

munist Party of Malaya (CPM) and influenced by the ideology of pan-Arab socialism, the BRN supported the establishment of a pan-Malay state that would be leftist (anticapitalist) in orientation. By 1984, the BRN had three discernable factions: BRN-Congress, BRN-Coordinate, and BRN-Uran. The BRN-Congress, which was led by Rosa Buraka (sometimes referred to as Rozak Burasoh or Abdul Razak Rahman), was the most militant of the groups. The BRN-Coordinate was a more political faction, and the BRN-Uran was headed by Haji Abdul Karan, who founded the group after he refused to accept his loss in a 1984 party election and led it until his death. In general, the BRN factions were more political and less engaged in military operations than PULO. (For a genealogy of major Thai separatist groups, see Figure 1.1.)

Beyond these three main separatist groups, a number of other fringe groups also emerged in the south, including Sabil-illah, which was founded in 1975 and bombed Bangkok's Don Muang Airport in June 1977; Tantra Jihad Islam; Black September 1902 (in Yala), which launched a bold attack on the king and queen in September 1977; the Haji Samae (in Yala); and the Dawlaw Taloh group.[36]

As this brief survey demonstrates, the primary failure of the Pattani Muslims from the 1940s to the 1990s was their inability to forge a broad-based alliance. The groups were highly fractious and divided on issues of ideology, tactics, and goals. Sporadic attempts were made to create umbrella organizations to coordinate their efforts, but none were successful. For example, the Muslim World League brokered an agreement among the groups in 1979 that led to a brief period of military cooperation, but it lasted only two years. The BBMP's attempt at unity in 1986 likewise failed.

Secessionism under Wraps

From 1968 through 1975, Thai forces launched major military operations against the separatist organizations with positive effect. Between October 1976 and December 1981, there were only 127 violent incidents, including a number of bombings of government buildings and schools. Committed principally in PULO's name, these attacks led to

---

36. Chaiwat, *Islam and Violence*, 9.

the deaths of 200 people and the wounding of roughly 300 others.[37] Although these attacks continued sporadically through the 1990s, this generation of Muslim separatist fighters, whose numbers were no more than three thousand at peak strength, realized almost no results. This proved to be the case for eight key reasons.

First, from the 1940s to the 1980s, there was considerable cooperation between Thailand and Malaysia in dealing with joint security issues along their common border. Many CPM insurgents had been driven out of Malaya by the British in the 1950s and had sought sanctuary in Thailand. The Thais, fearful of CPM cadres linking up with Communist Party of Thailand (Pak Komunist Haeng Prathet Thai, or CPT) members, sought to deny CPM rebels sanctuary. Under a 1964 agreement, the Thais reluctantly allowed Malaysian police to cross the border in hot pursuit of communist rebels.[38] In March 1970, a bilateral antiterrorism agreement was signed between the countries, although, at Kuala Lumpur's urging, it focused on the common threat posed by communists, not Muslim secessionists.[39]

While provincial politics have influenced the extent of Malaysia's role in Thailand, such as when the Kelantanese party and supporter of the Thai insurgents, Pantai Islam, lost power in 1978, the federal government of Malaysia has had its own reason to limit its support for the Thai Muslims. Although Malaysia is a predominantly Muslim country and a constitutional Islamic monarchy, it was and still is concerned about Islamic radicals in Thailand linking up with its own Islamist radicals. In short, Kuala Lumpur has valued its relationship with Bangkok more than its relationship with the rebels, minimizing its support for them

---

37. Ibid. 13.

38. Malaysian police were allowed to pursue CPM rebels eight kilometers into Thailand for up to seventy-two hours. Angered by a Malaysian military aircraft that entered Thai airspace in hot pursuit, the Thais withdrew this right in 1976. Border-security cooperation resumed in late 1976, following a military coup in Thailand that brought a staunch anticommunist government to power. Joint and coordinated attacks began in January 1977 and lasted into the 1980s. In 1981, the Thais drove several hundred PULO members into Malaysia, although the Malaysian government failed to provide the same degree of assistance to the Thai government. By 1981, the CPM's strength had declined by one-third, to only 2,000. In December 1989, the CPM and the Malaysian government signed a formal peace treaty, finally ending the forty-odd-year emergency.

39. Liow, "The Security Situation in Southern Thailand," 541.

much as it dropped support for the Moro rebels in the southern Philippines. As a result, the two countries established the Thai-Malaysia General Border Committee in 1977. That year also saw joint military operations between them. Partly because of this increased cooperation, only 300 to 500 Muslim guerrillas were left in the south by the late 1980s, and nearly half of these remaining guerrillas laid down their arms in 1993 following the Thai government's offer of general amnesty.[40] After the 1997 establishment of the Malaysia-Indonesia-Thai Growth Triangle, the desire to maintain a positive government-to-government relationship only increased within Malaysia. Malaysian prime minister Mahathir Mohammed went so far as to yield to Thai demands and personally approve of joint police raids against secessionists believed to be operating from northern Malaysia.[41] This led to the arrest of several key Thai secessionist leaders, including Hadji Sama-ae Thanam (Haji Ismail Ghaddafi), head of PULO-PULA; New PULO chief Hayi Abdul Rohman Bazo; New PULO deputy Hadji Mae Yala; and Hadji Dato Thanan. In short, bilateral cooperation led to the virtual annihilation of both states' security concerns along the border, including those related to the CPM, the CPT, PULO, and the BNPP.[42]

Second, there was never any large-scale, deliberate Thai government repression of Muslims that would have created a broad anti-Thai movement in southern Thailand. The guerrillas were never able to capitalize on wide-scale public discontent. Even during counterin-

---

40. "A Long History of Resistance and Reconciliation," *Nation*, May 12, 2003.

41. Chalk, "Separatism and Southeast Asia," 245.

42. The CPT had only a small presence in the south (Yala, Pattani, and Narathiwat) along the Malaysian border, a region under the influence of the CPM, although it did have a strong base area in Surat Thani, Nakhorn Sri Thammarat, and Phatalung. The CPT was based predominantly in the northern and northeastern parts of the country, where it had closer ties to the Pathet Lao and the Vietnam Workers' Party. It received most of its funding from the Chinese Communist Party. Chinese aid declined dramatically in 1979, following the Vietnamese invasion of Cambodia and the ouster of the Chinese-backed Khmer Rouge. In a quid pro quo for Thai support of the Chinese efforts to rearm the Khmer Rouge and support an insurgency against the Vietnamese, the Thais demanded that Beijing cut support for the CPT. For more on the Sino-Thai alliance and the demise of the CPT, see Nayan Chanda, *Brother Enemy: The War after the War* (New York: Harcourt Brace Jovanovich, 1986), 348–349; Pasuk Phongpaichit et al., *Guns, Girls, Gambling, Ganjah* (Bangkok: Silkworm Press, 1998), 132–137.

surgency operations in the 1970s and 1980s, the Thai military was careful not to antagonize the local population by being heavy-handed or repressive. Surrounded by countries facing active armed insurgencies (Burma, Laos, Cambodia, Malaysia, and Vietnam) and having faced its own communist insurgency, the Thai military had ample experience in counterinsurgency warfare and employed effectively many of its tactics against the Muslim insurgents in the south. The Thai military also had ample financial and technical support from the United States to deal with its security issues,[43] and the number of Muslim leaders who assimilated and worked with the Thai state also worked against the insurgency.[44]

That noted, the Thai government never approached the south with a completely military mind-set. In 1981, for instance, Prime Minister Prem Tinsulanond, himself a southerner, established the Southern Border Provincial Administrative Committee (SBPAC) to govern the south and coordinate all economic development there. (He also established its armed wing, CPM-43, a unified military-police-civilian command in charge of all security operations in the south.[45]) The SBPAC was an important forum for raising local grievances and had significant influence in the Thai cabinet. It was also an important dispute-resolution mechanism on the ground, one through which the local population could demand redress for corrupt and abusive leaders and security personnel. In 1987, Prem further signaled the government's intent to shift

---

43. From 1946 to 1959, the United States provided US$292.9 million in military assistance, loans, and grants; military assistance skyrocketed to US$618 million in the 1960s because of the Vietnam War and the use of Thai military facilities. In the 1970s, the figure rose to US$654.5 million, primarily because of high levels of aid from 1970 to 1973. Funding tapered off in the late 1970s (US$32.1 million in 1979), but with the Vietnamese invasion of Cambodia in 1979 and the decade-long occupation, U.S. military aid to Thailand spiked to more than US$100 million in the mid-1980s. Total U.S. military aid in the 1980s was US$682 million. With the end of the Cold War, U.S. military assistance to Thailand dropped precipitously to only US$15.5 million in the 1990s; it was at this time that Thailand began to turn to China for weapons sales. U.S. assistance doubled after 9/11. See the United States Agency for International Development (USAID), *U.S. Overseas Loans and Grants* (The Greenbook), http://qesdb. cdie.org/gbk (accessed October 1, 2008).

44. Suhrke, "Loyalists and Separatists," 237–250.

45. CPM-43 established a joint civil-military-police headquarters to facilitate cooperation. It was first under the command of the Fourth Army but in 1996 was shifted to the Ministry of the Interior.

from a military to a political-economic approach by shifting the Internal
Security Operating Command from the military's Supreme Command
to the Office of the Prime Minister. Under Prem, the capability of the
bureaucracy in the south greatly improved—as it did in the rest of the
country. In addition, the Thai government implemented some successful development programs and invested heavily in the physical infrastructure of the region. The 1980s represented a transformative time in
which law and order was imposed there.

Third, Thailand's rapid and sustained economic development helped
raise the standard of living of the majority of the population, even most
of the Muslims in the south. Beginning with Prime Minister Sarit
Thanarat in the late 1950s, the government has had a stated goal of
bringing development to all parts of the country. In the 1980s, the government made particular efforts to remedy disparities in health care,
education, and welfare. Despite these efforts, Muslim-majority areas are
by every measure less developed than greater Bangkok and the central
region. Although the fourteen provinces of southern Thailand rank
higher than the north and northeastern provinces on most measures
of socioeconomic development (per capita GDP, longevity, infant
mortality), the three provinces of Yala, Narathiwat, and Pattani are
among the poorest in Thailand.[46]

Fourth, the insurgent groups were never able to develop a political
platform other than secessionism. Through the mid-1990s, the various insurgent groups were woefully divided in terms of both ideology and goals, and the lack of a cohesive social, political, and economic objective and plan kept them from developing a mass
following. This is so, in part, because the Thai government worked
very hard to deprive the movement of oxygen by addressing many of
the local population's grievances. Additionally, the crown has been
very active in the south and arguably has led development projects
longer than the government has. Furthermore, there exists considerable religious freedom and pluralism within the country. Islam is not
at all repressed, and there is no limit on mosque construction. The
constitution requires the government "to patronize and protect Bud-

---

46. For more information, see the data in the *2000 Population and Housing Census*
(Bangkok: National Statistical Office, 2000).

dhism and other religions," meaning it must support Islamic education, provide allowances for Muslim clerics who hold administrative and senior ecclesiastical posts, fund the renovation and repair of some mosques, and provide the daily upkeep of the Central Mosque in Pattani.[47] Thai officials estimate that there are up to 8,000 *ustadz* in the south, some 2,000 mosques around the country, including 434 and 309 in Narathiwat and Yala provinces, respectively, and some 200 registered *pondoks*.[48]

While many Muslims chafed at the government's imposition of the national curriculum at all schools, roughly 80 percent of pondoks received some government assistance to support these curriculum upgrades.[49] The Thai government has also offered intensive training so that teachers are capable of instructing in both the secular and religious curricula.[50] Furthermore, the government has an advisory board for Muslim issues, the National Council for Muslims, which advises the Ministry of Education and the Ministry of the Interior.[51] The government has also financed Islamic educational institutions and pilgrimages to Mecca, and has supported several hundred Islamic primary and secondary schools. Likewise, a parallel system of Islamic law is permitted: imams of local mosques are allowed to try simple cases of family law, while more complicated cases are referred to each province's Islamic Religious Committee Council (IRCC). Although the IRCCs are not formal Islamic courts, Sulaiman Doroh notes that "this mode of dispensing advice grew and developed to fulfill people's requests for assistance" and that the IRCCs actually decide cases on the basis of a set of 1941 codes.[52] Muslims also successfully demanded

---

47. U.S. Department of State, "Thailand: Country Report on Human Rights Practices, 2005," March 8, 2006, 17, www.state.gov/g/drl/rls/hrrpt/2005/61628.htm (accessed October 1, 2008).

48. "A Long History of Resistance and Reconciliation," *Nation*, May 12, 2003.

49. Catharin Dalpino and David Steinberg, eds., *Georgetown Southeast Asia Survey, 2003–2004* (Washington, D.C.: Georgetown University, 2004), 61.

50. Dalpino and Steinberg, *Georgetown Southeast Asia Survey*.

51. The king appoints the five members. The head of the National Council runs a division in the Department of Religious Affairs in the Ministry of Education.

52. Doroh, "Enforcement of Shar'iah in Thailand," 62–63.

Islamic banking, which was established in September 2001.[53] Moreover, foreign funds for Islamic education and da'wah were able to flow into the country completely unchecked until 2001.

Fifth, Muslims are not politically marginalized and have held influential positions at the national level. They traditionally have had strong representation in the Democrat Party (notably, former foreign minister Surin Pitsuwan), and the Wadah faction of the ruling Thai Rak Thai Party (which emerged from the Chart Thai Party) under former interior minister Wan Muhammad Noor Matha was a key Muslim political group. In the two houses of parliament, Muslims have had a slightly smaller share of the seats than their population would suggest, but the proportions do not suggest that they are marginalized. In the parliament elected in 2001, for example, there were eight Muslim senators (4 percent) and sixteen Muslim MPs (3.2 percent). In the parliament elected in February 2005, there were eight Muslim senators (4 percent) and twenty-four Muslim MPs (5 percent).

Sixth, although the insurgents received some financial and military sponsorship from Libya and Syria in the 1970s (especially the BRN, with its Islamic-socialist platform), state sponsorship was very limited and most weapons were purchased from illegal brokers within Thailand itself.[54] One PULO official acknowledged that, in the late 1970s to early 1980s, "around 10 people went to Libya every year for four or five years for a variety of short and long courses."[55] The BRN sent more members to Syria, and one returnee said that he was in a class of fifty Pattani militants.[56] Despite these relationships, there was a sharp decline in other sources of international support during this period. In 1984, the Saudi government shut down the offices of PULO, arrested

---

53. Supara Janchitfah, "Southern Muslims Plead for Understanding," *Bangkok Post*, September 2001; "Muslim Anger Festers in Thailand's South," Al-Jazeera, January 12, 2002.

54. Dominic Whiting, "Thai Muslim Guerrillas at Peace Despite Fears of Unrest," Reuters, November 20, 2002; "Thailand Probes Local Groups for Terrorist Links," Agence France-Presse, December 27, 2002; "PULO and the Middle East Connection," *Far Eastern Economic Review*, October 9–15, 1981.

55. Yousuf Longpi, who claims to have been PULO's representative in Libya from 1979 through 1981, quoted in Whiting, "Thai Muslim Guerillas at Peace."

56. "A Rebel Changes His Stripes," *Nation*, May 12, 2003.

and deported its leaders, and forced other Thai groups out of the kingdom. The Saudis were unhappy with PULO for collecting zakat (compulsory Muslim charitable donations) and issuing identity papers to Thai Muslims, as well as for having ties to the Baathist regime in Syria and for opening offices in Iran.[57] Moreover, unlike the Moro National Liberation Front (MNLF) in the southern Philippines, none of the Thai groups have ever had the active support of the Organization of the Islamic Conference (OIC) or have had permanent representation in the organization.

Seventh, insurgents are constrained by the physical geography of the Malay Peninsula. Although many commentators note that the porousness of the Thai-Malaysian border aids insurgents, great physical obstacles exist that constrain insurgent activities. The border itself is only 506 kilometers long and runs between the Gulf of Siam on the east and the Straits of Malacca on the west. To the north, past the Isthmus of Kra, is the Thai Buddhist majority. Directly to the south, in Malaysia, is a fairly inhospitable operating environment, especially in the BRN-controlled states. While the forest cover is dense and the terrain mountainous, the region is small enough that the Thai military's superior mobility makes a difference in countering insurgent activities.

Eighth and finally, building on the government's successful use of amnesties to quell the communist insurgency in the north and northeast, Prime Minister Prem issued Order No. 65/2525 in 1984 to grant amnesty for Malay separatists. This followed the Communist Act of 1952, which offered a blanket amnesty for communist insurgents, and a general amnesty (Order No. 26/23) for the CPT and militant leftists in 1982. A second offer of amnesty in 1993 further depleted PULO's ranks. PULO was dealt another blow in September 1994 when Thai police arrested a senior commander, the Syrian-trained Da-o Krongpinang. In 1995, PULO had a soul-searching congress in which members acknowledged that their movement had suffered serious setbacks between 1988 and 1994 and that it had lost popular support. The congress elected new leaders who decided that the way to rekindle the movement was to launch a

---

57. ICG, *Southern Thailand: Insurgency, Not Jihad*, 13.

series of military attacks to draw attention to the organization's cause, a campaign known as Operation Falling Leaves.[58] By the end of 1997, PULO claimed to have killed 146 Thai soldiers and wounded more than eighty in thirty-three separate attacks.

Despite this brief paroxysm of violence, by 1998 the Thai insurgency under PULO was in its death throes. On January 14, 1998, Malaysian authorities arrested Haji Sam-ae Thanam and turned him over to Thai authorities, which was terribly demoralizing for PULO's fighters.[59] Then, in February 1998, Abdul Halim, a senior PULO commander, turned himself in after fifteen years on the run, taking advantage of the government's amnesty program, as did some 900 combatants who had sought refuge in northern Malaysia and felt betrayed by the Mahathir administration.[60] Haji Sama-ae Thanam was ultimately put on trial along with Haji Dato Thanam and Haji Buedo Betong. All three were convicted in October 2002 of waging insurgency and were sentenced to life in prison.[61] Two of New PULO's leaders, Abdul Rohman Bazo and Haji Mae Yala, were also captured and turned over to Thai authorities.[62] These developments collectively caused PULO to become a very weak and fractious organization, little more than a Web site. Other leaders—such as Tunku Bilor Kortor Nilor and Haji

---

58. The attacks may have included elements of New PULO. There is some evidence that the umbrella organization Bersatu was established in 1997–98 and that this was one of its first coordinated operations. PULO, "The Year of National Reorganization (1998–1999)," www.pulo.org/reorg.html (accessed in the early 2000s).

59. "KL Decides It's Time to Help," *Bangkok Post*, February 5, 1998; "Arrests in South Boost Malaysian Ties, Security," *Nation*, January 24, 1998; Julian Gearing, "Southern Discomfort," *Asiaweek*, March 20, 1998.

60. "Southern Rebels Meet Deadline to Surrender," *Bangkok Post*, March 10, 1998; Leslie Lopez and Shawn Crispin, "Fighting Back," *Far Eastern Economic Review*, April 22, 2004.

61. The three were sentenced to death, but the sentences were commuted to life imprisonment because they pleaded guilty and offered confessions. In the same trial, the court acquitted two other PULO members, Abdul Rahman bin Abdul Gadar and Kami Maseh (Yamil Maseh), because of inadequate evidence. See "Thai Muslim Separatists Sentenced to Life Imprisonment," Kyodo, News, October 15, 2002.

62. "Separatists Arrested in Malaysia," *Bangkok Post*, January 20, 1998.

Lukman B. Lima, the deputy president—are currently living in exile. The BNPP and the BRN likewise collapsed.[63]

Although low-level and sporadic attacks continued in 1998–99, Thai authorities became increasingly confident that the security situation in southern Thailand was steadily improving. The era of ethnonationalist struggle, led by the old Malay aristocrats, had largely come to an end. But as in the Philippines, where the Datu-led MNLF gave way to the distinctly Islamist movement of the Moro Islamic Liberation Front (MILF), a new generation of insurgents in southern Thailand would soon emerge and adopt an Islamist jihadist stance.

Internal Colonialism: The Southern Thai Economy

According to the Thai government's National Economic and Social Development Board, Muslim communities dominate two of the four poorest provinces. Narathiwat, the poorest province in the country, had a poverty rate of 45.6 percent in 2002, while Yala had a poverty rate of 37.9 percent.[64] This was significantly higher than the national poverty rate of 13 percent. Further, roughly 21 percent of the population of the three provinces earned less than Bt820 (US$17) per month. The latest available statistics suggest that the per capita income in the predominantly Muslim provinces is about Bt40,000 (US$829) a year, which is less than half of the national average of Bt81,000 (US$1,679).[65] And considering that the Buddhist and ethnic Chinese communities dominate the economy, retail and wholesale trade, and professional positions in the south, the Malay community specifically remains plagued by unemployment and underemployment. The government provision of health care, education, and welfare has also been inadequate. According to Aurel Croissant, an assistant professor at the Naval Postgraduate School, the southern region is dramatically worse off than it was forty years ago relative to Thailand as a whole (see Table 1.1).[66]

---

63. New PULO's leaders, Ar-rong Moo-reng and Hayi Abdul Rohman Bazo, likewise went into exile. See "Separatists in Malaysia Flee Abroad," *Bangkok Post*, February 22, 1998.
64. Janchitfah, "Southern Muslims Plead for Understanding."
65. "Muslim Charities in the Spotlight," *Bangkok Post*, May 4, 2007.

Table 1.1: Relative Economic Status of the South versus Thailand as a Whole

	Household Income (percentage)		Gross Regional Product (percentage)	
	1962	2000	1962	1999
Whole Kingdom	100	100	100	100
Southern Region	120.7	091.8	126.2	68.7

Note: Entries represent relative percentages, with 100 as a baseline.
Source: Croissant, "Unrest in Southern Thailand."

Although the south is poor, the insurgency has never been just about economic marginalization. There is a strong sense of internal colonialism and relative deprivation. The Thai Malays seem more concerned with protecting their way of life and their identity than with developing the economy. For example, in one well-known case, the Muslim community (as well as some Buddhists) has held up a major development project that the Thai government believes would be a boon to the south's economy, citing environmental and other concerns.

And although there has also been some interest in establishing large-scale palm oil plantations in the south and talk of developing southern Thai ports and of establishing a halal food processing plant there to increase exports to the Middle East,[67] the security situation has deterred most investment there.[68]

At present, the provinces of Narathiwat, Yala, and Pattani contribute only 1.4 percent to the country's GDP. There is almost no industry in the region. Tourism accounts for about 30 percent of the regional economy; rubber accounts for 40 percent to 50 percent; and the remainder is from agriculture and fishing.[69] The region is overwhelmingly agrarian. According to 2003 census data, the latest available, 56.9

---

66. Aurel Croissant, "Unrest in Southern Thailand: Contours, Causes, and Consequences Since 2001," *Strategic Insights* 4, no. 2 (February 2005): 6.

67. David Fulbrook, "An Economic Battle, Too," *Asia Times*, December 14, 2004.

68. "Investor Interested in Pattani's Palm Oil Industry," Thai News Agency, December 20, 2004.

69. Fulbrook, "An Economic Battle, Too."

percent of the population is engaged in agriculture.[70] While 91.5 percent of the farmers own their own land, the average landholding of 17.3 *rai* (seven acres) is less than the national average of 19.8 rai.[71] Only 1.5 percent of the labor force in the three provinces identifies itself as an employer; people identify themselves principally as being either self-employed (33.5 percent), an unpaid family worker (24.3 percent), or an employee (40.3 percent).[72] Just as much of the economy is dominated by the rubber industry, so too is much of the employment. However, rubber tappers work for only a few hours a day, around dawn, hence there are high rates of underemployment. No sector is terribly strong. The tourism industry in Sungai Golok and Hat Yai, for example, is heavily reliant on sex tourists from Malaysia and Singapore. Moreover, of all tourism-related jobs, locals hold only 60 percent of them. Further, within the first two years of the insurgency, tourism dropped by 24 percent in Narathiwat alone.[73] More recently, economists estimated that tourism in Hat Yai, the center of wholesale trade and finance in southern Thailand through which much of the world's latex rubber passes, would decline by 13 percent because of the violence—which would account for more than Bt2 billion (US$50.7 million) in lost revenue.[74]

Additionally, fisheries in the Gulf of Thailand already have been depleted by large trawlers from the north and by foreign ships, and there has been a lack of investment in agribusiness, despite the region's fertile lands. With 57 percent of the land in the south under rubber cultivation, the three southern provinces produce 600,000 tons of natural rubber annually, 20 percent of the national total.[75] Although rubber markets have been booming in recent years, small-scale producers (the majority in southern Thailand) do not have enough land to replant trees, which take roughly seven years to become productive. In fact, rubber output in the south was down 6 percent in 2005, and land prices have fallen by 50 percent.

---

70. *2003 Agricultural Census* (Bangkok: National Statistical Office, 2003).

71. Ibid.

72. *2000 Population and Housing Census.*

73. Martin Petty, "Bombs Take Their Toll on Sex Tourism," *Thai Day*, January 10, 2006.

74. "Violence Affects Tourism in South," Thai News Agency, February 25, 2007.

75. "Militant Order Keeps Thai Rubber Tappers Home," Reuters, July 9, 2005.

Perhaps the most important part of the south's economy is the remittances from the nearly 230,000 people (one-fifth of the south's workforce) working in Malaysia, who remit an estimated Bt6 billion (US$152 million) annually.[76] Further, aside from security concerns, there is very little prospect of the southern Thai region successfully courting foreign investment and developing a manufacturing base because of a lack of education among the potential workforce. According to the 2003 census, 37.5 percent of the population in Yala, Narathiwat, and Pattani between the ages of six and twenty-four were not in school.[77] The situation has only gotten worse as schools and teachers have been systematically targeted by insurgents for more than three years, keeping schools shuttered for months on end.

Given these statistics, perhaps it is not surprising that former prime minister Thaksin saw the insurgency as an economically driven one: "[The] Thai government realized that southern border provinces have been underdeveloped and we now plan to change that by promoting the regional economic growth, which would narrow the gap in economic status between people in the deep south and those in other parts of the nation. We would improve their education, their skills, and their economic opportunity."[78] To that end, he pledged US$300 million in aid for the south, believing that anything could be resolved through cash disbursements.

Lingering Grievances

Despite the government's attempts to address the underlying causes of the previous generation's insurgency, the Muslim community in the south still has numerous grievances. These grievances relate broadly to (1) education and language, (2) assimilation, (3) social justice, (4) morality, and (5) institutionalized racism.

First, the Muslim community has complained that it has few domestic religious higher education facilities and that the Ministry of Education gives academic recognition to only a handful of Islamic universities

---

76. Ibid.

77. *2000 Population and Housing Census.*

78. Quoted in "Thai Leader Kicks off Paper Birds for Peace Campaign," Thai News Agency, November 18, 2004.

abroad, making it hard for returning graduates to find work. The government also requires all Islamic schools to be registered and, thus, to use the government curriculum. Graduates from the roughly three hundred unregistered schools cannot sit for civil service exams, enter the military, or apply for tertiary education,[79] so unless they farm or have a family business, all they are capable of doing is running their own madrassas. Further, Thai Muslims have always resented the Ministry of Education's refusal to have a bilingual curriculum in the south's public schools.

Second, the Muslim community is angered by the government's campaign to assimilate them. The three pillars of Thai national identity are monarchy, state, and religion. While the monarchy is held in surprisingly high esteem in the south, owing to its long-standing presence and development projects in the region, the Thai monarch is still perceived as a Buddhist god-king. The state religion, Theravada Buddhism, is anathema to Islamic values. As a community that has traditionally identified more with Malaya, Thai Muslims especially resent more than a century's worth of forced assimilation through policies targeting education, clothing, language, and legal reforms. This resentment was only heightened in 2007 with debates over whether Buddhism would be named as the official state religion in the new constitution. Thais always refer to the Muslims of the south as "Thai Muslims," a complete misnomer. They are ethnic Malays.

Third, there is a very strong sense that the state operates in a culture of impunity, in which government, police, and military abuses are not properly dealt with, reinforcing the Muslims' notion that they are second-class citizens. Concerns about social justice are reinforced by levels of state violence in the south that are higher than national levels. Of the 2,500 people killed during Prime Minister Thaksin's war on drugs, the majority were in the south. No charges were ever filed against the government, police, or military, and the government continues to assert that the deaths were all related to violence among drug lords. Since the insurgency began, the culture of impunity has only become more embedded. Under the 2005 Emergency Decree, for example, government forces are totally immune from prosecution, a factor that further

---

79. Dalpino and Steinberg, *Georgetown Southeast Asia Survey*, 61.

drives a wedge between the Muslim community and the Thai state. Muslims have low levels of trust toward the judicial system.

Fourth, the Muslim community in the south is deeply concerned about the alarming spread of Thai "values"—that is, secularism and real and perceived vices, such as prostitution, drugs, gambling, and karaoke. Muslims believe that these "values" represent corrupting influences that, like the Thai language, are eroding their cultural identity. The irony, of course, is that Malays from the neighboring state of Kelantan, which is controlled by the Islamist opposition party, tend to comprise most of the tourists to the region, a market force that is driving the surge in vice.

Fifth, Thai Buddhists tend to be very disparaging toward Muslims and have little trust toward them. Thais, including Thai government officials in the south, often refer to southerners as *khaek*, a term that is usually translated as a visitor or resident alien—that is, they imply that the Muslims are not Thai. While the Thais believe that the term is not a pejorative, the Muslim community clearly believes it is. For the Muslims it is ample evidence that they are the victims of institutionalized racism and that the Thais are prejudiced. This prejudice likely makes it more difficult for Muslims to identify with the Thai state. As Robert Albritton found, more than half of the Thai-speaking Muslims and one-fourth of the Malay-speaking Muslims self-identify as being Thais first.[80]

Although the government initiated a successful counterinsurgency campaign that led to a decade-long cessation of hostilities during which a generation of insurgents reentered normal civilian life, its inability to address these grievances created the needed space for a small group of hard-core militants to indoctrinate and recruit a new generation of militants—just as a new, widely popular Thai politician, a former policeman and successful entrepreneur, rose to power.

---

80. Albritton, "The Muslim South in the Context of the Thai Nation," 15.

2

Populism, Politics, and the War on Terror

P rime Minister Thaksin Shinawatra came into office in 2001 as a populist and staunch nationalist and as a candidate with a healthy dose of anti-American rhetoric. Accordingly, he was slow to respond to the 9/11 attacks,[1] hiding for several days behind the Association of Southeast Asian Nations' (ASEAN's) collective statement condemning the attacks. He initially stated that Thailand would be "neutral" in the war on terror and even equivocated on the issue of military overflight. As Deputy Prime Minister Thammarak Isarankul na Ayuthaya explained at the time, "We [Thailand] would not want to help the U.S. in perpetrating a war . . . [as] Thailand could become vulnerable to terrorists if it showed a strong alliance with the U.S."[2] But Thaksin came under immediate attack from many high-ranking bureaucrats in the Ministry of Foreign Affairs and the leadership of the Royal Thai Army (RTA) for not living up to Thailand's treaty commitments with the United States.[3] Pressured to be more supportive of the United States, Thaksin changed his tune within days, stating, "Thailand will cooperate with the United States and the United Nations to eliminate

---

1. Although the events of 9/11 clearly served as a catalyst for the insurgency, the insurgency in southern Thailand is largely independent of the global war on terror and would have erupted around the same time even without the terrorist attacks on the United States. This does not mean, however, that the Thai government's response to the insurgency was not colored by the global war on terror. The political calculus of one has affected the other, with the war on terror framing the Thai reaction to the insurgency.

2. The United States did not publicly request the use of Thai military facilities as it did during the 1991 Gulf War, when U.S. bombers used Thai airfields, but when the bombing of Afghanistan began on October 8, 2001, there were reports that U.S. forces used the U-Tapao airfield. "Thailand Will Stay Strictly Neutral," *Nation*, September 15, 2001.

3. Thailand and the United States are bound by two agreements: the 1954 Manila Pact and the 1962 Communiqué. In addition, the two countries hold the annual Cobra Gold military exercises, the largest bilateral exercises in the region.

terrorism."[4] Additionally, the Ministry of Foreign Affairs announced that, as a "longtime friend and treaty ally," Thailand would "render all possible assistance to the United States as Thailand has done consistently in the past."[5]

Although Thailand agreed to implement UN Security Council Resolution 1368,[6] its support of the U.S. campaign was halfhearted, both for fear of the impact such support would have on the insurgency in the south and because of lingering anti-Americanism that had developed within Thailand in the late 1990s. Members of parliament were particularly resentful toward America's tepid response to Thailand's economic crisis in 1997–98. The head of the Thai Senate Foreign Relations Committee, Kraisak Choonhavan, angrily remarked, "The U.S. did nothing to help when the economic crisis started with Thailand." He warned that the prime minister had to get parliamentary approval before "making any military commitment." Another senator demanded that the government confirm whether U.S. forces were using the U-Tapao airfield and expressed outrage that Thailand was "being dragged into what could be a prolonged war."[7] Some legislators even considered scrapping the 1996 Thai-U.S. acquisition and cross-servicing agreement, which was to expire in 2003.[8]

In October 2001, Thailand ultimately joined with its ASEAN partners Malaysia, Indonesia, and the Philippines to create an antiterror network, although it publicly downplayed the threat posed by Islamist terrorism within its borders for fear of hurting the country's investment climate and international tourism. The Thai intelligence sector also played a role in the country's tepid response, as it did not take the threat of Islamist terrorism very seriously either. As one Thai critic put it,

---

4. "Thailand Gives Support to War on Terrorism," *Bangkok Post*, September 17, 2001.
5. Ibid.
6. UN Security Council Resolution 1368 committed all nations to assist in efforts to combat al-Qaeda.
7. "Thailand Gives Support to War on Terrorism."
8. The agreement obligates Thailand to provide bases, refueling services, communications equipment, repair and maintenance facilities, and warehouses. In return, the United States provides weapons and training for Thai military personnel through the Foreign Military Sales program. See Wassana Nanuam, "US Military Pact Could Be Scrapped Before Expiry Date," *Bangkok Post*, October 13, 2001; "Utapao Explanation Demanded," *Bangkok Post*, October 10, 2001.

"Obviously, the Thai intelligence agents had full knowledge of the presence of an al-Qaeda network in Thailand, even before the 11 September bombings. But they did not say so publicly, as they believed that this network . . . was a benign one: . . . [The al-Qaeda presence] did not target the Thai people. As such, the government was reluctant to adopt pro-active and tough counter-measures."[9] For example, following al-Qaeda's January 2000 planning meeting in Kuala Lumpur, Malaysia, two of the 9/11 hijackers, Khalid al Mindhar and Nawaq al Hazmi, passed through Thailand but were not adequately tracked. Admittedly, this could have been the fault of U.S. intelligence officials, who may not have requested assistance from their Thai counterparts.[10]

Despite Thailand's initial equivocation, some Thai officials did begin to publicly acknowledge or at least recognize the terrorist threat as the government became increasingly aware that countries in the Middle East were providing "training, education and financial support for fundamentalist groups in the south [of Thailand]."[11] As a result, Thailand quietly began to respond to the United States in several positive ways, particularly with regard to combating al-Qaeda. Thai supreme commander Gen. Surayud Chulanont, for one, admitted that military intelligence was monitoring a "small number" of operatives in Thailand.[12]

Then, in March 2002, Thai authorities arrested twenty-five Middle Eastern men suspected of laundering al-Qaeda funds in the kingdom, charging several of them with forging travel documents, passports, and visas for al-Qaeda members.[13] Thai authorities also shut down three al-Qaeda front companies—Jallil Trading Ltr Co. Ltd., Al Amanah Enterprise Co. Ltd., and Sidco Co. Ltd.—and tipped off U.S. and Canadian officials about an al-Qaeda operative[14], Muhammad Man-

---

9. Kavi Chongkittavorn, "Al-Qaeda in Thailand: Fact or Fiction?" *Nation*, January 13, 2003.

10. *The 9/11 Commission Report* (New York: W. W. Norton, 2004), 181–182.

11. John McBeth, "The Danger within," *Far Eastern Economic Review*, 22–23.

12. Ibid.

13. "Thailand a Transit Point for Terror Funds," *Straits Times*, March 11, 2002.

14. For more, see Zachary Abuza, "Funding Terrorism in Southeast Asia: The Financial Network of Al Qaeda and Jemaah Islamiyah," *NBR [National Bureau of Asian Research] Analysis* 14, no. 5 (December 2003): 39.

sour Jabarah, as he left Thailand for the United Arab Emirates, where he as arrested.

Further, in late 2003, Thai and U.S. security officials analyzed Thai immigration data and found that 128 "followers of al-Qaeda," including six Jemaah Islamiyah (JI) members, had passed through the country.15 Although a watch list of some 220 individuals was established, in some cases the Thai government was unable or unwilling to track JI operatives. For example, one of bin Laden's top deputies, Walid Muhammad Salih bin Attash (Khallad bin Attash), who masterminded the USS Cole attack in Yemen on October 12, 2000, lived in Thailand and Cambodia from early 2002 to August 2003.

Generally speaking, Thai officials seemed fairly blasé about the possibility of an attack on their country throughout this period, yet the information provided by detained al-Qaeda operatives makes it clear that as far back as mid-2000 Thailand was being considered as a target.[16] In 2000, Khalid Sheikh Muhammad discussed the possibility of attacks in Thailand, Singapore, and Indonesia with Muhammad Atef, al-Qaeda's chief of military operations, and ordered senior al-Qaeda and JI operational coordinator and regional operations chief Riduan Isamudin (also known as Hambali) to select "Jewish targets in Thailand." Video of potential target sites was shot and tapes were sent to the al-Qaeda leadership in Afghanistan.[17] *The 9/11 Commission Report* contends that Osama bin Laden approved of these plans but wanted Muhammad to concentrate on the 9/11 attacks.[18]

If the Thai government gave some support to operations against al-Qaeda, Thai cooperation was much less forthcoming with regard to JI. Following the crackdown on JI in Malaysia and Singapore in late fall

---

15. The six Singaporean nationals were Mas Salamat Kastari (now detained in Indonesia), Ahmed Sahgi, Hassan bin Islamial, Zainal Abidin, Muhammad Rashid, Ishak Muhammad Noohu, and Muhammad Hassan bin Sayudin. Prayuth Sivayaviroj and Kavi Chongkittavorn, "Key Terrorists Passing through Kingdom," *Nation*, November 26, 2003.

16. Thailand had earlier been the focus of a March 1994 Hezbollah plot to blow up the Israeli Embassy in Bangkok, but the plot went awry in its final stages and was not executed.

17. *9/11 Commission Report*, 150.

18. Ibid.

2001, large numbers of JI members crossed into southern Thailand, where they were able to take advantage of kinship, friendship, and mosque and madrassa networks to lie low. JI senior operative Ali Ghufron (Mukhlas), for one, spent time in southern Thailand before traveling to Indonesia to take part in the Bali bombing. Around the same time, Singaporean JI senior leader Mas Salamat Kastari also passed through Thailand before traveling to Indonesia.[19] Some JI members, such as Wan Min bin Wan Mat, were captured, but only after they crossed back into Malaysia. Hambali is believed to have held a major policy meeting in Bangkok in January 2002 that laid out the plan for the October 2002 Bali attack. Although they acknowledge that Hambali and other JI officials passed through the kingdom, Thai authorities assert that no such meeting took place. According to Thailand's top counterterrorism official, Maj. Gen. Tritot Ronnaritivichai, "The only plans they were making in Thailand were where to run next."[20] Although he further asserted that Thai officials tracked the JI operatives, they did not arrest any of the operatives or their Thai liaisons.

Despite the rhetoric, cooperation between Thailand and the United States continued. In 2002 the fully U.S.-funded Joint Counter-Terrorism Intelligence Center (CTIC) was jointly established by Thai intelligence agencies and the Central Intelligence Agency (CIA).[21] That same year, Thailand signed the ASEAN-U.S. Joint Declaration on Counter-Terrorism. Thailand's offer of an airbase at U-Tapao for operations in Afghanistan indicated closeness at the operational level, if not at the political level.[22] But arguably the most important cooperative initiative stemmed from a secret 2002 agreement that opened up a Thai military facility (believed to be Sattahip naval station) for the secret rendition and interrogation of high-level al-Qaeda suspects. As Dana Priest of the

---

19. For more, see Andrew Perrin, "The Hard Cell," *Time–Asian Edition*, June 23, 2003.

20. Shawn W. Crispin, "Thais Clash With the FBI," *Far Eastern Economic Review*, February 13, 2003; Crispin, "Thailand Tracked Terrorists, Official Reveals," *Far Eastern Economic Review*, February 13, 2003.

21. "CIA, Thai Agencies United Against Terrorism," *Australian Financial Review*, October 2, 2002.

22. Raymond Bonner, "Thailand Tiptoes in Step with American Anti-Terror Efforts," *New York Times*, June 7, 2003.

Washington Post wrote in her exposé of the CIA's network of clandestine interrogation centers,

> Pakistani forces took Abu Zubaida, al Qaeda's operations chief, into custody and the CIA whisked him to the new black site in Thailand, which included underground interrogation cells. . . . Six months later, Sept. 11 planner Ramzi bin al Shibh was also captured in Pakistan and flown to Thailand. . . . But after published reports revealed the existence of the site in June 2003, Thai officials insisted the CIA shut it down, and the two terrorists were moved elsewhere.[23]

Later media reports revealed that the CIA interrogation centers in Thailand were where senior al-Qaeda members had been waterboarded.[24]

Thailand cooperated in other ways, most notably in border security. The U.S. government helped finance a major computerization effort to document (including photographs) all foreign nationals entering and leaving the kingdom, as well as a new generation of passport scanners. Thailand also stepped up efforts to investigate document fraud and smuggling.[25]

---

23. Dana Priest, "CIA Holds Terror Suspects in Secret Prisons," *Washington Post*, November 5, 2006. Thaksin accused journalists who wrote about Priest's exposé of being "unpatriotic."

24. "CIA Lawyer Reaffirms Torture Jail Did Exist," *Nation*, January 18, 2008; "Tortured in Thailand," *Bangkok Post*, January 18, 2008.

25. These efforts included the arrest in August 2005 of two ethnic Algerians who had 638 passports between them: Mahiededine Daikh was arrested on August 2 at Bangkok's airport in possession of 452 fake passports; Atamnia Yachine was arrested in Bangkok shortly thereafter in connection with the Daikh investigation and had possession of 186 fake French and Spanish passports. Yachine had long been a suspect in the sale of forged documents. According to press reports, British authorities issued a warrant for Yachine's arrest in 1995 when his fingerprints were found on a parcel that contained two hundred passports. British police believe that Yachine supplied fake travel documents to the July 7, 2005, London bombers. Despite a British government request for Yachine's extradition, "He pleaded guilty in court and got a three-year jail term," a Thai police spokesman said. The British government's extradition request for Daikh is still being processed. In March 2006, two South Asian men were arrested in Bangkok for allegedly making forged passports—and selling them for Bt50,000 (US$1,349) each. They were caught with twenty-three passports in their possession—twenty-one of them were copies of Indian passports, one was a copy of a Hong Kong passport, and one was a copy of a German passport.

Cooperation between Thailand and its ASEAN counterparts also increased greatly. Several JI operatives, including Arifin bin Ali (John Wong Ah Hung) and Zubair Muhammad, were captured in joint Singaporean-Thai operations in May and June 2003, respectively.[26] More notably, Hambali was captured in the central Thai city of Ayutthaya on August 11, 2003, along with two accomplices, Bashir bin Lap (Lillie) and Awang Ibrihim, a Thai member of a local jihadist organization, Jemaah Salafi.[27]

Explaining Thaksin's Behavior

Although Thailand could have offered stronger cooperation to the United States and done much more to stem Islamist militancy in the south in the 2002–04 period, Thaksin simply did not have the political will to offer or do more. As the CIA succinctly reported to Congress in 2003,

> Although Thai officials have privately given strong support for US counterterrorist efforts, Thailand's efforts are limited by legal limitations on tackling terrorist-related offenses, resource shortfalls, and a porous border with Malaysia. Cultural barriers also pose a problem; the vast majority of Thai security personnel are Buddhist, do not speak the local Malay dialect used by the southern Muslims, and are mistrusted by the Muslim population. The Thai government also is concerned about sparking unrestrained dissatisfaction

---

26. Arifin bin Ali was arrested on May 16, 2003, at the request of the Singaporean Internal Security Department. A Chinese convert to Islam, he often went by his given name, John Wong Ah Hung. He married a Thai Muslim and was a senior Singaporean JI member and trainer who had spent time in MILF camps in Mindanao. He fled to Malaysia in December 2001 and then to Thailand in January 2002. He was wanted along with Mas Salamat Kastari for plotting to hijack an Aeroflot jetliner from Bangkok and crash it in Singapore. The Thai government announced that he had also plotted to blow up Western embassies during the Asia Pacific Economic Cooperation (APEC) summit in Bangkok in October 2003. Currently, he is detained under Singapore's Internal Security Act. Zubair Muhammad was an important finance operative for JI and a close personal assistant to Hambali. "Bangkok Plays Terror Cards Close to Its Chest," *Nation*, July 29, 2003; "Thaksin Discloses Plot to Bomb Embassies," *Bangkok Post*, June 15, 2003; "Jemaah Islamiyah (JI) Special, Part III: Suspects Squeezed out to Thailand," *Nation*, July 31, 2003.

27. Awang Ibrihim was married to the sister of Sman Ismail, a Thai national living in Cambodia who was a close associate of Hambali. Neither was a member of JI, but they were loyal to and worked directly for Hambali.

among Muslims in the south, with whom they have made efforts over the past decade to integrate into the national polity.[28]

In truth, Thaksin's erratic behavior regarding the global war on terror and the southern situation was driven largely by political self-interest, with his policies reflecting his nationalist and populist platform. He was not so much anti-American as he was pro-Thaksin, particularly with regard to his economic and political agendas.[29]

The cornerstone of Thaksin's administration was the rehabilitation of Thailand's economy in the wake of the Asian economic crisis of 1997–99. Thaksin was especially wary of adopting policies that would make Thailand a terrorist target. He knew that a Bali-like attack would devastate the Thai tourism industry, which in turn would have major and immediate spillover effects on foreign direct investment, banking and finance, consumer and investor confidence, and ultimately on the economic health of the still-fragile Thai economy. While Indonesia's financial markets had already factored in the possibility of a terrorist attack, Thailand's had not, meaning a terrorist incident would have had an especially devastating effect on its financial markets.

But to truly understand Thaksin's behavior, one really has to understand his political calculus. Thaksin's Thai Rak Thai Party (TRT) won a landslide election in January 2001. He dominated Thai politics as few political leaders had. By 2005, he had not only won re-election but his party had also become the first to ever win an outright majority of seats in the Thai parliament. Even so, Thaksin rarely showed up before parliament, governing by decree. He was out to totally dominate Thai politics, paying only lip service to democratic norms, and the south was his *bête noire*.

Since 1975 the south has been the stronghold of the Democrat Party, currently the country's leading (and only real) opposition party.[30] In the 2001 elections, for example, of the south's fifty-four parliamentary seats, the Democrat Party controlled forty-eight, the New Aspiration Party

---

28. CIA, "Unclassified Responses to the Worldwide Threat, [Congressional] Hearing of February 11, 2003," August 18, 2003, 159–160.

29. Pasuk Phongpaichit and Chris Baker, *Thaksin: The Business of Politics in Thailand* (Bangkok: Silkworm Books, 2004).

30. McCargo, "Southern Thai Politics," 14–16.

controlled five, and Thaksin's TRT controlled only one.[31] The Democrat Party's two best-known politicians—former prime minister Chuan Leek Pai and former foreign minister Surin Pitsuwan—hail from the south, as does its previous leader, Banyat Bantadtan. As Duncan McCargo of Leeds University put it, "Thaksin saw the deep south as hostile territory for his Thai Rak Thai party, a sub-region dominated by officials loyal to Prem, the Palace and the democrats."[32]

Thaksin was determined to win the south by undermining the Democrat Party. He wooed a group of Thai Muslims, the Wadah faction, which had split from the Democrat Party and then the New Aspiration Party, to become the face of the TRT in the south. Wadah's leader, Wan Muhammad Noor Matha, became Thaksin's minister of interior. Wan Muhammad and Thaksin feared that overt cooperation with the United States would inflame Muslim hostility in the south and hurt the TRT's electoral standing. Thaksin was particularly averse to any policy that would be unpopular there, as he sought to erode the Democrat Party's base of support in the run-up to the February 6, 2005, election.[33]

This political calculus played itself out with devastating effect when Thaksin dismantled the long-standing bodies that had helped quash the insurgency. The south traditionally has been under the army's control and since 1981 had been administered through the SBPAC.[34] Beginning in the 1990s, however, as the insurgency ebbed, the Ministry of the Interior began to push the military to relinquish control of the south. With Thaksin's election, the ministry finally had high-level political support for its position. In May 2002, he transferred security authority in the south from the army to the Ministry of the Interior and the police and dissolved the SBPAC and its joint security command, CPM-43.[35] He even purged or relocated the majority of the officers of these bodies,

---

31. See www.ect.go.th/english (accessed October 1, 2008).

32. Duncan McCargo, "Network Monarchy and Legitimacy Crises in Thailand," *Pacific Review* 18, no. 4 (December 2005): 514.

33. "The Real Problems of the Muslim South," *Nation*, April 7, 2002.

34. The SBPAC was at first a Ministry of the Interior inspectorate that grew to include security, governance, and dispute resolution.

35. Prof. Srisompop Jitprimosi attributes the spike in violence to the dissolution of the military-run agencies. See Noppadol Phetcharat, "Major Spike in Violence under This Government—Study," *Nation*, December 20, 2004; Lopez and Crispin, "Fighting Back"; "Trouble Down South," *Economist*, January 17, 2004.

largely because of his suspicion that they were too close to the Democrat Party. The army was furious about the loss of prestige, prime assignments guaranteeing visibility and promotion, and control over the lucrative cross-border trade and smuggling routes, and perceived Thaksin's policy as police-oriented favoritism. Making matters worse, Thaksin then appointed three political allies from the TRT to the governorships of the three southern provinces. None had experience in the south or understood the complexities of the situation, and none were respectful of the Muslim communities. This infuriated the local population. If the citizens of Bangkok could elect their own governor, why would southerners not be allowed to elect theirs?

Despite its failings, the SBPAC served as an important dispute-resolution forum where citizens could raise complaints about corrupt and abusive officials and express their grievances. As McCargo explained, "Although ostensibly motivated by a desire to rein in the excesses of the Fourth Army, which had long been a law unto itself in the deep south, Thaksin's actions undermined a delicate local social contract, and quickly precipitated a wave of extrajudicial killings and disappearances."[36] For example, in 1981, the SBPAC, under the leadership of Charoenjit na Songkhla, a former Songkhla governor, succeeded in bringing southern violence under control by ordering a mass transfer of more than two hundred officers, mostly police, who were alleged to have mistreated locals, giving people a small sense of social justice.[37]

More important, this dissolution created a terrible loss of intelligence gathering, as the police had no human intelligence (HUMINT) network comparable to the one established by the military over the previous thirty years. "[The Royal Thai Army's] HUMINT [apparatus] was very capable," noted one Thai security adviser.[38] As Panitan Wattanayagorn of Chulalongkorn University explained at the time, "The transitional period [between the military and the police] has led to a power vacuum, and the police are having a terrible time seeing the big picture."[39] The police were complacent and notoriously corrupt. The police arrested and systematically killed many of the army's informers,

36. McCargo, "Network Monarchy," 514.

37. "Southern Unrest/Chavalit's Comments," *Bangkok Post*, January 4, 2006.

38. Author interview, Bangkok, March 16, 2005.

39. Quoted in Lopez and Crispin, "Fighting Back."

further crippling their intelligence mechanism. When the National Intelligence Agency (NIA) reported on police hit squads in 2003, the police raided the NIA's southern headquarters and seized all of its documents. The close interagency collaboration and coordination under the SBPAC had given way to turf wars.[40]

By many accounts, the military withheld intelligence from the police and appeared to be content to watch the police fail. As the insurgency began to unfold in 2003, the military sat tight, watching the police struggle with the situation. When martial law was declared in January 2004, the military wasted no time stepping back in and assuming total control.[41]

Om al-Qura and the Thai-Cambodian Nexus

One case in particular demonstrated Thai resistance to dealing with JI. As noted, Arifin bin Ali was arrested in May 2003 in a joint operation with Singapore.[42] But Singaporean security officials later complained that it took them eight months to convince their Thai counterparts to arrest him. Similarly, critics of the Thaksin administration complained that although the interrogation of Ali revealed an important al-Qaeda presence in both Thailand and Cambodia,[43] Thai security officials waited to act on the information, only doing so on the day that Thaksin met with President George W. Bush at the White House and Thailand received major non-NATO ally status.

The Arifin bin Ali interrogation resulted in the arrest of six Thai citizens in southern Thailand and Cambodia in May–June 2003. The arrests centered around a relatively unknown Saudi charity, the Om al-Qura (OAQ) Foundation, and the better known Saudi charity Al

---

40. Author interview, Pattani, August 15, 2005.

41. "Thai Troops Sent to Troubled South," BBC, April 29, 2004.

42. "Bangkok Plays Terror Cards Close to Its Chest," *Nation*, July 29, 2003.

43. The traditionally Muslim ethnic Cham community in Cambodia was decimated under the Khmer Rouge, but the influx of Malaysian and Persian Gulf funding (Saudi and Kuwaiti, in particular) has led to a revival of the community. There are now 269 mosques and 400 madrassas in Cambodia. This funding has also led to the spread of Wahhabism: approximately 20 percent of Chams belong to the Saudi sect, and it is the fastest growing segment of the Muslim community.

Haramain.[44] However, the politically motivated timing of the arrests led to a popular backlash against the government.

The OAQ, which has offices in Bosnia, Somalia, Cambodia, and southern Thailand, ostensibly was established to address the needs of the minority Muslim populations in those countries. In Cambodia, the foundation ran an Islamic school in Kandal Province, Al Mukara, for grades seven through ten. The school enrolled approximately 580 students and was 100 percent funded by OAQ. The teachers hailed from Yemen, Sudan, Egypt, Nigeria, Pakistan, and Thailand. Al-Qaeda used the OAQ for "significant money transfers" for both itself and JI,[45] and the foundation is believed to have laundered several million dollars for al-Qaeda through its network of offices.[46] Al Mukara was receiving US$10,000 wire transfers each month into its account at the Cambodian Public Bank.[47] The men behind the operation were the founders of the OAQ: an Egyptian named Yaser Elsayed Mohamed Rousha and a Malaysian named Zubair Muhammad, who joined al-Qaeda as a student in Karachi, Pakistan.[48]

On May 28, 2003, following Arifin bin Ali's interrogation, three employees of the foundation—an Egyptian, Esam Mohamid Khadir Ali, and two Thai Muslims, Haji Thiming Abdul Aziz and Muhammad Jalludin Mading—were arrested for plotting to carry out terrorist attacks in Cambodia, including one against the British Embassy.[49]

---

44. Al Haramain's offices in Indonesia were designated as a terrorist front by the United Nations in January 2004. For more on the OAQ, see Noy Thrupkaew, "Follow the (Saudi) Money," *American Prospect* (August 2004), 58–61.

45. Quoted in Perrin, "The Hard Cell."

46. Author interview, Bangkok, July 31, 2003; Ker Munthit, "3 Muslim Foreigners Arrested in Cambodia," Associated Press, May 28, 2003; Ek Madra, "Cambodia Cracks Down on Foreign Muslims," Reuters, May 28, 2003.

47. For more, see Perrin, "The Hard Cell."

48. Zubair's July 2003 arrest led authorities to the capture of Hambali, who was the brains behind laundering al-Qaeda money through schools, nurseries, and orphanages throughout the region. The most important vehicle for money laundering was the OAQ. In Malaysia, he ran Aliran Salam Sdn. Bhd., a kindergarten and nursery that was also involved in money laundering.

49. The threat of terrorism in the predominantly Buddhist nation was already high. On the basis of Omar al-Faruq's confession and the confession of Mohammed Mansour Jabarah, both in U.S. custody, U.S. embassies in Malaysia, Indonesia, Cambodia, and Vietnam were shut down for the first anniversary of the 9/11 attacks. There was also

Soon after, a fourth suspect, a Cambodian Muslim named Sman Ismael, was arrested.[50] Haji Thiming was the conduit of money to the JI cells in southern Thailand and was linked to four suspected Thai JI members who were controversially arrested in June 2003.[51]

Although the four arrests were made as a result of investigations into the OAQ and the debriefing of Arifin bin Ali, they took place in southern Thailand on the eve of Prime Minister Thaksin's meeting with President Bush at the White House, leading to charges that the arrests were simply Thailand bowing to U.S. pressure.[52] The first arrest was of Waema Hadi Wae Dao, a doctor and owner of a pharmacy who was a respected elder in the community. A 1986 graduate of Prince of Songkhla University in Pattani, he studied in Egypt at Azahase Islamic College, where he became involved in radical Islamic politics.[53] International donors helped fund his twelve-bed hospital in Narathiwat. He denied being a member of JI but admitted that he forged passports for JI members. A Thai academic explained that Waema Hadi appeared on the radar screen of security services because he treated JI members and militants; without being a member, he was sympathetic and provided assistance.[54] The second and third arrests were of Maisuri Bozoru Haji Abdullah, a religious schoolmaster at Islam Burana Tohno, and his son, Muyahi Haji Doloh.[55] The father and son at first admitted to being

---

concern that the ASEAN Foreign Ministers' Meeting, to be held in Phnom Penh in June 2003, would be targeted. Hambali later confessed that the U.S. Embassy in Cambodia had been discussed as a possible target. By September 2003, Cambodian authorities were considering releasing the Egyptian, Esam Mohamid Jhadir Ali, because of a lack of evidence. See Romesh Ratnesar, "Confessions of an Al Qaeda Terrorist," *Time*, September 16, 2002; Raymond Bonner, "Plan to Attack Embassies in South Asia Cited for Terror Alert," *New York Times*, September 1, 2002; Indonesian National Intelligence Agency (BIN), "Interrogation Report of Omar al-Faruq," June 2002.

50. Sman, who was educated in southern Thailand, revealed to Cambodian authorities that Hambali was in Cambodia.

51. The Thai detainees were Maisuri Haji Bozoru Abdollah, Maisuri Muyahi Haji Doloh, Waemahdi Wae-dao, and Samarn Waekaji.

52. For more, see Perrin, "The Hard Cell"; Supara Janchitfah, "Insecurity in the South," *Bangkok Post*, June 15, 2003.

53. For more on Waema Hadi Wae Dao, see Janchitfah, "Insecurity in the South."

54. Author interview, Bangkok, August 13, 2005.

55. The school has approximately two hundred students and is being monitored closely by Thai security forces. Maisuri Haji Abdullah announced his intentions

members of JI, but they later denied it during their trial, stating that their confessions were coerced.[56] The fourth arrest was of Samarn Waekaji, Arifin bin Ali's liaison and the key planner of an attempted bombing of five Western embassies in Bangkok.[57] He turned himself in.[58] At the time, authorities announced that they were looking for five more suspects, that eighteen other suspects were under close watch, and that eighteen pondoks were being scrutinized.[59]

Critics of Thaksin contend that there was not one convincing arrest based on Arifin bin Ali's interrogation. Waema Hadi's allegations that his confessions were coerced received the support of leading politicians such as Sen. Kraisak Choonhaven.[60] Indeed, the court case against the four collapsed in June 2005. The court ruled that "no evidence was found that they were setting up a JI network or gathering people to launch a terrorist attack."[61] Security officials still believe the four were guilty, but the major piece of evidence against them—the confession of Arifin bin Ali—was thrown out on a technicality.[62] In April 2006, Waema Hadi was elected to the Senate.

The Hambali Fallout

In August 2003, Hambali, along with two of his key aides, Bashir bin Lap (Lillie) and Awang Ibrihim, were arrested in the Thai city of Ayut-thaya by a joint CTIC-CIA team. In the course of Hambali's interroga-tion, several issues related to Thailand emerged. Most notably, Hambali was planning to execute a major bombing in Bangkok. The alleged tar-

---

to run for parliament on the newly founded Thai Peace Party slate in the October 2006 elections.

56. Maisuri Haji Abdullah admitted to renting houses for JI members but not to being a member himself. "JI Terror Suspect Denies All Charges," *Nation*, February 2, 2005.

57. For more, see Perrin, "The Hard Cell."

58. "Terrorist Cell: 3 'JI Members' Arrested in the South," *Nation*, June 11, 2003; Nirmal Ghosh, "JI Timed Bomb Attacks for APEC Summit," *Sunday Times*, August 18, 2003; "Jemaah Islamiyah (JI) Special, Part III," *Nation*, July 31, 2003.

59. "Terrorist Cell," *Nation*, June 11, 2003.

60. "Kraisak: Bomb Plot Doctor Tortured to Confess," *Bangkok Post*, April 30, 2005.

61. "Thailand Terror Case Collapses," BBC, June 2, 2005.

62. Arifin bin Ali's confession was ruled hearsay and was thus inadmissible in Thai courts. The government decided not to appeal the verdict. "JI Acquittal Won't Be Appealed," *Nation*, July 7, 2005.

get was the J. W. Marriott Hotel on Sukhumvit Road, although other potential targets—such as Western embassies and the El Al (Israeli airlines) counter at Don Muang Airport—had been discussed. When this plot was abandoned, Hambali considered a smaller-scale attack (a firebombing) in the backpacker district of Bangkok known as Khao San Road. He dispatched Malaysian JI member Yazid Sufaat to Thailand to identify targets. Sufaat was accompanied by a local Thai mujahideen, Abu Hisham, who was reportedly in charge of logistics, including renting houses for Hambali.

Hambali coordinated these efforts with Abdul Fatah (Muhammad Haji Jaeming), a leading Thai jihadist and the head of a small radical group, Jemaah Salafi, whose assistant was a courier to the MILF in the southern Philippines. Abdul Fatah had attended the three JI-sponsored Rabitatul Mujahideen (RM) meetings in Malaysia in 1999–2000, which included members of other Salafi jihadist groups from the region and were designed to broaden JI's network and forge strategic alliances. Hambali entrusted him—as JI's emergency banker—with the safekeeping of al-Qaeda funds.

Hambali also approached Thailand's leading Wahhabite cleric, Ismail Lutfi Japagiya, to recruit personnel for the bombing campaign. Lutfi is the rector of Yala State University and president of the new, privately owned Yala Islamic College (YIC).[63] His followers are thought to number in the tens of thousands, many more than the 800 students at Yala State University and the 1,500 at Yala Islamic College (which, like many Islamic schools in southern Thailand, is funded primarily by Saudi money). Most of the Saudi funding comes through the Muslim World League (Rabitat al-Alam al-Islami, MWL) and its sister organization, the Islamic International Relief Organization (IIRO).[64] As a councillor

---

63. Lutfi is a graduate of Imam Muhammad bin Daud Islamic University, a hard-line Wahhabite institution in Riyadh, Saudi Arabia. The YIC has a staff of more than a dozen Arab teachers.

64. The Saudi royal family established the MWL in 1962 to support the propagation of Wahhabism. Most MWL officers travel on Saudi Arabian diplomatic passports or have diplomatic visas, as the MWL is directly connected to the Saudi government. The second Thai representative to the MWL is the TRT politician and former minister of the interior Wan Muhammad Noor Matha. The IIRO is believed to be the largest donor, not just in terms of aid but also in terms of the number of recipients of its largesse. The Thai minister of defense has accused the IIRO of donating more than

of the Muslim World League, Lutfi openly admits its financial support: "The Council of the Muslim World League has supported Muslim education in Thailand. It joins with other charity organizations around the world to give scholarships to poor Thai students to study abroad and donate money to build public properties in Thailand, including over 30 mosques and Yala Islamic College."[65] In a 2003 interview with the respected Thai English-language daily the *Nation*, Lutfi also admitted that he received some US$7.8 million for his school from Kuwait; much of that money is thought to have come through the OAQ.[66]

Although many of the regional security services describe Lutfi as a leading member of JI, there is no evidence to support this assertion. To be sure, he has provided logistical support to JI, such as transportation, safe houses, documents, and money transfers, and he has clear connections to members of the terrorist organization. For example, he hosted Mukhlas when the latter fled Malaysia in late 2001. He is also possibly a "talent scout" for the terrorist organization. When it came to Hambali's request, however, he demurred and refused to support their planned terrorist campaign. But why offer JI sanctuary and then keep it at bay?

As Sidney Jones of the International Crisis Group has demonstrated with regard to Indonesia, many Salafis believe that violent jihad distracts from the primary goal of full inculcation of Salafist Islamic principles and teachings.[67] However, Lutfi is overtly political—what pure Salafis term a "Sururist."[68] (Indeed, evidence suggests that Lutfi gets funding from the Sururiyah network.) His decision was not based on Islamic principle. Rather, as a shrewd politician, he recognized that a violent jihad would be counterproductive. For him, the potential for mass

---

Bt100 million (US$2 million) to Thai organizations. See John R. Bradley, "Waking up to the Terror Threat," *Straits Times*, May 27, 2004.

65. "Interview with Ismail Lutfi Japagiya," *Krungthep Thurakit* [Business Bangkok], n.d.

66. Author interview, Bangkok, June 24, 2005.

67. ICG, *Indonesia Backgrounder: Why Salafism and Terrorism Mostly Don't Mix*, Asia Report No. 83 (Singapore/Brussels: ICG, September 13, 2004).

68. Sururiyah networks are Salafi groups (such as the Muslim Brotherhood) that espouse advancing their agenda through political involvement rather than only through da'wah.

arrests, disappearances, and extrajudicial killings of Muslim clerics and community leaders was ultimately persuasive. Lutfi saw a low-level insurgency as more effective than a Bali-like bombing against a soft target that would result in a major crackdown by Thai forces.

Recognizing that such a crackdown would be disadvantageous to both himself and his ultimate goals, Lutfi instructed Abdul Fatah and his group, Jemaah Salafi, to stop supporting Hambali and deterred other Thai organizations from assisting JI. In the absence of central leadership over the mujahideen, respected figures, especially religious leaders such as Lutfi, held sway. Lutfi also encouraged JI to support the insurgency in the south in lieu of a terrorist campaign aimed at Western targets. Hambali reportedly told Khalid Sheikh Muhammad that the Thai insurgents were not supportive of his efforts. As a result, JI's subsequent efforts focused on Indonesia, the Philippines, and Singapore. In short, although Lutfi supports JI's ultimate goals, he finds its strategy—fighting the "far enemy," as defined by Abdullah Azzam, Osama bin Laden, and Ayman al-Zawahiri—to be less effective than concentrating on the "near enemy."

Despite evidence linking Lutfi to JI, as well as pressure from both U.S. and regional security services to detain the radical cleric, the Thai government has refused to move against him, or others. For instance, although the U.S. government has identified Abdul Fatah as a JI leader and offered a reward for his capture, he continues to live openly—if quietly—in the south. Moreover, as a slap in the face to both the Americans and Thailand's ASEAN counterparts, Thaksin approved the crown prince's attendance at the opening of new buildings at Lutfi's YIC in February 2003. With this high-profile meeting, Lutfi was accorded protection from prosecution. In return, Thaksin expected Lutfi to publicly denounce JI and terrorism. According to Thai journalists, Lutfi became immune to public criticism.

The Thais came to see Lutfi as an important ally: in early 2004, he was appointed to both the National Reconciliation Commission (NRC) and the Southern Border Provinces Peace Building Command (SBPPC). Although NRC chairman Anand Panyarachun demanded that Lutfi publicly denounce the militants' violence, he continued to refuse to do so. While he has publicly failed to denounce both terrorism and JI and at times has engaged in anti-American polemics, he has maintained a lower profile. In recent interviews, he has portrayed himself as a victim: "We are between the violence of the people and violence from the state. We are caught between two guns, not only volleys of verbal abuse."[69] Yet, there is a growing belief within the government that Lutfi is not part of the solution.[70]

The Politicization of Thai Security and Its Consequences

So many of the problems in the south emerged because of Thaksin's attempt to consolidate TRT power in the main opposition party's regional stronghold. His decisions and policies were based solely in terms of what would undermine the popular basis of support for the Democrat Party. He dismantled effective organizations, such as the SBPAC, transferred authority from the army to the police because he thought they were too close to the Democrat Party's power structure, and replaced competent managers with political cronies. With regard to the global war on terror, when it was clear that JI was using Thailand and violence was growing in the south, the government's policies were based not on security concerns but on political ones. As a result, when the insurgency finally erupted in January 2004, the government was caught completely off guard.

---

69. Anuraj Manibhandu, "Power-Sharing, Not Self-Rule—Anand," *Bangkok Post*, August 10, 2005.

70. Author interview, Bangkok, January 10, 2006; author interview, Bangkok, January 20, 2006.

3

Violence Erupts

Although the media's common reference point for the start of the insurgency is January 4, 2004, the current violence really dates to 2001, the year, ironically, that Thaksin declared the insurgency resolved.[1] The same groups that are responsible for today's insurgency were active then and operating in similar patterns, but their activity was at a low-enough level that it blended into the overall criminality endemic to the region. In 2001, for example, there were 50 insurgent-related incidents of violence, including the bombing of the Hat Yai train station and a hotel in Yala and the killing of nineteen police officers. In 2002, there were 75 such incidents, including several major raids on police stations and the bombing of the Yala train station. And in 2003, there were 119 violent incidents, including two bombings.[2] Dating the start of the insurgency to a specific date in early 2004 was—like a lot of reporting—in part politically motivated and journalistically convenient.

Although these pre-2004 incidents included several raids by militants on government arsenals, most analysts at the time viewed the raids as criminal in nature and, as a result, little attention was paid to them or to the dramatically growing levels of violence.[3] From 1993 to 2003, there were only 722 recorded incidents of separatist-linked violence in the three Muslim provinces, but in 2004 alone there were 3,027 violent incidents, of which 867 were linked to separatism. In 2005, with an average of more than one bombing per day, these numbers rose further still

1. While much of the insurgent violence stopped by the late 1990s, small hard-line groups that never accepted the government's amnesties, particularly the Gerakan Mujahideen Islamiya Pattani (GMIP) and the BRN-C, continued to commit the occasional violent act.
2. Anthony Davis, "Ethnic Divide Widens in Thailand," *Jane's Terrorism and Security Monitor*, November 17, 2004; Anthony Davis, "Thai Militants Adopt New Bombing Tactics," *Jane's Intelligence Review*, May 1, 2005.
3. Liow, "The Security Situation in Southern Thailand," 542–543.

to 3,300 and 1,017, respectively.[4] Even in the six months following the introduction of the Emergency Decree in July 2005, more than 300 people were killed and more than 300 were wounded.[5] In January 2004, violent incidents averaged 30 per month; in December 2004, they averaged 250 per month. By mid-2006, more than 1,300 people had been killed since the generally recognized start of the insurgency, a rate of roughly 42 per month or more than one per day.[6] By the end of 2007, more than 3,400 people had been killed. Although the unrest has not yet escalated to a full-scale communal conflict, the potential for one exists.

The violence has come in several waves, with the overall level, lethality, coordination, and technical proficiency increasing with each wave. There are spikes in the violence and then distinct lulls (see figures 3.1, 3.2, and 3.3). Although there is no proof of why these spikes and lulls occur, they probably have much to do with issues related to the militants' resources and their reactions to government investigations and

---

4. "Two Police Killed in Rail Bomb Blasts," *Bangkok Post*, October 3, 2005.

5. Waeda-oh Harai, "Death Toll Near 300 Since Executive Decree Introduced," *Bangkok Post*, October 24, 2005.

6. There is a vast discrepancy in the actual number of deaths. On June 30, 2005, the Royal Thai Police announced that 790 people had been killed and 1,217 wounded since January 4, 2004; yet on August 22, the government announced that only 586 people had been killed and 1,211 wounded through mid-July 2005. Anand Panyarachun, the head of the NRC, said in an interview, "Official statistics say 730 persons died during the past two years, my guess is more than half [of these deaths] do not involve southern violence." One prominent local businessman agreed with Anand and said that the official numbers were overinflated. Another businessman explained that many victims' families report victims of crimes as insurgent-related casualties so they will be eligible for government compensation and insurance programs. Others have hypothesized that the police have labeled some violent acts as insurgent related to cover up their own corruption. Much of the killing is personal and business related, reflecting the vigilante culture of the south. But while some deaths can be attributed to personal and business score-settling, the numbers since January 2004 far exceed the annual average of violent deaths before the insurgency began. Press reports indicate that, from January 2004 through mid-August 2005, only 380 deaths were immediately attributed to militants. This number is low, as press reports did not include people who were originally categorized as wounded and later died. This author estimates that by mid-2006 militants had killed some nine hundred people and security forces were responsible for the deaths of several hundred Muslims. Two incidents—Krue Se (April 2004) and Tak Bai (October 2004)—account for almost 120 deaths. See "All MPs Told to Support Decree," *Nation*, August 23, 2005; Sanitsuda Ekachai, "What's Lacking in the News? The Truth," *Bangkok Post*, August 10, 2005; author interview, Pattani, August 8, 2005.

Figure 3.1 Number of Attacks by Type, January 2004–November 2007

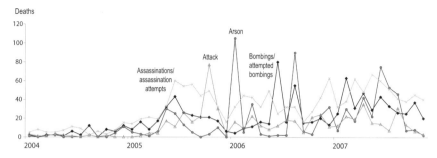

Figure 3.2 Number of Deaths by Cause, January 2004–November 2007

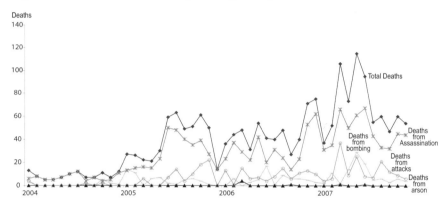

Figure 3.3 Lethality of Bombings, January 2004–December 2007

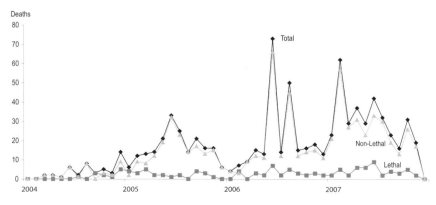

counterinsurgency operations. There are also spikes and lulls in the types of attack: while bombings may go down in a certain period, for example, assassinations and arson attacks may spike. The insurgents clearly think about the type of attack that they should execute and how best to respond to government countermeasures. For the purpose of this study—and the author's database—attacks are organized into four broad categories: bombings, targeted assassinations, arson attacks, and raids on police/army outposts.

The First Wave: The Insurgency Takes Hold

On January 4, 2004, a group of roughly one hundred unidentified Muslims torched twenty government-run schools in Narathiwat and raided a Thai army camp, killing four soldiers and making off with more than four hundred weapons, including rocket-propelled grenades (RPGs), machine guns, and semiautomatic rifles. It was a very well coordinated attack, with plenty of training and intelligence. Two bombings in Pattani Province on that same day and an attack on a police post in Yala forced the Thai government to impose martial law and dispatch an additional three thousand troops to the south, bringing the total to almost thirty thousand. Three cabinet ministers and the army's commander were sent to investigate.[7]

Thai officials were uncertain about who was behind the attacks. Although it issued thirty-three arrest warrants ten days after the raids—including for three known Gerakan Mujahideen Islamiya Pattani (Pattani Islamic Mujahideen Movement, GMIP) members and one BRN member—the suspects' affiliations were mostly unknown.[8] The intelligence failure was glaring and resulted in a knee-jerk crackdown on the former separatist organizations but not on the current generation of separatist groups, which were considered to be fringe Islamist organizations.

Simultaneous attacks conducted at geographically dispersed locations demonstrated extensive planning, command and control, coordi-

---

7. Shawn Crispin, "Strife down South," *Far Eastern Economic Review*, January 27, 2004.

8. GMIP members included Nasori Saesaeng (Awae Kaelae), Karim Karubang, and Jehku Mae Kuteh (Doromae Kuteh). The BRN member was Masae Useng. For more, see ICG, *Southern Thailand: Insurgency, Not Jihad*, 17.

nation, and strict operations and communications security. Indeed, the operation was very well organized: the militants had oxyacetylene torches, bolt cutters, and winches. Moreover, they knew the compounds well. This was a meticulously planned and well-executed series of attacks, not something conducted by a ragtag criminal element, as initially suggested by the government. As a very senior Thai intelligence official confided, "There was a long planning period [for the attack]."[9] Even Prime Minister Thaksin acknowledged, "The assailants are not ordinary bandits. They are professional and well trained."[10]

Of greater concern to Thai security officials was why the attacks occurred. They surmised that it was for three reasons. First, they believed that the attackers had grown frustrated with the previous generation of Pattani leaders, most of whom had laid down their arms.[11] Second, they believed that Malaysian crackdowns on JI, the Kumpulan Mujahideen Malaysia (KMM), and their associates had forced the insurgents' hand. Third, they believed that Thai complacency was also to blame. "We didn't crack down. We invited the radicals in," said one official.[12]

Thai officials believed that the January 4 instigators fled into Malaysia and, without showing any real understanding of the organizational structure of the insurgency, presented their Malaysian counterparts with a list of eighteen names. Few arrests were made on either side of the border, and small-scale attacks continued through February and March. The one semisignificant arrest, by Malaysian authorities at Bangkok's request, was of Poohsu Ismael, a radical cleric believed to be the author of a short booklet titled *Ber Jihad Di Pattani* (Waging Jihad in Pattani), which had been found on the bodies of several militants killed in early 2004.[13]

---

9. Author interview, Bangkok, March 16, 2005.

10. "Southern Violence: Pattani Hit, Martial Law Declared," *Nation*, January 6, 2004.

11. Author interview, Bangkok, March 16, 2005.

12. Ibid.

13. Malaysian authorities have been reluctant to turn him over to Thai officials. He allegedly holds dual Thai-Malaysian citizenship. There is some question about his authorship of the pamphlet, which is supposed to be a seven-day sermon by an unidentified "deceased" Thai cleric.

Although the Thaksin administration offered an economic aid program worth US$300 million to the four southern provinces (including Satun), local resentment over martial law, mistrust of Thai security forces, and memories of the past army "occupation" only heightened tensions.[14] Much of the southerners' anger was directed toward the March 12, 2004, abduction of Somchai Neelapaijit, a respected human rights lawyer and advocate for the four JI suspects arrested in June 2003 and nine other militants.[15] Somchai, himself a Muslim, had lodged a complaint with the Thai National Human Rights Commission, stating that his clients had been tortured in conjunction with the January 4 raid on the army post even though all of them had been in police custody for seven months. Although the government put five police officers on trial in June 2004 in connection with the lawyer's abduction, the charges were minor. In the end, only one of the five—Police Maj. Ngern Thongsuk—was found guilty of any crime and sentenced to three years for the minor charge of "physically forcing others into submission"; the other four were acquitted for lack of evidence.[16] The case reinforced the intense feeling among Thai Muslims that they could not enjoy any

---

14. Andrew Perrin, "Hearts and Pockets," *Time–Asian Edition*, May 17, 2004.

15. Somchai was the head of the Muslim Lawyers Association and vice chairman of the Human Rights Committee of the Law Society of Thailand. For more on his disappearance, see Human Rights Watch, "Thailand: Lawyer's Disappearance Darkens Rights Climate," March 18, 2004, http://hrw.org/english/docs/2004/03/17/thaila8127_txt.htm (accessed October 1, 2008).

16. Amy Kazmin, "Thai Police Deny Abduction of Muslim Lawyer," *Financial Times*, June 22, 2004. For criticism of the government's handling and lack of concern about the case, see "Missing Lawyer: Time for Action from the Premier," *Nation*, June 21, 2003. For more revelations about the Somchai case, see Bhanravee Tansubhapol, "Police under Sant May Have Met Somchai," *Bangkok Post*, July 26, 2005; "Panel to Try to Determine Lawyer's Fate," *Nation*, August 11, 2005. Despite the fact that prosecutors presented a record of seventy-five phone calls made by the five defendants on the day Somchai was abducted, the courts found no evidence of a conspiracy to abduct him. "The failure to support a truly independent investigation raises serious concerns about the ability of the Thai police force to investigate itself," said the Observatory for the Protection of Human Rights Defenders. Ismail Wolff, "Issue of Police Impunity Revisited," *Thai Day*, January 12, 2006; "Thai PM Says Missing Lawyer Dead," BBC, January 14, 2006; "Somchai Was Killed by Govt Officials, Says Premier," *Nation*, January 14, 2006.

degree of social justice. Somchai is still missing, and Thaksin announced in January 2006 that he was dead.

The violence gradually picked up steam, and the quality and size of the bombs increased. On March 28, 2004, a bomb exploded outside a bar in the Thai border town of Sungai Golok, wounding twenty-nine people.[17] A few days later, ten armed men raided a quarry in Yala Province and made off with 1,300 kg (2,866 lb.) of ammonium nitrate, 58 sticks of dynamite, and more than 100 blasting caps.[18] Militants were becoming increasingly emboldened by the lack of arrests and any government understanding of their identity.

From January 4 to April 27, 2004, the militant attacks were quite limited and were remarkable for their lack of sophistication. Although thirty-one people died and forty-two were wounded, there were only five bombings (with one attempted bombing) and three arson attacks. One bombing left three policemen dead and two other bombings left a total of twenty-eight people wounded; the remaining three bombings caused no casualties whatsoever. The rest of those killed in this period were assassinated in either drive-by motorcycle shootings or machete attacks. Although the majority of attacks were directed at agents of the state—five soldiers, one policeman, and ten local government officials were killed—three Buddhist monks were also killed and one was wounded, raising the specter of sectarian conflict. Due to a public backlash, monks would not be directly targeted again until October 2004.

The First Catalytic Event: The Krue Se Siege

Fighting peaked on April 28, when security forces killed 108 machete-wielding militants who were attempting to storm a number of police positions and military armories; seventeen militants were arrested.[19] The worst massacre in the eight-hour conflict occurred when Thai soldiers attacked the sixteenth-century Krue Se mosque in Pattani,

---

17. "Thailand Tightens Security in South after Bombing," Reuters, March 28, 2004.

18. "Thailand on High Alert," Australian Broadcast Corporation, March 31, 2004.

19. Unofficially, the death toll was 120. Three Thai policemen and two soldiers were killed, and fifteen policemen were wounded. See Human Rights Watch, "Thailand: Probe Use of Lethal Force in Muslim South," April 29, 2004, http://hrw.org/english/docs/2004/04/28/thaila8512_txt.htm (accessed October 1, 2008); Nopporn Wong-Anan, "Thai Army Knuckles down in Troubled South," Reuters, April 29, 2004.

in which thirty-one heavily armed gunmen had sought refuge. All thirty-one were killed, and another gunman was shot to death at a police checkpoint.[20] An independent investigation later conducted by the NRC found that government forces "failed to launch genuine negotiations for surrender of the militants."[21] Although the NRC also found that the militants had engaged in extensive planning for the operation and that they walked knowingly into certain death,[22] the siege became a catalytic event, fueling the insurgency. The local population saw these individuals as martyrs and the state as butchers. Interestingly, the local population even turned on the army, which it had always held in higher regard than the police. After Krue Se, the two were considered equally bad.[23]

The Thai government downplayed the incident. Thaksin asserted that it was the work of "local bandits" who had no links to "international terrorist groups like Jemaah Islamiyah." The minister of defense, Chetta Thanajaro, said it was the work of "drug addicts." Scholar Joseph C. Liow similarly suggested that the attacks were

---

20. Lt. Gen. Proong Bunphandung, the regional police commander, said, "The security forces were tipped in advance about the highly coordinated attack and waiting for the poorly armed assailants, most of whom carried only machetes." Local Muslims and human rights groups condemned the police for not trying to negotiate the militants' surrender. The independent commission that investigated the incident concluded that the level of force used in the April 28 attack on the Krue Se mosque was "disproportionate to the threat posed by the militants" and that "the tactic of laying siege to the Mosque, surrounding it with security personnel, in tandem with the use of negotiation with the militants, could have ultimately led to their surrender." For more, see Human Rights Watch, "Thailand: Prosecute and Discipline Officials Responsible for Southern Violence," August 5, 2004, http://hrw.org/english/docs/2004/08/05/thaila9188_txt.htm (accessed October 1, 2008); Human Rights Watch, "Thailand: Probe Use of Lethal Force in Muslim South." The man in charge of the assault—Gen. Pallop Pinmanee, deputy director of the Internal Security Operations Command—was transferred to a position in Bangkok for "insubordination," although he was not further disciplined. See "Pallop Moved for Insubordination," *Nation*, April 29, 2004.

21. For the report, see www.nationmultimedia.com/specials/takbai/p2.htm (accessed October 1, 2008).

22. On April 20, some twenty militants—including Isma-ae (Ustadz Soh) Rayarong, Samae Lateh, Sakariya Yusoh, Abdulroha Sana, and Mana (Baeka) Madiyoh—met to plan the assault. "Militants Met to Plan Attack," *Nation*, April 26, 2005.

23. Author interview, Yala, January 14, 2006.

carried out by unaffiliated youths, arguing that the attackers were hired but that they "shared little, if any, affinity to the ideological cause of their paymasters."[24] In all, most Thai politicians and analysts of Southeast Asia were very dismissive of the insurgents, their political agenda, and religious indoctrination.

But the assertions put forth by Thaksin and Chetta were dangerously naive and have not been supported by the evidence. The *Nation* dismissed the pair outright in its March 25, 2004, editorial: "What the two leaders do not see, or pretend not to see, is that this is not about addiction or banditry; this is about a fanatical ideology that none of us knew existed on such a large scale."[25] Even the normally proadministration *Bangkok Post* concurred: "Denying that a more serious problem exists appears to be a deliberate strategy of this image-focused administration. This is folly of the most perilous sort."[26] The dress of the militants themselves makes this plain: some wore Hamas-style headbands, and one had stitched "JI" into his clothing. Although such dress was likely only symbolic in nature, it demonstrated the aspirations of the young insurgents and the direction that they, at least as individuals, hoped to take their movement. As Chaiwat Satha-Anand, a Muslim member of the NRC, explained, "Their weapons of choice, primarily knives and machetes; and their willingness to use them against the authorities' guns, represented their willingness to die fighting."[27] According to the independent NRC report, the insurgents were buried as martyrs and their gravestones include the word *shaheed*, Arabic for "martyr." These men were willing martyrs, marking a clear ideological shift. Such acts of martyrdom likely came only after a sustained process of ideological indoctrination.

Why did the government make the assertions it did? Obviously, it wanted to downplay any unrest, which would have had negative economic repercussions and put the Thaksin administration and its policies in a bad light. The region has been home to many bandit groups and

---

24. Liow, "The Security Situation in Southern Thailand," 543.
25. Editorial, *Nation*, March 25, 2004.
26. Editorial, *Bangkok Post*, March 25, 2004.
27. See Chaiwat Satha-Anand, presentation at the Asia Foundation, Washington, D.C., April 7, 2005.

politically connected gangsters (*jao pho*, or godfathers).[28] The majority of the militants were young men—fifteen to twenty years of age—who for the most part were lightly armed with sticks and machetes. Regarding the drug allegations, it appears true that many of them were high on methamphetamine, but it is unclear whether the drugs were taken willingly or given by the ringleaders.[29] This point suggests an interesting phenomenon: although Wahhabism is making inroads, it is being built on the traditional base of Sufi mysticism.[30] Drugs were allegedly provided to give the young militants a sense of invulnerability. Moreover, a similar pattern can be seen in other militant Islamist organizations in Southeast Asia. Recruitment takes place in pondoks among troubled and very aggressive young males, many of whom have petty criminal pasts and have used drugs. The government points to such criminal records as evidence that the movement is criminal in nature. What the government fails to understand is that entry into a pondok can be an opportunity for a young man to ritually cleanse himself; devotion allows him to atone for past sins. The intense and secluded nature of the pondoks creates bonds between unquestioning students and their infallible masters, who become father figures to them. The students are soon willing to do anything to prove their loyalty and devotion. In Indonesia, JI frequently recruited *premen* (thugs), with jihad serving as a form of spiritual absolution for them.

Although the young militants may have been poorly armed, their superiors were not; many carried M-16s and AK-47s.[31] The attacks were well coordinated, if not operationally secure: six separate police stations were charged simultaneously in Yala and Songkhla. Simultaneous attacks by cells across a large swath of territory indicate centralized authority, meticulous planning, and centralized command and control. The intended goal of the militants was to increase their arsenal, clearly

---

28. McCargo, "Southern Thai Politics," 8–9, 16–17.

29. According to the minister of public health, Sudarat Keyurphan, "The autopsy results show that these people took drugs before launching their operation." See "Tested Positive," *Nation*, April 29, 2004.

30. According to detainees, they mixed Wahhabite preachings with Sufi prayer chants to "protect [themselves] from bullets." See Simon Elegant, "Southern Front," *Time–Asian Edition*, October 11, 2004.

31. "Thai Troops Sent to Troubled South," BBC, April 29, 2004.

fitting the pattern of GMIP raids in 2002–03. Indeed, the government later announced that a GMIP commander, Jehku Mae Kuteh (Doro-mae Kuteh), was wanted in conjunction with the attacks.[32] Additionally, the group was highly disciplined and had a compartmentalized cell structure. One detainee told journalist Simon Elegant that when a fellow militant picked him up, the militant realized that he was an old neighbor; he had no idea who was in the organization.[33] PULO issued a statement on its Web site denying responsibility for the attacks but warning that there would be reprisals for the crackdown.

The Second Wave: The Summer of Discontent

The Krue Se mosque siege served as a catalyst that led to a significant increase in both the rate and scope of the violence, which escalated dramatically through the summer of 2004. Between April 28 and October 24, the militants killed fifty-one people, including both Buddhists and Muslim "collaborators," and wounded seventy-eight others. Among those killed were seven soldiers, fourteen police (eighteen wounded), and eleven local government officials. Although the victims were primarily agents of the state, two important trends began: the violence was increasingly directed toward fellow Muslims— and the population at large. Fifteen civilians were killed and forty-four were wounded. Additionally, four teachers were assassinated and a fifth was almost killed. Three of the five teachers and most of the civilians who were attacked were considered to be moderate Muslims. One victim was described in the press as a police informant. A new and discernable trend was emerging: in addition to agents of the state, the militants had begun to target those whom they believed to be collaborators or unsupportive of the insurgency.

Although most of the victims were killed by assassination, the number of bombings also dramatically increased. There were seventeen bombings, one double bombing, and six attempted bombings, causing sixty-two casualties, including two fatalities. The sophistication of the bombs increased, too. For example, police defused one bomb that consisted of a

---

32. "Muslim Group 'Behind Thai Raids'" BBC, January 8, 2004.
33. Simon Elegant, "Southern Front."

car packed with cooking gas cylinders and Powergel.[34] On August 3, the first roadside improvised explosive device (IED) in southern Thailand hit Thai special operations forces, wounding three. The bomb was made of Powergel surrounded by nails and pellets and was detonated by mobile phone. On August 4 another IED exploded in a remote district of Yala as a truck carrying eight policemen passed, wounding two. A third roadside IED was detonated on August 5.[35] In the first week of October, five soldiers were killed and a dozen were wounded in separate attacks. In one attack, a bomb hit a truck full of soldiers.[36] Coordination was also becoming a hallmark of the violence: on August 5, four separate bomb attacks targeted government buildings.

As a result of the increased attacks, the Thaksin administration dispatched additional troops to the region. That seems to be exactly what the militants had hoped for, as locals began to complain about an "occupation." Although the Thaksin administration took a step toward ameliorating some Muslim anger in May by establishing an independent commission to investigate the Krue Se mosque massacre,[37] the specter of greater sectarian conflict quickly reemerged. Three bombs were placed outside Buddhist temples on May 17, and in late October militants targeted groups of monks collecting alms in one bombing and one attempted bombing. By then, the Thai military had already begun to provide protection to monks during their daily alms collection.

The attacks also forced Thaksin to improve bilateral relations with Malaysia. In April 2004, he traveled to the Malaysian city of Putrajaya to meet with his counterpart, Abdullah Badawi, to reestablish joint border patrols. In turn, Malaysian deputy prime minister Najib Razak traveled to Bangkok in May 2004 to discuss border security coordination efforts. Although Malaysia refused to close the border, it did pledge more men and equipment for its security forces in the four provinces bordering Thailand.[38]

---

34. Concern was raised in January when a large number of gas cylinders were reported stolen. See "Bomb-Plot Fears after 40 Gas Cylinders Stolen," *Nation*, January 21, 2005.

35. Anthony Davis, "Thai Insurgents Turn to Roadside Bombings," *Jane's Terrorism and Insurgency Centre*, August 18, 2004.

36. Elegant, "Southern Front."

37. "Thailand Probes Mosque Shootout, Malaysia Talks End," Reuters, May 4, 2004.

38. Nopporn Wong-Anan, "Thai Army Knuckles Down," Reuters, April 28, 2004.

The Second Catalytic Event: The Tak Bai Incident

The Tak Bai incident represents the most important catalytic event to date in the insurgency. As one senior Thai intelligence official lamented, "This incident will haunt us for many decades."[39] On October 25, 2004, approximately two thousand Muslim youths (most but not all unarmed) demonstrated against martial law in the Thai border village of Tak Bai. By the end of the day, eighty-five protesters were dead—seventy-eight of them died from asphyxiation after being crammed into unventilated army trucks to be taken for interrogation. Videos of the event are very disturbing and show Thai soldiers and security officials severely mistreating the demonstrators.[40]

The callous nature of the deaths was compounded by the defiant reaction of Prime Minister Thaksin and his unqualified defense of the military, which asserted that the demonstration turned into a riot and that the security forces responded with an acceptable measure of force. Furthermore, Thaksin's assertion that the deaths were the result of the detainees' weakness brought on by their Ramadan fast provoked enormous outrage, a spike in violence, and a surge in revenge killings.[41] Nearly thirty people were killed in revenge attacks within two weeks of the incident.[42] Targets included not just police, soldiers, and judges—the normal targets of the militants—but also Buddhist civilians.

Although the government paid Bt10,000 (US$256) in initial compensation to the family of each victim with the promise of more to come, the government's own inquiries into the incident were met by the local population with suspicion and cynicism and reinforced the sense that the government acts with impunity. The Thai government's independent commission on Tak Bai completed its report on December 17, 2004. Although the full report was not released to the public, it found that "among those responsible are Fourth Army Regional Commander Lt. General Pisarn Wattawongkiri, Assistant National Police Chief Lt. General Wongkut Maneerin and Interior Ministry

---

39. Author interview, Bangkok, March 16, 2005.

40. The government has sought to suppress independent videos of the incident. "Police Crackdown on 'Illegal' Tak Bai VCD," *Nation*, December 9, 2004.

41. "Thai PM Defiant amid Anger over Deaths," Associated Press, October 17, 2004.

42. "Thai King in Southern Peace Plea," BBC, November 18, 2004.

Deputy Permanent Secretary Siva Saengmanee." The report also found that the Fifth Battalion commander was "in charge" at Tak Bai but that the deaths were not a "deliberate act."[43] Although the chairman of the commission, Pichet Soonthornpipit, stated that "piling the detained protestors on top of one another in a crowded truck was in the least negligence," the report did not assign individual blame or call for dismissals. The government announced in January 2005 that the Ministry of Defense would establish its own panel to determine "whether disciplinary action is to be taken against the senior military officers found by the independent committee to have been responsible for the high death toll of the Muslim protestors due to their negligence."[44] While none of the responsible commanders have been disciplined to date, they have been passed over for promotions and Pisarn stepped down voluntarily from his command.[45]

Between October 25, 2004, and mid-March 2005, the violence surged. There were forty-eight bombings (including four double bombings and one triple bombing); five firebombings; twelve attempted bombings; thirty-two assassinations; and more than thirty arson attacks. In total, more than sixty people died in the attacks (thirty-one by bombs), including fifteen police and four soldiers, and more than four hundred people were injured.

The Third Wave: Spiraling out of Control

The reaction to the Tak Bai massacre, the proliferation of bomb-making technology to new bomb makers, and the confidence gained in the face of the government's incompetence and failure to make any meaningful arrests led to a surge in violence in 2005. Attacks became more frequent, spectacular, coordinated, and sophisticated. In July, the government replaced martial law with an Emergency Decree that gave it even greater powers of arrest and control, yet to little effect.

---

43. "Official Tak Bai Inquiry: Report Stops Short of Blame," *Nation*, December 18, 2004; "Independent Committee on Tak Bai to Conclude Investigation," Thai News Agency, December 1, 2004.

44. Wassana Nanuam, "Top Officers Face Tak Bai Inquiry," *Bangkok Post*, January 26, 2005.

45. Wassana Nanuam, "Tak Bai Brass Miss out on Promotion," *Bangkok Post*, March 16, 2005.

The first six months of 2005 saw some 115 bombings and attempted bombings and 179 deaths. Alarmingly, the insurgents beheaded fifteen people in 2005, eight in June alone—apparent copycat actions of beheadings by Iraqi insurgents.[46] Starting in March 2005, monks once again became targets, with two bombs exploding outside temples.[47] The triple bombings of April 3 in Songkhla and Yala, which killed two and wounded more than eighty, further demonstrated that the insurgents had the capacity to carry out near-simultaneous bombings and to target key aspects of the economic infrastructure, such as the Hat Yai Airport. What was less reported in the press was that nine bombs had actually been set that day.[48] In May, there were twenty-six bombings, or almost one per day. A quadruple bombing occurred in Yala in June.[49] That month witnessed thirty-six bombings and attempted bombings—more than one a day—with 207 people killed and 601 wounded in Yala, Narathiwat, and Pattani.[50] In July, sixty militants staged a well-planned raid in Yala City, blowing up four electric transformers and plunging much of the province into darkness. They then set out through the city, setting bombs and burning rows of shops and warehouses. This type of attack was repeated throughout the second half of 2005. Although only two policemen were killed and nineteen people wounded, the brazenness of the attack, near the Fourth Army base, was a psychological blow.

An analysis of the bombings demonstrates increased technical proficiency.[51] There were fewer duds, and the bombs were becoming more technologically sophisticated. Roadside IEDs became standard, as did

---

46. "South Beheadings Inspired by Iraq," *Nation*, July 5, 2005.

47. "Monk and Soldiers Injured in Yala Bomb Blast," *Nation*, March 24, 2005; "Army Chief, Abbot Targeted in Attacks," *Nation*, March 25, 2005.

48. Two bombs were found in the car park of the airport and one bomb was found outside a large shopping complex (this was similar to the earlier bombing of the Carrefour store). Author interview, Kuala Lumpur, April 18, 2005; author interview, Bangkok, April 21, 2005.

49. "Four Bombs Detonated in Yala," *Nation*, June 24, 2005.

50. Fifteen of the dead and seventy-four of the wounded were police; soldiers accounted for 6 of those killed and 78 of those injured. Civilians accounted for 186 of those killed and 449 of those injured. "South Beheadings Inspired by Iraq," *Nation*, July 5, 2005.

51. Davis, "Thai Militants Adopt New Bombing Tactics."

cell–phone–detonated explosives. One bomb was rigged to a car door, detonating when the intended victim got into his vehicle. While most of the bombs were approximately 2 kg (4.4 lb.), a number of them were in the 10 kg (22 lb.) range and above (by comparison, the bombs used in the 2005 London attacks were roughly 5 kg, or 11 lb., each). On February 17, a car bomb composed of 100 kg (220 lb.) of ammonium nitrate and diesel fuel was detonated in Sungai Golok, Narathiwat, killing seven and wounding forty.[52] Car bombs of 50 kg (110 lb.)were used on two other occasions. In several cases, the insurgents used delayed bombs to target police and military investigators drawn by a smaller initial explosion.[53] The bombings themselves increasingly targeted railways and other pillars of the local economy, such as banks, and not just bars. [54]

Two car bombs in Yala detonated by cell phone destroyed fourteen vehicles and wounded five people.[55] One of the car bombs was in front of the provincial capital, the first time a provincial capital had been targeted. In addition to the increased precision of the attacks, there also was an increase in the number of coordinated attacks. On October 26, 2005, for example, thirty-four coordinated nighttime attacks left six people dead.[56] In another incidents, eighteen locations in six different districts were hit in one night, while another night saw militants hit two dozen outposts, killing five people and seizing forty-two firearms.[57] In November and December 2005 alone, militants stole more than a hundred government weapons.

Because the bombings had become so effective, the government took the unprecedented countermeasure of blocking all unregistered prepaid

---

52. Insurgents had tried but failed to detonate car bombs in 2001 and 2002.

53. "Policeman Killed, 24 Injured in Twin Blasts," *Nation*, October 30, 2004; "8 Injured by Yala Bomb, Schools Burnt," *Nation*, January 1, 2005; "More Deaths, Injuries and Rebel Arson," *Bangkok Post*, January 26, 2005.

54. A mid-May 2005 report prepared for the prime minister found that sixty-five bombs had been set by militants since Tak Bai; twenty of them were planted alongside railroad tracks, and thirty-five others were planted near the railway station. "More Than 60 Bombs Set off over Six Months," *Nation*, May 17, 2005.

55. "Two Car Bombs Rock Yala," *Nation*, November 8, 2005.

56. "Six Reported Dead in Southern Thailand Attacks," Associated Press, October 27, 2005.

57. "Militants Raid Guns," *Nation*, October 27, 2005.

mobile phones—the detonator of choice.[58] This was a very successful move that contributed to a precipitous drop in bombings in December 2005 and January 2006. Since the ban, militants have returned to command-detonated bombs using wires. Authorities also have evidence that the militants are now experimenting with infrared devices such as detonators, although they have not consistently deployed these bombs, which entail greater risk because they require closer proximity.[59]

The government's November 15, 2005, ban on unregistered subscriber identity module (SIM) cards had an immediate effect on the bombings. In the first half of November, there were thirteen bombings, roughly one a day. In the second half of the month, there were just three bombings.[60] In retaliation for the ban, insurgents began to target mobile-phone towers and relay stations, severely disrupting service across the troubled south in much the same way that they caused blackouts in the summer of 2005 by targeting electric transmission grids.

While overall the bombs are still fairly small and simple and the kill ratio (casualties per bomb) remains low, the same could be said about the bombing campaign that Jemaah Islamiyah launched in 2000. Indeed, the primary reason that few people die in the Thai bombings has less to do with the size of the bombs than with the type of mobile-phone network that is in place: the network has a time delay, so bombs against moving targets often fail to detonate at the right moment.[61] Also, the bombings take place in open areas rather than in close quarters, where the effects of a blast are intensified. That noted, the professionalism and technical proficiency of southern Thai bomb makers has improved dramatically—and very quickly. The Thai militants are also learning

---

58. There are some 22 million prepaid phone users in Thailand—more than 100,000 in the south. Although the ban is technically feasible, the phone companies (including the Thaksin family's own AIS) balked at the time and expense required to implement it. Thaksin called on mobile-phone operators to set up separate exchanges in the three border provinces so that authorities could better monitor communications. "Unregistered Prepaid Phones in South to be Blocked," *Nation*, May 5, 2005; "Thaksin Wants Mobile Phone Operators to Set up Exchanges in the Deep South," *Nation*, August 23, 2005.

59. "Army Fears Infra-Red Bomb Devices," *Nation*, November 29, 2005.

60. Martin Petty, "Southern Bombings Continue Despite Security Measures," *Thai Day*, February 10, 2006.

61. Davis, "Thai Militants Adopt New Bombing Tactics."

techniques from abroad. "They have stolen cement kilometer road markers to make bombs, for which we have seen instructions posted on some web sites in the Middle East," noted a senior intelligence official.[62] There is clearly some technology transfer occurring, as evidenced by the use of newer IEDs similar to ones employed in Iraq that are designed to go through metal and destroy trucks.[63] The expertise and the "cookbooks" are out there should any Thai insurgents want to escalate further the degree of violence.

While the bombs make the headlines, it is the daily assassinations that have created a sense of fear in the three provinces. In fact, more than six times more people have been killed in drive-by shootings than in bombings. The insurgents "don't care about headlines," a local journalist said. "They just want to spread fear and make the region ungovernable."[64] One Thai analyst stated that among the insurgents there are different bounties for different types of victims (judges, government officials, police, and soldiers).[65] Two suspected militants arrested on May 16, 2005, confessed that they were paid Bt1,000 (US$25) for each arson attack that they committed.[66]

During this third wave, there was particular concern that the violence was spreading beyond the ten (of thirty-three total) districts that the Ministry of the Interior had conceded were "plagued by violence."[67] While Narathiwat accounted for roughly 45 percent of the violence (down from a high of 57 percent in August 2005), the rate in Yala rose steadily, reaching 24 percent in mid-2005 (see Figure 3.4). Most alarming for the Thai government was the spread of the insurgency to the "upper south." In November 2005, the Fourth Army extended martial law to Songkhla's Chana and Thepha districts, because separatist violence had spilled over into this province.[68] This was the day after several

---

62. "Muslim Thai South Rebels Copying Iraq Insurgents," Reuters, October 6, 2005.

63. Author interview, Bangkok, December 30, 2005.

64. Author interview, Pattani, January 15, 2006.

65. Author interview, Bangkok, April 20, 2005.

66. "Two Suspects Held for Pattani Attacks," *Bangkok Post*, May 17, 2005.

67. "Army to Take Control of 10 Districts," *Nation*, June 28, 2005.

68. "Martial Law Issued for Songkhla's Chana and Thepha Districts," *Bangkok Post*, November 3, 2005.

Figure 3.4 Deaths by Province, January 2004–November 2007

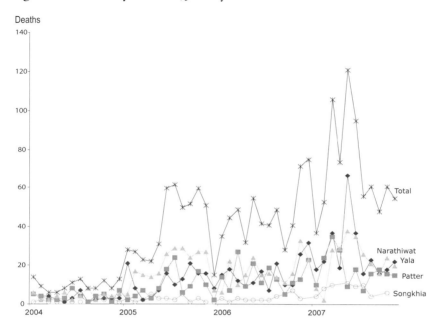

bombs blacked out the provincial capital.[69] Songkhla Province and its main city, Hat Yai, are economic hubs of the entire southern region and represent a psychological threshold. Moreover, because Hat Yai and Songkhla do not require registered cell phones, local security officials were bracing for a wave of bombs detonated by cell phone.[70] Another cause for concern was the number of incidents in spring 2005 in Narathiwat's Bacho District, an area that the army had highlighted as a "model district."[71]

As in the other periods of the insurgency, the victims in this period represented the normal range of insurgent targets (see Figure 3.5). Police and soldiers remain opportune targets; militants target them when available. "They have become more sophisticated with bombings and assassinations, and have a real aversion to risk," explained Davis of

69. "Thai Districts Put under Martial Law," Associated Press, November 3, 2005.

70. Author interview, Hat Yai, January 15, 2006.

71. Author interview, Bangkok, June 25, 2005.

Figure 3.5 Deaths by Victim Type, January 2004–November 2007

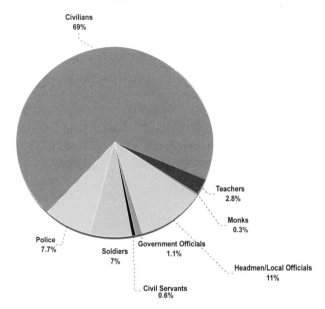

Jane's Defense Weekly, "That makes them good guerrillas who only hit when they know they can get away with it."[72] Militants also try to target government officials and civil servants. But much of the targeting focuses on civilians, teachers, and local government officials. Among them are a large number of Muslims deemed by the insurgents to be collaborators. Most of the village headmen and local government officials who are killed are Muslim. For example, on May 4, 2006, a gunman shot and killed a unit commander of the border patrol police while the commander was taking part in the weekly Friday prayer at a local mosque with scores of fellow Muslims.[73] Indeed, since March 2005, a majority of the militants' victims have been fellow Muslims, including imams. According to the *Nation*, "Ninth Police Region records [through 2005] show that more than half of the nonsecurity personnel assassinated . . . are Muslims."[74]

---

72. Martin Petty, "Climate of Fear Intensifies in South," *Thai Day*, January 3, 2006.

73. "Police Commander Was Shot at Close Range in Pattani," *Nation*, May 5, 2006.

74. Supalak Ganjanakhundee and Don Pathan, "From Guerrillas to Terrorists: New Face of Violence," *Nation*, January 9, 2006.

Leaflets have warned Muslims not to work for the government, and militants have assassinated fellow Muslims working in new government-run job-creation schemes.[75] Leaflets have also warned people not to serve as informants. "Those who cooperate are merely loyal dogs to their rulers. You are not the enemy of the mujahideen fighters for Pattani, but if you still cooperate and support the Siamese rulers who invaded our sovereignty, it is the equivalent of declaring war against us," reads one pamphlet.[76] In August 2005, a headman who was a government informant, some employees of the SBPPC, a village headman who negotiated the surrender of eleven militants, and two former militants–turned–government informers were all targeted.[77] One Thai academic has found that militants leave a "warning sign" to let potential victims know that they are on the militants' hit list: they leave sand, rice, white cloth, or eggs (all symbolic items in Muslim burial rites) at the door of the victim's house before the attack.[78]

The militants also target Buddhists, whom they hope to drive away. There is ample evidence to suggest that this plan is working: according to household registration statistics compiled by the *Nation*, 34,523 residents, mainly Buddhists, fled the three provinces between January 2004 and May 2005.[79] More than sixty teachers have been killed and nearly a hundred wounded or assaulted by militants. Teachers are often the only manifestation of the state in rural communities—and are often perceived as agents of Thai-Buddhist assimilation. Thus, to the militants, they represent an assault on Islam. Arson attacks have totally destroyed twenty-eight schools and damaged tens of others. Almost two thousand teachers have sought transfers to other regions, and one thou-

---

75. "More Deaths as Gunmen Target Southern Job Creation Workers," *Bangkok Post*, June 28, 2005; Leaflets Tell Muslims to Quit Government Jobs or Die," *Bangkok Post*, July 7, 2005.

76. "Leaflets Tell Muslims to Quit Government Jobs or Die," *Bangkok Post*, July 7, 2005.

77. Amornrat Khemkhao, "Insurgents Surrender, More Likely to Follow," *Nation*, August 9, 2005; "Three Shot, Government Claims Progress," *Nation*, August 11, 2005; "PM Tells Businesses to Ignore Death Threats," *Nation*, August 14, 2005; "Soldiers May Replace Police," *Nation*, August 29, 2005.

78. "Insurgents Leave Warnings," Issara News Centre, October 17, 2005.

79. "Thousand Teachers and Residents Flee Deep South," *Nation*, July 5, 2005.

sand have asked to be moved from rural to urban schools.[80] Militants recently sent more than a hundred letters to teachers at thirty-seven schools under military protection, calling on them to expel the soldiers or face the consequences.[81]

Another notable feature of the attacks in this period was that they increasingly became more shocking and brutal. As Davis said, "The militants are using shock tactics like beheadings and attacks on mosques, designed to incite revulsion and fear." [82] As of February 2006, there had been twenty-four beheadings, one of which was performed in front of a crowded teahouse. In October 2005, fifteen militants stormed a Buddhist temple (Wat Promprasith in Pattani), hacked a monk to death, killed a novice monk, and set the bodies and the monastery's living quarters on fire. The incident gripped the nation.[83]

The Fourth Wave: A Lull and Resurgence

As noted, there was a significant downturn in bombings and violence in December 2005 and early January 2006. Although the government was quick to take credit, the drop was principally due to the weather—the south was plagued by torrential rains and severe flooding. As a result, despite the assertion by Lt. Gen. Ongkorn Thongprasom, the commander of Thailand's Fourth Army, that "the situation in the three southern border provinces should improve since the militant network has been weakened by the arrest of its top members,"[84] the violence returned to its November 2005 rate by February 2006. By April, the insurgency was spiking back to the peak levels reached in June–July 2005, when an average of sixty people were being killed per month.

---

80. The torching of schools is not new. Chaiwat Satha-Anand found twenty-six cases of schools being torched or bombed between January and March 1979. "Teachers Abandon School after Attack," Issara News Center, 17 January 2006.

81. Waedao Harai Maluding Deeto, "Insurgents Tell Teachers to Oust Troops from Schools," *Bangkok Post*, January 7, 2006.

82. Martin Petty, "Climate of Fear Intensifies in South," *Thai Day*, January 3, 2006.

83. "Pattani Temple Murders: Monk and Two Teenagers Slain," *Nation*, October 17, 2005.

84. Cited in Wassana Nanuam and Waedao Harai, "Weak Mobile Phone Signal Saves Lives," *Bangkok Post*, April 17, 2006.

The first ten days of February saw a spate of bombings at a rate of one per day. This was the first surge in bombings since the November 15 ban on unregistered prepaid SIM cards. The deadliest of these bombings was a February 2 car bomb that killed two local officials in Narathiwat. Determined to counter the government's jamming, the militants began to steal mobile phones, and near the border, they were able to use Malaysian SIM cards. This enabled them to detonate a 5 kg (11 lb.) bomb by mobile phone at an open market in Sungai Golok, wounding nine people.[85] Many of the bombings occurred in remote parts of the countryside where wire-detonated bombs could be used without attracting attention. In one afternoon in May 2006, for example, two separate bombs targeted soldiers patrolling remote country roads in their Humvees.[86]

Insurgents struck a demoralizing blow on June 15 when they launched an unprecedented number of bombings across thirty-one of the thirty-three southern districts. In the course of four days, some seventy-four bombs were detonated, including fifty on the first day alone (twelve in Yala, eighteen in Pattani, and twenty in Narathiwat).[87] On June 17, another twelve bombs were detonated and at least ten more were defused. The bombs were quite small and the vast majority weighed 2 to 3 kg (4.4–6.6 lb.). Some were larger and demonstrated new detonating technologies and tactics (several of the bombs were detonated by new digital alarm clocks and remote-control devices). Remote-controlled detonating devices were employed in two roadside IED attacks (weighing roughly 5kg and 10 kg or 11 lb. and 22 lb.) against police convoys, which wounded ten police and two civilians. One 7 kg (15.4 lb.) motorcycle bomb was detonated in a market.[88]

Although the death toll over the four days was surprisingly low—less than ten people were killed—the unprecedented scope of the attacks said far more than the damage wrought. The organizational capacity of the militants to perpetrate so many attacks, many simultaneously,

85. "Bomb Injures 9 at Sungai Kolok Market," *Nation*, March 1, 2006.
86. "Four Shot Dead as the South Bleeds," *Nation*, May 9, 2006; Martin Petty, "Six Killed in Militant Attacks in South," *Thai Day*, May 10, 2006.
87. "Fifty Bombs Kill Three in South," *Bangkok Post*, June 16, 2006.
88. "Fresh Wave of Bombings Leaves Five Badly Injured," *Thai Day*, June 18, 2006.

proved to be greater than previously acknowledged by the government. While many bombs were left in public places (train stations, public toilets, etc.), half of them were detonated inside major public office buildings, including four city halls, two provincial offices, two district police stations, and two municipality office buildings.[89] According to the *Nation*, "Half of the bombs were planted just a few meters from the work desks of district chiefs and mayors," and one came close to the acting deputy prime minister, who was on an inspection tour.[90] The government claimed that they had some forewarning of the attacks, and yet they were still powerless to stop or prevent them. This show of force by the militants was a stunning rebuke to the Thai security forces that continually asserted that the insurgency was under control and that the government's policies were working.

Despite the government's announcement that they had intelligence that a second wave of attacks would hit in late July, they were again caught flat-footed.[91] On August 1–2, militants perpetrated 128 near-simultaneous violent acts in 12 southern districts. These attacks included more than 70 bombings and acts of arson on public buildings and Buddhist temples. A 5 kg (11 lb.) bomb placed on a train track in Songkhla's Chana District killed three border patrol policemen, while twenty other bombs along the rail line were defused. Militants also began to target more systematically the economic infrastructure of the south. On July 1 they attacked a rubber factory in Pattani, destroying 100 to 500 tons of rubber sheet worth Bt30 million (US$790,500).[92]

---

89. "Lull Ends in Savage Wave of 44 Blasts," *Nation*, June 16, 2006.

90. "Bombings Spark a Scramble for Excuses," *Nation*, June 19, 2006.

91. Interior Minister Kongsak Wanthana said security forces were expecting the attacks, having received prior warning from military intelligence. "Most of the bombings we knew would occur as we were informed earlier," he told reporters. "The intelligence has also warned of more attacks soon, so we have ordered an immediate tightening of security." Quoted in Ismail Wolff, "Govt Still Fails to Heed Warnings," *Thai Day*, August 3, 2006; see also Muhammad Ayub Pathan and Wassana Nanuam, "Intelligence Sources Warn of Major Strike Late This Month," *Bangkok Post*, July 13, 2006.

92. "Militants Launch Attacks in Thai Muslim South," Reuters, August 1, 2006. Surapan Boonthanom, "Bomb in Thailand's South Kills 3, Hits Rail Traffic," Reuters, August 2, 2006.

The insurgents also proved to be very adaptive in 2006. For example, they responded to the government's blockage of prepaid cell phones by launching a spate of arson attacks.[93] January 2006 witnessed more than a hundred arson attacks, a form of attack that had diminished throughout 2004–05 as the insurgents' bombing tactics became more proficient. In the early hours of March 3, militants torched some eighteen locations in eight districts of Pattani and in the Saba Yoi and Thepha districts of Songkhla, including more than nine cell-phone signal towers in seven districts.[94] There were also two reported thefts of large numbers of SIM cards from mobile-phone shops by alleged militants.[95] Likewise, militants increased the number of drive-by assassinations. May 2006 saw more than forty-two people gunned down by insurgents, the highest rate of any month in the insurgency.

The insurgents also grew bolder and began to operate in daylight hours in larger numbers.[96] For example, in late January 2006, about twenty gunmen in two pickup trucks attacked a train station in Yala, killing a policeman in a ten-minute daytime firefight.[97] In another attack, militants engaged soldiers in a roughly twenty-minute firefight; where as previously all encounters had lasted less than five minutes. In yet another attack, some ten militants in a pickup truck sprayed a police kiosk with AK-47 and M-16 assault rifles, killing three officers and wounding one.[98] On June 19 nine rebels attacked a police station. Perhaps the boldest attack came on July 23, when a militant disguised as a student gunned down a teacher in front of a classroom of terrified students in Narathiwat Province. This attack led local education

---

93. Ron Corben, "Southern Thai Militants Target Mobile Phone Network," Voice of America, January 22, 2006.

94. "Flames Spread over 8 Districts," *Nation*, March 3, 2006; "Rebels Target Songkhla, Pattani in Arson Spree," *Bangkok Post*, March 3, 2006.

95. Martin Petty, "Govt Admits Violence Is on the Rise," *Thai Day*, July 18, 2006; "Teacher Shot Dead in His Class," *Bangkok Post*, July 25, 2006; "Village Raid Nets 2 Men Linked to Blast Targeting Peace Team," *Bangkok Post*, July 29, 2006; "Chidchai Orders Unregistered Mobiles Cut Off," *Bangkok Post*, August 1, 2006.

96. "Six Killed When Militants Raid Office," *Thai Day*, March 16, 2006.

97. "Attackers Hit Train Station, Killing One," *Nation*, January 30, 2006.

98. "Muslim Militants Kill 3 Police in Thai South," Reuters, July 20, 2006.

authorities to briefly close 100 of the 199 schools in the district.[99] In August 2006, militants fired guns into a motorcycle repair shop, killing its owner. Once security personnel arrived on the scene, a pre-positioned bomb killed two civilians and wounded eleven others, including six soldiers.[100]

As part of this growing boldness, August saw a new direction in targeting. Militants attacked Fadruddin Boto, a fifty-two-year-old caretaker senator from Narathiwat. This was the first time that militants had targeted a top-level Muslim politician.[101] The following day, the Narathiwat governor, Pracha Tehrat, disclosed that militants had sent five-man hit squads to each province to assassinate political leaders, although the army leadership denied this.[102] During this period, the insurgents also appeared to begin employing women. A woman was suspected of having parked and exploded a motorcycle laden with several kilograms of TNT in front of a tea shop in a May 2006 attack, killing two women and a soldier and injuring sixteen others.[103] Although seventeen people, including an Indonesian, were detained in raids following the attacks, public confidence in the government plummeted.[104]

The attacks also took on a more ominous sectarian tone. In a coordinated assault, thirty armed men raided a Buddhist village in Pattani's Yaring District, torched two houses, and shot dead three villagers; two others were gunned down that night in a nearby village.[105] There was also growing concern in the summer of 2006

---

99. "Extremists Gun down Teacher in Classroom," *Bangkok Post*, July 24, 2006.

100. "South Thailand Rebel Attack Kills 2, Wounds 10," Reuters, August 13, 2006.

101. Fadruddin Boto is also the director of Darusalam Islamic School, the biggest in Narathiwat with nearly 5,000 students. "Narathiwat Caretaker Senator Shot and Seriously Injured," *Nation*, August 7, 2006; "Senator Shot at in Narathiwat," *Nation*, August 7, 2006.

102. "Former MP's Sister Shot in Far South," *Bangkok Post*, August 8, 2006.

103. Don Pathan, "Blast Kills 3, Injures 16," *Nation*, May 11, 2006.

104. Waederamae Mamingji, the chairman of the Islamic Committee of Pattani Province, said the bombings undermined the government's repeated assurances that its policies were effectively resolving the conflict: "Is this what they call the right track or an improving situation? They need to consider where the mistake lies." "People 'Losing Confidence,'" *Bangkok Post*, June 16, 2006.

105. "Violence Grips Pattani," *Nation*, March 3, 2006; "Two Killed and Houses Torched in Coordinated Attack," *Thai Day*, March 6, 2006.

that insurgents would attack Hat Yai again. Local intelligence reports suggested that Faisal Hayeesama-ae, who had conducted the airport bombing in 2005, was back in Hat Yai planning more operations.[106] The bombing in Songkhla that killed three border patrol police raised additional fears that the insurgency was moving out of its heartland.

Along with this growing boldness, the sophistication and capacity of the insurgency improved markedly beginning in 2005. "The first year was disorganized and uncoordinated," said Panitan Wattanyagorn. "They lost lives and lost legitimacy. But now there are car bombs of more than 50 kg; they can derail trains and target infrastructure, water supplies and electricity. They attack community leaders who cooperate with the government, showing they have good human intelligence too."[107] The same could not be said about the government, which continued to have an appallingly poor understanding of who was behind the insurgency. That, or it was unwilling to publicly admit who was behind the unrest for fear of scaring away tourists. With roughly one thousand leading insurgents active in the south, according to Lt. Gen. Ongkorn Thongprasom's estimations, the government did little to dismantle the organizations or the insurgents' infrastructure.[108]

Despite its poor understanding of the insurgency, the government did make some progress in seizing arms caches and recovering stolen weapons in the first five months of 2006. In one raid, five hundred security personnel raided a house and unearthed twenty-three firearms, including two AK-47 assault rifles, four M-16 assault rifles, ten sticks of dynamite, eleven bags of fertilizer, C-4 explosives, and more than three hundred rounds of ammunitions.[109] In another raid police found a large quantity of bomb-making materials, including eight sets of detonators,

---

106. Martin Petty, "Bombarded by Alerts, Hat Yai Is Starting to Feel a Lot Less Bustling," *Thai Day*, July 11, 2006.

107. Petty, "Climate of Fear."

108. Wassana Nanuam and Muhammad Ayub Pathan, "Sonthi Orders Troops to Focus on Mission," *Bangkok Post*, March 10, 2006.

109. The M-16s were among those stolen from the government in January 2004. Martin Petty, "Stolen Army Weapons Found in Cache Seized in Narathiwat," *Thai Day*, February 21, 2006.

iron boxes, steel sheets, and 25 kg (55 lb.) of ammonium nitrate. In a third raid, police recovered six M-16 rifles, three AK-47s, other small arms, and a fully assembled 10 kg (22 lb.) bomb.[110] In a raid on a militant training ground along the border of Narathiwat's Rueso and Bacho districts on July 9, police recovered five guns and a bag of urea nitrate and cell phones. Police divers located an M-16 and an AK-47 assault rifle hidden in a canal behind Sasana Withaya Pondok School in Pattani's Saiburi District. Then, following a raid on a Pattani police post in which three police and two militants were killed, police netted three suspects and seized four HK33s, four M-16s, one AK-47, one 38 mm pistol, and 180 rounds of 5.56 mm ammunition. The five M-16s recovered in these latter two raids are believed to have been stolen from the army camp in Narathiwat in January 2004.[111]

Although Pol. Lt. Gen. Adul Saengsingkaew, the head of Region 9, insisted that the situation had improved, stating that the number of violent incidents had declined from three hundred in the first six months of 2005 to two hundred in the first six months of 2006,[112] his data were appallingly inaccurate. In that time period, the number of deaths increased by 37 percent, from 185 to 253; bombings increased by 45 percent, from 124 to 180; and arson attacks increased by 22 percent, from 124 to 151. At the same time, the government increased its assessment of the number of insurgents to three thousand, making it hard to take claims of success seriously.

The Fifth Wave: Responding to the Coup

On September 16, 2006, the twenty-first anniversary of the founding of GMIP, a series of six bombs detonated at five-minute intervals down the main street of the southern Thai commercial hub of Hat Yai. Detonated by cell phones, the bombs killed six people, including the first Western victim of the insurgency, a Canadian teacher, and wounded at least fifty,

---

110. Rapee Mama and Ismail Wolff, "Suspected Stolen Weapons Found," *Thai Day*, May 13, 2006.

111. "Kongsak Confident about Southern Bomb Detectors," *Thai Day*, July 10, 2006; "Search in Pattani's Saiburi District Turns up M-16, AK-47, Magazines," *Nation*, July 22, 2006; "Insurgents Wore Soldiers' Uniforms," *Bangkok Post*, July 23, 2006.

112. Muhammad Ayub Pathan, "More Help for Bomb Disposal Unit," *Bangkok Post*, July 1, 2006.

precipitating concerns that the violence was spreading beyond the three Muslim-dominated provinces. The targets included three department stores, a marketplace, a massage parlor, and a hotel.

Three days later, Royal Thai Army chief Gen. Sonthi Boonyaratglin ousted Prime Minister Thaksin Shinawatra in a bloodless coup. Although the coup was ultimately about elite contestations in Bangkok, Thaksin's mishandling of the south was clearly one of the justifications for it.

There were high expectations that the coup leaders would do a better job in tackling the south than the Thaksin administration. Gen. Sonthi and Prime Minister Surayud Chulanont announced a two-pronged strategy for dealing with the insurgency: winning back the support of the moderates and improving the capacity and interagency relations of the security services. Attempts at the former included a public apology by Surayud for the Thaksin administration's policies; the dropping of charges against fifty-eight Tak Bai protesters; a renewed pledge to solve the disappearance of human rights lawyer Somchai Neelapaijit, now labeled a "murder"; the abolition of blacklists; an end to the culture of impunity; and promises to adopt Malayu as a working language. Attempts at the latter included reinstating the SBPAC, having more consistency in personnel and policies, and improving coordination with Malaysia. The government announced plans to negotiate with the insurgents and would go on to consider offering amnesties. To date, few of those promised initiatives have actually been implemented.

Rather than dropping, the violence spiked dramatically. The daily average rate of killing almost tripled in the six months after the coup to more than four per day. More than 800 people died in the nine months after the coup. The increased violence was indicative of the fact that the insurgents believed that they were winning and gaining momentum, that they had little to gain from negotiating, and that they were out to eliminate all political opposition to them within the Muslim community. Aside from the dramatic escalation in the number of people killed, six discernable trends emerged in the aftermath of the coup.

First, while most people had been killed by gunshot in drive-by motorcycle shootings, the death toll from explosions climbed markedly.

When the insurgency began in 2004, most bombs were small black-powder pipe bombs, usually under 2 kg (4.4 lb.). By 2006, the average bomb was a 4–5 kg (8.8–11 lb.) ammonium nitrate bomb; the average IED also increased in size. Soldiers also died in higher numbers. For example, five soldiers in an armored personnel carrier were severely wounded while patrolling a rural road when a 15 kg (33 lb.) IED buried in the dirt road exploded.[113] In January 2007, a 15 kg antipersonnel mine, triggered by a detonation wire, targeted an eighteen-member armed patrol unit traveling on a truck.[114] That same month, ten policemen escorting a convoy of teachers were injured when a 15 kg IED buried in the road exploded. On April 20, a 10 kg (22 lb.) roadside bomb tore through a military pickup truck carrying five soldiers on patrol. The following day, three military officers were killed and two others critically injured from a 20 kg (44 lb.) command-detonated IED attack on their Humvee.[115] Another 15 kg roadside IED killed seven soldiers on May 9. As the police lieutenant colonel investigating the attack put it, "It appeared that the bomb was assembled extremely well."[116] On May 31, the Royal Thai Army suffered their single greatest loss, when twelve soldiers were killed in a single IED attack and ambush.

Insurgents also stepped up their use of booby-trapped bodies and second bombs intended to target first responders. Most notably, Narathiwat's deputy police chief lost a leg and hand while inspecting a bomb scene on April 18. In mid-June, fourteen police were wounded when a bomb went off at a soccer game, and a powerful roadside bomb killed a district chief, Chayaphat Raksoyos, and a high-ranking officer from the Internal Security Operation Command (ISOC), Col. Surasak Phosutha.[117] In another attack, militants killed seven soldiers protecting teachers. The soldiers, who had been thrown from their truck by an IED blast, were then shot in the head execution style.[118]

On occasion, insurgents also got hold of high explosives—usually mining-grade plastic. In February 2006, for example, a Malaysian-

---

113. "Three Bomb Attacks Rock Narathiwat," *Nation*, November 16, 2006.
114. "Army Chief, Teachers to Meet," *Bangkok Post*, November 29, 2006.
115. "Roadside Bomb Kills 3 Soldiers," *Nation*, April 22, 2007.
116. Don Pathan, "Seven Killed in Brutal Attack," *Nation*, May 10, 2007.
117. "Chayaphat's Death Is a Great Loss," *Nation*, June 19, 2007.
118. "Patrol Bombed, Shot in Head," *Bangkok Post*, June 16, 2007.

sold high explosive called Emulex was employed in two consecutive days of bombings.[119] Detonators continued to include command-detonated cell phones, but digital watches and other timing devices were increasingly being used. There was also some continued experimentation with infrared detonators, and IED technology proliferated, as did the number of bomb makers. As a senior Thai military intelligence official stated in early 2007, "the list is so long that we cannot even begin to identify individual bomb makers."[120]

Another interesting development was the involvement of women in the insurgency. For the first time, a woman was confirmed to have delivered a bomb. A convenience store closed-circuit camera caught a woman in a black head scarf placing a 3 kg (6.6 lb.) IED by a food stall in a Yala market in March 2007. The bomb exploded minutes later, injuring three, including a female police officer.[121] So many women have become involved in the insurgency—principally in the organization of demonstrations—that the Thai army has opened a separate prison for Muslim women. Thai officials estimated in 2007 that Permuda, a youth movement thought to be an arm of the BRN-C, had recruited some five thousand women into its ranks.[122]

Second, the attacks grew far more provocative both in terms of the type of attack and choice of targets. While insurgents stepped up their attacks on police and soldiers, civilians, monks, women (including pregnant women), and children were also killed with appalling frequency. The attacks on civilians became painfully brutal. In an act reminiscent of the savagery of Algeria and Kashmir, in March 2007 a group of militants threw a small bomb in front of a small passenger van, disabling the vehicle, then opened the side door and shot execution style all nine Buddhist passengers, including three women and two girls. That same month, insurgents opened fire on a class of fifth graders, leaving an eleven-year-old in a coma. The following day two female

---

119. "South Thai Bombs Used Malaysian Explosive: Police," Reuters, February 21, 2007.

120. Author interview, Bangkok, February 9, 2007.

121. "Yala Bomb Planted by a Woman, Police Say," *Nation*, March 13, 2007.

122. Wassana Nanuam, "Fourth Army to Open Jail for Muslim Women," *Bangkok Post*, March 28, 2007.

high-school students were gunned down on their way to class.[123] In May, a man and his two children, an eleven-year-old daughter and seven-year-old son, were shot at point-blank range.[124] Monks also continued to be targeted. In October 2006, a 7 kg (15.4 lb.) bomb killed a soldier and wounded five monks collecting alms.[125]

Many other killings were equally horrific, with people being hacked to death by machetes. The rate of beheadings also increased markedly: nearly 50 percent of all beheadings since the insurgency began occurred in 2007. In November 2006, insurgents doused a man and his house with oil and set them ablaze.[126] In December 2006, suspected Islamist militants shot two Buddhist teachers and then set their bodies ablaze near their school.[127] In February 2007, a teenage boy was shot, hacked apart, and then set on fire.[128] That same month, insurgents beheaded a villager and then burned the remains of his body, leaving a sarcastic note: "This is the work of do-gooders." A Buddhist man was beheaded while his fourteen-year-old nephew was shot; both bodies were set on fire. The man's head was found 5 km (3.1 miles) away at a government school where three bombs had been planted at the entrance.[129] In April 2007, a Buddhist woman was shot and then burned alive. Her death sparked mass protests among Buddhists demanding that the state do more to quell the violence.[130] In May 2007, a family of four was killed and their bodies set on fire.[131] That same month, a Muslim man was

---

123. "Insurgents Kill Two Female Students," *Bangkok Post*, March 2, 2007.

124. "Father, Two Children Gunned Down," *Nation*, May 6, 2007.

125. "Soldier Killed, 5 Monks Hurt in Blast During Morning Rounds," *Nation*, October 23, 2006.

126. "Extremists Burn Villager in His Home," *Bangkok Post*, November 30, 2006.

127. "Two Teachers Killed, Set Ablaze in Thailand's Muslim South," *Nation*, December 28, 2006.

128. Muhamad Ayub Pathan Waedao Harai, "South Teenager Shot Dead and Burned, Nitya Admits Violence Is Not Being Stopped," *Bangkok Post*, February 18, 2007.

129. "Two Buddhists Set Ablaze in Thai Muslim South," Reuters, April 30, 2007.

130. Surapan Boonthanom, "Buddhist Woman Burned Alive in Muslim South Thailand," Reuters, April 11, 2007; "Yala Demonstrators Refuse to Move Woman's Coffin," *Nation*, April 14, 2007.

131. "Rebels Murder Family, Then Burn Their Bodies," *Bangkok Post*, May 23, 2007.

hacked to death by militants in public view at a Yala market, and a rubber tapper was cut apart and burned after being shot.[132]

In total, more than forty people were beheaded and some fifty people were hacked to death with machetes between 2004 and 2007. Why the gratuitous violence? A note left by the bodies of a decapitated rubber tapper and his wife who had been shot execution style seemed to sum it up: "As long as you don't leave our country Pattani, we will kill all of you crazy Buddhists."[133] The goal has been to terrorize the population: to force the Buddhists to leave and to compel the Muslims to support the insurgents. By 2007, 15 percent of the Buddhist community had fled the region; those who have stayed were clustered in towns and small cities.

Insurgents also stepped up their attacks on fellow Muslims whom they deemed to be collaborators. In February 2007, suspected insurgents walked into a mosque during Friday prayers and shot a village headman.[134] An Islamic religious teacher, Hamsah Yakariya, was gunned down in broad daylight. In Narathiwat, a prominent local Muslim leader, Kawee Prachumkayohmas, known for his tough stance against extremism, was also shot dead as he left a cemetery.[135] Another Islamic teacher was shot dead on July 16 allegedly because he was helping the authorities.

There were also some notable attacks on the broader Muslim *ummah* (community). For example, a bomb was detonated along the motorcade route of a delegation of foreign ministers from Qatar, Kuwait, and Saudi Arabia, who were accompanied by Thai interior minister Aree Wong-searaya, himself a Muslim. Although the motorcade passed by the site fifteen minutes before the bomb exploded, it was a clear political statement by the militants. Likewise, there was a spate of violence the day before the secretary-general of the OIC, Ekmeleddin Ihsanoglu, began his first official visit to Thailand. Many questioned why Muslim insur-

---

132. "Father, Two Children Gunned Down," *Nation*, May 6, 2007; "Buddhist Shot Dead, Burnt in Yala," *Nation*, May 8, 2007.

133. Muhamad Ayub Pathan, "'Pattani Warriors' Warn Buddhists," *Bangkok Post*, January 15, 2007.

134. "Insurgents Shoot Official inside Mosque," Thai News Agency, February 18, 2007.

135. "Yala Schools Won't Open Till Monday," *Bangkok Post*, January 4, 2006.

gents would target fellow Muslims this way, but it is clear that the militants were angered by the OIC's continued endorsements of Thailand's policies and were offended by the diplomatic whitewash.

In addition to the ongoing attacks on soldiers, police, and civilians, there were four attacks on members of royal entourages in 2007, a critically important development in the Thai context. The head of Crown Prince Vajiralongkorn's advance team, a police colonel, was shot in the head by a sniper in February.[136] Then, a police team discovered an IED planted in the road in Narathiwat's Bacho District along the route that the crown prince's motorcade was to take the following month.[137] Also in February, some twenty insurgents opened fire on the convoy of the queen's aide-de-camp, Thanpuying Viriya Chavakul, in Yala's Krong Pinang District, nearly killing her.[138] Most audaciously, insurgents placed a bomb about a hundred meters from a parking area where a helicopter was about to land to pick up the beloved Crown Princess Maha Chakri Sirindhorn.[139] As a senior army officer attached to the royal security detail noted, the attacks on royals were meant "to provoke the army into a real crackdown," which would further alienate the security forces from the broader Muslim community.[140]

Third, teachers and schools continued to be prime targets of the insurgents. On June 11, 2007, insurgents entered a school in Narathiwat and executed three Buddhist teachers, including two females, while roughly a hundred children played in front of the library after their lunch.[141] On June 13, insurgents torched thirteen schools in nearly simultaneous arson attacks in Yala and Pattani provinces.[142] Many teachers began to state that they only go to work because the military makes them.[143]

136. "Ice Cream Vendor Beheaded in Thai Muslim South," Reuters, February 1, 2007.

137. "Queen Vows to Protect Southerners," *Bangkok Post*, March 18, 2007.

138. "'I Was about Seconds from Death,'" Thanpuying Viriya," *Nation*, February 22, 2007; "Queen's Aide Escapes Death in South Attack," *Nation*, February 22, 2007.

139. "Bomb Detonates Before Princess' Arrival," *Bangkok Post*, February 7, 2007.

140. Author interview, Bangkok, March 19, 2007.

141. "Teachers Shot Dead in Narathiwat," *Nation*, June 11, 2007.

142. "Muslim Killed, 13 Schools Burned in Southern Thailand," *Nation*, June 14, 2007.

143. Author interview, Bangkok, February 25, 2007.

Fourth, there were more concerted attacks on economic targets, a trend that really began in mid-2006. For example, on November 9, 2006, eight bombs went off simultaneously at different car and motor-cycle showrooms in Yala's Muang District, injuring thirteen people and damaging twenty-two vehicles. That same month a series of bombs ripped through six stores in Rangae District's main shopping area, including a liquor store.[144] On Lunar New Year's eve, the ethnic Chi-nese community, the region's economic mainstay, was targeted in a wave of attacks across the four provinces—twenty-four bombings, more than twenty arson attacks, and numerous shootings—that killed eight and wounded almost seventy. On February 19, 2007, a bomb was placed in a Chevrolet showroom in Pattani's Muang District; it injured seven people, including a police officer, and damaged twenty automobiles, causing some Bt50 million (US$1,481,000) in damage.[145] On the night of April 13–14, four cell towers were targeted. One of the largest rubber factories in southern Thailand, Southern Land Rubber Co., was attacked on February 21, causing the destruction of more than Bt600 million (US$17,772,000) in inventory.[146] The attacks on the factory, where 80 percent of the 400 workers are Muslim, as well as the routine murders of rubber tappers, led to a 15 percent decline in rubber produc-tion, the driving force of the economy. Eight months after the Septem-ber 2006 coordinated attacks on Hat Yai, insurgents again set off bombs in the busy downtown neighborhood, targeting department stores, two hotels, and a pharmacy with seven bombs. The following day, two bombs were planted in a crowded marketplace in Songkhla's Saba Yoi District.[147] The attacks in Songkhla, which caused greater consterna-tion in Bangkok than similar attacks in Narathiwat or Yala, killed three and wounded twenty-five.

Fifth, militants began to use more boldly small arms and improved their ambush tactics. An attack on October 24, 2006, was indicative of the type of concerted attack the insurgents started to employ: militants

144. "PM Seeks Way to Resolve Injustice in South," *Bangkok Post*, December 14, 2006.
145. "Utter Mayhem in South," *Nation*, February 20, 2007.
146. "Suspected Rebels Set Fire to Rubber Warehouse in Yala," *Nation*, February 22, 2007.
147. "New Bombing Kills Three, Injures 10 in South," Deutsche Presse-Agentur, May 28, 2007; "13 Hurt as Bombs Rock Hat Yai," *Bangkok Post*, May 28, 2007.

fired three rounds from an M79 grenade launcher at a police station in Tambon Sakor before spraying it with bullets and escaping.[148] The militants no longer cut and run. For example, in March 2007, heavily armed insurgents opened fire on a unit of ten patrolling soldiers, provoking a ten-minute firefight; one Thai officer was killed.[149] In April, some fifty insurgents ambushed military vehicles, injuring eighteen soldiers in a series of coordinated predawn gunfights and roadside bombings that overturned two military trucks in Sungai Padi District.[150] In another April attack, a group of insurgents ambushed officers traveling back to their camp. The exchange of gunfire injured nine officers. In May, two police officers manning a sandbag bunker in Rangae District were killed by six insurgents in an attack in broad daylight. The insurgents made off with two pistols and an AK-47. Because the insurgents do not have a steady supply of ammunition, obtaining ammunition and weapons seems to be the main calculus for attacks on police and army posts.[151] On July 4, a group of ten insurgents attacked teacher escorts and engaged them in a five-minute firefight.[152] Perhaps the most audacious of these attacks occurred in early August, when insurgents engaged some eighty government forces in a three-hour firefight. Although they lost three cell leaders, that attack represented the longest sustained fight for the insurgents.[153]

Sixth, there was a large increase in the number of civil disobedience cases, generally involving women and children. In the past, protesters would march on police stations demanding the release of suspects. Authorities tended to acquiesce for fear of a violent confrontation, but this only emboldened the protesters. They not only began to demand that police release certain suspects but they also began to escalate their demands and call for entire units to be withdrawn.

---

148. "Cabinet Gives Its Approval to Revive SBPAC," *Bangkok Post*, October 25, 2006.

149. "Toy Sellers Killed in Front of Hundreds," *Bangkok Post*, March 21, 2007.

150. "18 Soldiers Injured in Attacks in South," *Nation*, April 24, 2007.

151. Waedao Harai and Wassana Nanuam, "Two Police Killed in Broad Daylight Raid," *Bangkok Post*, May 12, 2007.

152. "Sonthi Orders Warfare Handbooks Published," *Bangkok Post*, July 5, 2007.

153. "Three-Hour Clash in Narathiwat Kills Three Militants," *Nation*, August 10, 2007.

The protests really picked up in mid-November 2006, when the deputy governor of Yala removed some forty border patrol policemen from Ban Bajoh to avoid confrontation with protesting local residents.[154] Encouraged by this move, villagers elsewhere in Yala began their own protests. Roughly a hundred people, mainly women and children, demonstrated to demand the removal of a security checkpoint from their village.[155] Three days later, more than three hundred villagers in Yala held a mass protest for two days in front of a border patrol police outpost demanding that the unit leave the area.[156] Another three hundred villagers demonstrated at a mosque in Yala's Than To District after a sixteen-year-old boy was shot dead in an exchange of gunfire between a group of young people and village defense volunteers. And roughly a hundred women and children paraded the body of a Muslim man whom they alleged had been killed by authorities.[157]

From December 2006 to January 2007, at least six suspected insurgents who had been arrested—an Islamic teacher at Ban Kubae Tadika Islamic School and five others, Isma-ae Kuteh, Sama-ae Jeha, Mahama Mubala, Mahuseng, and Mayadee Samah—were released on bail due to protests by women and children. During one protest, individuals tried to escalate the situation by planting explosives and by putting down road spikes, prompting authorities to allege that the militants had organized the demonstrations.[158] "It's a set-up, it's been planned. Most of the women are wives and relatives of the insurgents, not the victims," explained Chidchanok Rahimmula, a professor of political science at Prince of Songkhla University in Pattani, who tracks events in the south.[159] For its part, the army threatened to take legal

154. Editorial, "War on Insurgents Enters a New Phase," *Nation*, November 7, 2006.

155. Chalee Boonsawat, "Thailand: More Violence," Reuters, November 19, 2006.

156. "Restaurants in Malaysia Aiding Rebels," *Bangkok Post*, November 22, 2006.

157. "Villagers Parade Body of Slain Muslim Man," *Nation*, November 30, 2006.

158. Abdulloh Benjakat, "Protesting Women Win Freedom for Teacher," *Bangkok Post*, December 19, 2006; "Murder Suspect Freed on Bail," *Nation*, January 6, 2007; "Villagers Protest to Demand Releases of Suspected Militants," *Nation*, December 26, 2006; "Protest after Detainees Set Free," *Bangkok Post*, December 28, 2006; "Women, Children Protest against Arrest of Muslim Man," *Nation*, January 26, 2007.

159. Simon Montlake, "Thailand Enlists Women to Battle Insurgency," *Christian Science Monitor*, April 4, 2007.

action against the Muslim women for their pressure tactics. Stated army spokesman Col. Akkhara Tipparoj, "I would like to warn women groups, who like to resort to violent protests, to stop their illegal actions. They should turn to use peaceful negotiations under the scope of the law. Such protests are wrongdoings warranting punishments."[160] The government also responded to the protests in a more clever way, creating an all-female ranger force trained specifically in negotiation and crowd control.[161]

But despite such warnings and initiatives, with each success, the rate of protests only increased. In Narathiwat's Raman District, for example, roughly two hundred women and children demanded that soldiers be moved out of the area and that a soldier who was suspected of killing a villager be prosecuted. The villagers won compensation and the district officials gave in to their six demands, including the demand that security forces would need to secure permission before entering the village.[162] On March 8, 2007, there were three separate demonstrations. In one, three hundred Muslim women, children, and masked teenagers blocked a major road in Bannang Sata District demanding the expulsion of rangers.[163]

More disturbingly for authorities, the protests became increasingly violent, which is exactly what the insurgents had hoped for. In a March 10 protest, a hundred Muslim women and children gathered at a police station in Pattani's Khok Pho District to demand the release of three suspects, Sufyan Jehteh, Ali Doloh, and Hamdan Hajibula, and blocked the highway. A Buddhist counterdemonstration, in which protesters demanded that the police uphold the constitution and that the suspects be tried, led to a fracas. Some 150 soldiers, rangers, and police were dispatched to the scene. A larger conflict was averted only following the intervention of the Pattani Islamic Committee chairman, Wae-

---

160. "Army Spokesman Threatens Legal Action against Female Southern Protesters," *Nation*, January 9, 2007.

161. "Southern Violence: Royal Visit, Women Rangers in Training," *Bangkok Post*, February 2, 2006; Simon Montlake, "Thailand Enlists Women to Battle Insurgency," *Christian Science Monitor*, April 4, 2007.

162. "Security Forces Ambushed," *Bangkok Post*, February 16, 2007.

163. "Angry Protesters Block Roads," *Bangkok Post*, March 9, 2007.

duramae Mamingji.[164] More protests erupted in Saba Yoi District after gunmen sprayed bullets and threw grenades at the Bamrungsart Wittaya Islamic boarding school, killing two students and injuring eight others. The government originally blamed insurgents for the attack, stating that they were trying to exacerbate tensions between the authorities and villagers, but it was later leaked that rangers had committed the attack.[165]

After a group of Buddhist village defense volunteers (VDVs) shot and killed four Muslim students and wounded six others, three large antigovernment protests erupted. The army at first defended the VDV actions, arguing that they had acted under the rules of engagement and in self-defense, but as the protests grew it reversed its positions the following day. "It should not have happened," army spokesman Acra Thiproj said, adding that the incident was "regrettable."[166] Under pressure, the border patrol police removed its forces from the area, even though insurgent infiltration into Songkhla's Saba Yoi District had never been greater.[167]

Following the government's imposition of a mandatory curfew in Yala after a wave of attacks, more demonstrations broke out. Authorities were convinced that the demonstrations had been organized by insurgents to end the curfew, because the curfew had actually been a success, driving down the rate of violence.[168] In late April 2007, mass demonstrations erupted across the three provinces following the arrest of twenty-four suspected insurgents. The twenty-four suspects included six individuals who had allegedly confessed to having participated in the February 21 attack on the queen's aide.[169] Despite the evidence against the men, Yala's deputy governor Natapol Wichianplert promised during his negotiations with the protesters that all the detainees would be set free within one month and that the rangers would gradually withdrawal

164. "Muslim Protesters Clash with Buddhists," *Nation*, March 11, 2007.

165. Vichayant Boonchote and Wadao Harai, "Attack on School Leads to Standoff," *Bangkok Post*, March 19, 2007.

166. "Army Admits Fatal Shooting Blunder," *Bangkok Post*, April 11, 2007.

167. "Three Dead in Bomb Attack on Army Humvee," *Bangkok Post*, April 11, 2007.

168. "New Protest Blocks Southern Road," *Bangkok Post*, April 27, 2007.

169. Wichayant Boonchote and Wadao Harai, "Market Blast Victim's Body Returned Home," *Bangkok Post*, May 2, 2007.

from the Krong Pinang subdistrict.[170] The arrest of Yunu Ma-ae, a fifty-four-year-old religious teacher believed to be a local insurgent leader, sparked another wave of protests on May 29.

The Muslim protests and release of suspected militants triggered many counterprotests by the Buddhist community. In one instance, nearly 2,000 Buddhist villagers demanded that the authorities maintain their forces in the area to protect their safety and not give into Muslim demands. In May, the families of two villagers slain by insurgents held a funeral service in the middle of the highway to draw attention to the state's failure to ensure the safety of Buddhists. In Pattani Province, nearly a thousand people, mostly Buddhists, gathered in front of Provincial Hall in a display of force to pressure the government to commit itself to ending the violence.[171]

In probably the largest show of force, some five thousand protesters led by a group of Muslim students from Ramkhamhaeng University in Bangkok demonstrated against the army for three days in Pattani in June 2007. In turn, Buddhists organized a thousand-person counterdemonstration.[172] Such events helped validate fears that the communities were becoming irreconcilable.

More Aggressive Counterinsurgency Operations

Despite increased attacks, police and soldiers became more aggressive in raiding insurgent strongholds, seizing bomb-making equipment and arresting more than a hundred suspects in the first three months of 2007.[173] An important gunrunner, Chaiyan Thongkam, was caught while on his way to deliver heavy weapons to a cell.[174] Royalee Yagoh, described as a major insurgent suspect, was arrested in Tak Bai.[175] Thien Rodkhiew, an influential *kamnan* (subdistrict headman), was

---

170. "Authorities Agree to Protest Demands," *Bangkok Post*, May 7, 2007; "Muslims, Army in Pattani Standoff," *Bangkok Post*, May 8, 2007.

171. "Muslim, Buddhist Protesters Block Roads in South," *Nation*, May 5, 2007; "Tense Protests Face off along Religious Lines," *Bangkok Post*, May 6, 2007.

172. "Concessions End Pattani Mosque Standoff," *Nation*, June 3, 2007; "Buddhist Mob in Pattani," *Nation*, June 3, 2007.

173. "Seven Muslim Men Held in Thai Rebellious South," Reuters, April 4, 2007.

174. "49 Schools Close in Face of More Arson Attacks," *Bangkok Post*, November 8, 2006.

175. "Yala Residents Take Refuge," *Bangkok Post*, November 11, 2006.

arrested; his brother, Thong, had earlier been arrested for his role in the torching of five schools in September 2006.[176] As noted, Thai security forces also arrested twenty-four men in conjunction with the attack on the convoy carrying the queen's aide-de-camp, and eight men were arrested for their roles in the Lunar New Year bombings. The Fourth Army commander, Lt. Gen. Viroach Buacharoon, claimed that the men had had "intensive military training."[177] Security personnel also arrested thirteen suspects in the passenger van attack, recovering maps marking the location where the van was ambushed, 60 kg (132 lb.) of ammonium nitrate, an M-16 assault rifle, and other bomb-making materials.[178] Sugri Banhaning, an insurgent thought to be a bomb maker, was killed in a shootout.[179] Some fourteen suspects were detained in a raid on Tambon Tanyong Limo in Narathiwat's Rangae District. There, authorities recovered two M-16s, three guns, radio communications equipment, medical supplies, and about Bt80,000 (US$2,459) worth of Thai and Malaysian currencies.[180] In connection with the investigation of the woman who was shot and burned alive, eleven men were arrested in Yala; some five guns, hundreds of rounds of ammunition, and 200 kg (441 lb.) of fertilizer were captured.[181] Police and soldiers also raided a grocery shop in a mosque in Narathiwat Province. Although they made no arrests, they seized seven two-way radios, CDs, and sixty pistol bullets that were hidden in the store's ceiling. In a major raid on Mamuwoh village in Rangae District, police arrested five men and eight women after finding four M-16s, three bombs, four sacks of ammonium nitrate, mobile phones, twenty-one digital wristwatches, and other bomb-making materials.[182]

Perhaps the most important counterinsurgency operation was one against a training camp in a mountainous region of Narathiwat. Five

---

176. "Kamnan Arrested for Alleged Involvement in Arson Attacks on Five Schools," *Nation*, November 8, 2006.

177. "Thailand Says Arrests 3 Muslims for Southern Bombs," Reuters, February 20, 2007.

178. "25 Held over Yala Murders," *Nation*, March 19, 2007.

179. "Insurgent Killed in Yala Shootout," *Bangkok Post*, November 22, 2006.

180. "Killers Entrenched in Villages: Sonthi," *Nation*, March 29, 2007.

181. Surapan Boonthanom, "Buddhist Woman Burned Alive in Muslim South Thailand," Reuters, April 11, 2007.

182. "Police Detain 13 in South Bomb Centre," *Bangkok Post*, March 28, 2007.

suspected insurgents were killed, while some ten others were believed to have escaped. Two M-16s, a shotgun, and ammunition were found. The training camp, according to army officials, was equipped with a tent and ten beds and had an adjacent training field. Army spokesman Col. Akara Tip-roj stated that at least three groups of youths had received training at the camp and that each group completed thirty to forty-five days of training.[183] A total of twenty-two suspects were arrested in Yala's Bannang Sata District on June 22, 2007; government forces claimed that seven of the suspects were ranking members of an alleged insurgent group known as the Runda Kumpulan Kecil (RKK), including a younger brother of RKK leader Ma-ae Aphibalbae.[184] That same month, the army detained 160 Muslims after rebels intensified attacks on government schools, civil servants, and security forces.

Growing Frustration

Despite these successes, the increased violence in the months following the coup led to a palpable degree of frustration among Thai security officials. In their eyes, they had offered many inducements to negotiate and reversed many of the Thaksin regime's worst policies. And yet the situation had only gotten worse. In part, this was because much of what they had offered was not implemented on the ground. But it was also due to the militants' attempts to dissuade any other group from speaking to the government on their behalf. They were infuriated, for example, that the old guard—PULO, the BRN, the BIPP, and others—spoke to the government in the secret Malaysian-brokered peace talks known as the "Langkawi process" in 2006 even though the groups had no operational control over the insurgents. In many ways, the government was still in woeful denial about the problem. General Sonthi did not even believe that the militants were Islamist or secessionist: "Their goal is clear, that they want to establish an autonomous state by means of violence."[185]

Aside from the general increase in violence, soldiers and police were being killed and wounded at higher rates than ever. Frustration within

---

183. "Army Pursues Militant Unit in Narathiwat," *Bangkok Post*, March 2, 2007.
184. "PM Announces Plans to Head to South Again," *Bangkok Post*, June 23, 2007.
185. "Top Separatist Goes Unnoticed," *Bangkok Post*, May 17, 2007.

the government and security forces led to some catastrophic operations and possibly breakdowns in command and control. The clearest example of this was the attack by rangers on the dormitory at the Bamrungsart Wittaya Islamic boarding school. And on the evening of May 31, 2007, following an IED attack that killed twelve soldiers, gunmen opened fire on a mosque during prayer time, killing five. The government asserted that militants staged the attack in order to incite locals against the army and government. But it is just as likely that soldiers engaging in an indiscriminant retaliatory action perpetrated the attack.[186]

To be fair, the insurgents have systematically targeted Muslims; almost 55 percent of their victims have been fellow Muslims. As one army spokesman noted, "The insurgents want to scare away Muslims who may want to help authorities in quelling the violence."[187] But insurgents have also attacked Muslims in a deliberate attempt to frame government forces. For example, in April 2007, insurgents fired four M79 grenades into the Pedaeru Mosque's Tabliqhi Jamaat's Dawa Centre in Yala's Yaha District during morning prayers. The army was immediately blamed for the attack.[188] As one Muslim leader explained: "A significant portion of the local population think the attackers were government security officers. I think the authorities must move quick to explain what really happened."[189] Stated the army, "[The attackers] want to cause strife between Muslims and Buddhists and make the two communities distrust each other."[190]

Aside from the insurgent violence, there was also the looming specter of vigilante justice by the Buddhist community, which felt that the state was not doing enough to protect it. On the evening of the passenger van massacre, for example, a hand grenade was thrown into a Yaha mosque, wounding eleven people, and gunmen shot up a tea shop, killing two Muslims. The army said that both the mosque attack and the shooting were carried out by militants hoping people would

186. "Militant Attacks Kill 13 in Thai Muslim South—Army," *Reuters*, May 31, 2007.
187. "Grenades Fired at Islamic Centres," *Nation*, April 6, 2007.
188. "Insurgents Bomb Mosque, Burn Schools," *Bangkok Post*, April 5, 2007.
189. "Grenades Fired at Islamic Centres," *Nation*, April 6, 2007.
190. Ibid.

believe them to be retaliatory attacks by Buddhists.[191] It may very well have been insurgents trying to create a cycle of violence. But it may have just as easily been security forces or Buddhist vigilantes. If the latter, from where did they get the hand grenades?

Regardless, those Buddhists who stayed in the south were becoming more assertive in their right to self-defense. As a result, the cycle of violence was poised to get much worse. As a March 2007 editorial in the *Bangkok Post* put it: "The insurgents have plainly taken this softer government policy, along with statements favouring *samanchan* (reconciliation) as a sign of weakness. They have escalated attacks on security forces, and increased their intimidation of local businesses and population centres in the region."[192]

Operation Southern Protection

The overall security situation improved beginning in June–July 2007, when the army increased the number of troops deployed in the south to a total of forty thousand. This "surge," known as Operation Southern Protection, was in part a response to the overall spike in violence. But in large part it was a response to the rapid increase in deaths of soldiers because of the increased average size of IEDs and the militants' increased proficiency in small arms.

Despite this increase in the number of forces, the troops were concentrated mainly in the cities and along main highways. As a result, attacks in the large towns decreased considerably, improving the mood of the populations there. The pervasive sense of insecurity that this author witnessed in the years since the insurgency began was ebbing, yet the army was still sparsely deployed in the hinterlands and "red zones."[193] Most checkpoints remained static positions in front of police posts or small army encampments and one rarely saw patrols.

---

191. Nopporn Wong-Anan, "Curfew Imposed after Minibus Attack in Thai South," *Reuters*, March 15, 2007.

192. Editorial, "Southern Policy Is Not Working," *Bangkok Post*, March 16, 2007.

193. Thaksin initiated a policy that categorized 1,580 villages as red, yellow, or green on the basis of the number of violent incidents in them, the willingness of the local residents to support the security forces and their investigations, and the degree of sympathy the residents had for the insurgents. Those villages believed to be most sympathetic to militants were designated as "red zones." See Don Pathan, "PM's Remedy for Crisis in South: 'Red' Villages Face Sanctions," *Nation*, February 17, 2005.

Nonetheless, the rate of violence at the end of 2007 was half of the June 2007 peak. By January 2008, the average number of killings was down to three per day, while the average number of acts of violence per week had fallen by half, from forty to twenty. Further, since 2006 there have been few simultaneous multiple attacks across the three provinces. There have also been few technical innovations in the design of bombs and detonators, and the ratio of deaths by shooting—always high—has increased.

The government has claimed success in its Operation Southern Protection, citing the increased number of troops on the ground, more aggressive operations, and more arrests of suspected militants. Asserted Fourth Army spokesman Colonel Acra, "Many suspects are in our custody and the violence has peaked. Things could not get any more violent. We are on to the insurgents and we are well-equipped to deal with them."[194] In another interview, he stated with Cheney-esque bluster, "Our past actions have been very successful. We have ended their networks. What they are doing now are not coordinated like in the past. . . . They are putting up their last fight."[195] In mid-October 2007, the army claimed that the number of insurgents and their supporters had fallen by 30–40 percent.[196] Although the active service generals may have gotten what they wanted out of the coup and have finally been able to implement their desired strategy, there are three other factors that explain the drop in violence that have nothing to do with the government's policies.

First, in each of the first four years of the insurgency, the violence has come in waves after distinct lulls. For example, there has been an annual downturn in violence in December and January due to heavy rains and flooding, with violence tending to increase in the spring and peak in midsummer. Thus, any government claim of success after a short improvement in the security situation should be treated with caution.

Second, as in Iraq in mid-to-late 2007, the militants have achieved one of their goals: they have "cleansed" much of the countryside. As this

---

194. Waedao Harai and Muhamad Ayub Pathan, "53 Arrests in Raids in Far South," *Bangkok Post*, July 30, 2007.

195. "Army: Insurgents Have Their Backs to the Wall," *Bangkok Post*, November 10, 2007.

196. "Yawi Language, Rebel Activity," *Bangkok Post*, October 16, 2007.

author witnessed over several trips to the south in 2007, the Buddhists in once-mixed villages had simply been driven away.[197] More recent press reports indicate that Buddhist villagers continue to be driven away due to the intense sense of insecurity. The villagers in the small number of predominately Buddhist villages that do remain in the countryside are often heavily armed, giving fears of vigilante justice.

Third, the current rate of violence remains consistent with the four-year average and is certainly no less than the average level of violence across the insurgency. Knowing that an excess of violence would turn the community against them and force the government to intervene, the insurgent leaders may have consciously limited the violence to better achieve their goals: to make the region ungovernable, to drive away Buddhists, and to implement a parallel sociopolitical system in the countryside to supplant the state.

Additional explanations for the drop in violence relates to the army's decision to resume the practice of extrajudicial killings, which it had pledged to stop in mid-2006, and to the government's detention program, which deserves intense scrutiny in the wake of the surge. By November 2007, some 1,930 suspects had been detained in the government's concerted efforts against the insurgents. Despite the scale of the arrests, however, after the initial twenty-eight-day detention period as allowed under the Emergency Decree, more than 90 percent of those arrested had been released without charge or trial. According to a March 2007 Human Rights Watch report, only 15 of some 350 suspects who had been arrested had been charged.[198] This indicates that either the government sweeps have been too broad-based or that the security forces have been unable to gather sufficient evidence to charge the detainees.

Although the vast majority of those arrested were either collaborators or sympathizers who were ultimately released, many militants directly linked to acts of violence were among those netted, as some targeted raids demonstrated improved intelligence. For example, in a set of July 29, 2007, raids that saw the detention of fifty-one suspects, five were

197. This author met a number of Buddhists in the cities who had moved from the countryside. Several of them stated that their parents had returned to Issarn, in the northeast of the country.
198. "Villagers' Arrest Creating Resentment: Lawyers," *Nation*, July 24, 2007.

described as "core leaders," including Abdul Romae Pereesee, a midlevel commander, Samae Awae, Doromae Masae, Mamah Waecheleh, and Usman Asah.[199] An August 21 raid in Pattani's Thung Yang Daeng District led to the capture of three key militants, Hama Buenae, Usaman Awae-busa, and Sama-eh Makeroh, and nine others.[200] A raid in September led to the capture of two other midlevel commanders, Abdulloh Pasa Lar and Maropee Marae.[201] Raids also led to the capture of a number of bomb makers, including Nuradin Hasa and Manaseya, the target of a Bt2 million (US$62,700) bounty.[202] And on November 24, three high-level rebel suspects were arrested in Narathiwat. These included a commander of a female cell, Abdulrohmae Ali, and Abduloh Pirisee, a fund-raiser.

Although the surge and raids have had an impact on the insurgents' operations, they have proved to be resilient. For example, in retaliation for the late July raids, insurgents set off six bombs on July 31, killed two soldiers, three civilians, and one policeman, and wounded twelve others.[203] On August 15, insurgents staged simultaneous attacks in some twenty spots in Songkhla and Pattani provinces.[204] Two days later, they attacked more than forty locations across Narathiwat's eight districts and in Yala Province.[205] Government forces broke up a major attack that included some twenty-two bombs intended to be set across the city of Hat Yai on September 21–22.[206] On October 1, nine bomb blasts in five districts killed one soldier and wounded at least thirteen villagers. A 20 kg (44.1 lb.) bomb was used in an October 16 attack at a train station in Rusoh. On November 2, ten entertainment venues in

---

199. "Five More Key Insurgent Suspects Netted," *Nation*, July 30, 2007.

200. "Machete Attack Kills Guard at Store," *Nation*, August 22, 2007.

201. "Joint Operation Nabs More Insurgent Suspects," *Bangkok Post*, September 10, 2007; "Curfew Will Be Lifted in Yala for Ramadan," *Bangkok Post*, September 10, 2007.

202. The army described Manaseya as a mercenary terrorist and not as a member of a group, stating that he sold IEDs for Bt2,000–4,000 (US$66–132). "Army Holds Mercenary Terrorist," *Bangkok Post*, July 17, 2007; "45 State Schools Closed in South," *Nation*, June 21, 2007.

203. "Bombings, Shootings Leave Nine Dead," *Nation*, August 2, 2007.

204. "Raid Nets Suspected Militants," *Nation*, August 16, 2007.

205. "South Hit by Spate of Attacks at Night," *Nation*, August 17, 2007.

206. Wichayant Boonchote and Waedao Harai, "Busted: Hat Yai Bomb Plot," *Bangkok Post*, October 7, 2007.

Narathiwat's Muang municipality were hit by near-simultaneous bomb blasts. One man was killed and four others were injured. On November 5, insurgents killed seven, including two Muslim religious leaders, two teachers, and two village headmen, while a 3 kg (6.6 lb.) bomb went off in an open market in Yala, wounding twenty-five. Sixty-one schools in Narathiwat Province closed indefinitely as a result of attacks against teachers. By its third week, November had already become the bloodiest month of 2007, with fifty-six people killed and more than eighty wounded in some eighty-five attacks.

The shock attacks also continued, as did attacks on monks. On August 21, a man was hacked to death with a machete in Sungai Golok. Phra Sangkasit Pitak, the seventy-year-old abbot of Sangkasit Dharam Temple in Narathiwat, was shot and wounded in the abdomen.[207] A 5 kg (11 lb.) bomb was detonated in Muang District as monks collected alms, killing one and wounding two monks, three villagers, and six soldiers.[208] On October 27, a Muslim deputy village chief was killed and beheaded, becoming the thirty-third person decapitated in southern Thailand since January 2004.

And while small-arms encounters with security forces dropped after the surge began, there were still a number of intense firefights in 2007. On September 27, for example, separatists ambushed three soldiers, including Lt. Gen. Ekkawit Phandan, in their pickup truck in Pattani. All were shot execution style. On October 10, a handful of militants fended off 150 soldiers before retreating.[209] Eight days later, soldiers engaged militants in a ten-minute firefight in Sai Buri after their truck was disabled by an IED that wounded three.

Although large coordinated attacks have clearly been down since the launch of Operation Southern Protection, as has the daily death toll, it is still far too soon for the government to declare victory. The insurgents have proved to be patient and determined—and the government still has a poor understanding of the networks that make up the insurgency.

---

207. "Another 28 Suspected Insurgents Rounded up," *Nation*, August 5, 2007.
208. "South Blast Kills One, Injures 11," *Bangkok Post*, August 26, 2007.
209. "Pre-Dawn Fight Kills Key Insurgent in Narathiwat," *Nation*, October 11, 2007.

4

Who Is behind the Attacks?

An Appalling Lack of Understanding

Although Prime Minister Thaksin blamed PULO for the April 2001 and July 2002 bombings in Hat Yai and Yala Province, PULO denied responsibility for the attacks. Indeed, given the state PULO was in at the time, there is little likelihood that it was responsible: most of PULO's leadership was arrested in 1997–98, and most of its rank and file had participated in the government's earlier amnesty programs. But if PULO did not commit the attacks, who did? Joseph C. Liow suggested that they were conducted or orchestrated by corrupt officials, criminal elements, and rogue security officials, especially police.[1] This became the conventional wisdom at the time, but as this chapter will demonstrate, the attacks signaled the start of a campaign by a new generation of insurgents.

Indeed, one of the most troubling aspects of the unrest in southern Thailand is that the government has always seemed to have a poor grasp of who is behind the attacks.[2] For example, early in the insurgency, former prime minister Thaksin asserted that "criminal gangs" had perpetrated the attacks, while policymakers blamed "separatists with possible links to foreign Muslim extremists."[3] As the respected security affairs correspondent Anthony Davis wrote in 2004, "The authorities appear to have little understanding of [the insurgency's] organizational composition, command structure, or the nature and extent of its inter-

---

1. Liow, "The Security Situation in Southern Thailand," 542–543.

2. It is not just the Thai government that has had trouble pinpointing the network or the structure of the insurgents. As the CIA stated in a report to the U.S. Congress, "We are uncertain whether Muslim separatist groups—possibly with ties to international terrorists—or local criminal networks have been responsible for the violence." See CIA, "Unclassified Responses to the Worldwide Threat," 159.

3. Gen. Kitti Rattanchaya, the government's former top security official for southern Thailand, quoted in Alan Sipress, "Inspired by Anger a World Away," *Washington Post*, May 15, 2004.

national connections."[4] A member of the royal family active in the south frankly acknowledged this fact in 2005, "We don't know who the insurgents are."[5] General Sonthi echoed this statement in 2006, "I have to admit I don't know who is pulling the strings. They don't say who they are. Look at Iraq. There's no 'head,' yet violent attacks take place there every day."[6] By May 2007, the intelligence had not improved dramatically. Stated General Sonthi, "We don't know the exact structure of the leading organisation, but we know for sure they have laid spawn cells in villages in the three southernmost provinces."[7]

This intelligence failure within Thailand has been even broader. Despite numerous arrests since 2004, Thai authorities have had on only a few occasions advance warning of an attack. In April 2005, the government announced that in the previous six months there had been fifty-five important arrests of militants, stating that these arrests had given them a better understanding of the insurgency. But as NRC chairman Anand Panyarachun complained in 2005 with only a small amount of hyperbole, "From January [2004] until now, the authorities did not know who were responsible in 85 percent of the incidents recorded. They knew who were responsible for the remaining 15 percent, but made no arrests."[8] Although the government did not even make its first arrest of a suspected bomb maker until August 2005,[9] by January 2006, it was making the outrageous assertion that only about ten insurgents responsible for planning and carrying out attacks remained free.[10] In April 2006, as the insurgency started to spike back to the highest levels from 2005, Lt. Gen. Ongkorn Thongprasom declared, "The situation in the three southern border provinces should improve since the mili-

---

4. Anthony Davis, "Are Thailand's Southern Militants Moving to Soft Targets?" *Jane's Terrorism and Insurgency Centre*, April 5, 2004.

5. Author interview, Bangkok, March 16, 2005.

6. Wassana Nanuam, "Army Camp on Alert for Fresh Raid," *Bangkok Post*, January 5, 2006.

7. "Top Separatist Goes Unnoticed," *Bangkok Post*, May 17, 2007.

8. Mongkol Bangprapa, "Anand: Decree Condones Violence," *Bangkok Post*, July 23, 2005.

9. The suspect was Masaky Ma. See "Bombers Nabbed," *Nation*, August 22, 2005.

10. "Another 5,300 Police to Be Deployed to Restive South," *Nation*, January 1, 2006; "Violence Is on the Decline: Chidchai," *Nation*, January 2, 2006.

tant network has been weakened by the arrest of its top members."[11] By mid-2006, police had issued warrants for 466 individuals, asserting that they had detained 123 individuals, yet few were ranking members.[12] One government spokesperson, Surapong Suebwonglee, claimed that 604 suspected militants had been detained and 472 identified, although he would not disclose how many had been charged.[13]

Although more aggressive raids in 2007 led to the arrest of nearly two thousand suspects—and netted more weapons and matériel than in earlier years—most suspects had to be released due to a lack of evidence and very few were ever charged. Thus, the authorities were either arresting the wrong people with no connection to the insurgency or were arresting the right people within a highly compartmentalized network. Stated Sonthi, "Even after being arrested, insurgents are sworn to secrecy, so we don't know the masterminds of the violence. They don't expose who they are."[14]

This poor intelligence did not stop authorities from going after the last generation of insurgents when the crisis erupted, however. For example, in the days after the January 2004 attacks, Thai authorities arrested Doloh Sengmasu, a former head of an armed unit in PULO who laid down his arms in 1988 and was elected as a village headman that same year. He was sentenced to two years and has appealed the case, noting with great irony that militants have made repeated attempts on his life because of his PULO membership and accommodation with the Thai state.[15] In fact, the insurgents have killed many of the group's members.

It must be noted, however, that PULO has taken a degree of responsibility through Web site postings warning foreigners to stay away from southern Thailand and that some PULO members have claimed in the

---

11. Cited in Wassana Nanuam and Waedao Harai, "Weak Mobile Phone Signal Saves Lives," *Bangkok Post*, April 17, 2006.

12. "Chidchai Reaches out to Students," *Nation*, April 16, 2006.

13. "Group Slams Govt's Decree for South," *Nation*, July 19, 2006.

14. "Killers Entrenched in Villages: Sonthi," *Nation*, March 29, 2007.

15. "Taking up Arms Again: Ex-PULO Militant Cannot Leave Former Life behind Him," Issara News Service, August 12, 2007.

press that their organization was leading the insurgency.[16] Further, PULO held a watershed "reunification congress" in Damascus, Syria, in 2005 that brought together some forty leading PULO figures from Thailand, Europe, and the Middle East,[17] and a PULO spokesman has hinted at the possibility of a terrorist attack in Bangkok or Phuket: "I can't guarantee it won't happen."[18] Despite such talk, no one on the ground believes that the aging European-based leadership has ever had any control over the insurgency, and all the evidence suggests that PULO is playing only a limited role in the insurgency.

First, PULO has been formally defunct for years. Second, PULO has always been a very secular organization, emphasizing Pattani secessionism, not religion, and therefore does not have the ideological zeal needed to target civilians. As Lukman B. Lima, PULO's deputy vice president, told the press, "Our struggle is for our own people, to get back what is rightfully ours." He added that the group had no connection to al-Qaeda or JI.[19] Third, neither Lukman nor Kasturi Mahkota, the head of PULO's Foreign Affairs Department, has claimed responsibility for the violence. Most observers understand that the media bursts by PULO and its attempt to outline a political platform (for example, Lukman's call for a referendum) merely represent efforts to leverage its diminished influence in the south.[20]

As evidence of this diminished influence, even though PULO led the delegation of "insurgents" to the secret Langkawi talks, it could not

---

16. Ed Cropley, "Exclusive: Malay Separatists Say behind Southern Thai Unrest," Reuters, August 28, 2005; Tony Cheng, "Behind the Bombs," BBC, August 30, 2005.

17. The congress elected Tengku Bira Kotanila as titular president and head of a seventeen-member executive council. See Anthony Davis, "Interview: Kasturi Mahkota, Foreign Affairs Spokesman, Patani United Liberation Organisation (PULO)," *Jane's Intelligence Review*, August 8, 2006.

18. Quoted in Kate McGeown, "Search for Justice in Thai South," BBC, August 9, 2006. This was contradicted by Kasturi Mahkota, PULO's spokesman, who said, "We do not need to be on anyone's terrorist list. Once we are on that list, it is all over." See Davis, "Interview: Kasturi Mahkota."

19. Cropley, "Exclusive: Malay Separatists Say behind Southern Thai Unrest."

20. After the Tak Bai incident, PULO threatened to reward mujahideen who killed Thai police officers. It also issued the following warning: "Their capital will be burned to the ground like they did to our Pattani capital. Their blood will be shed into the earth and flood into the rivers. Our weapons are fire and oil, fire and oil, fire and oil." PULO and Bersatu, "Statement of Protest," October 31, 2004.

deliver one day of peace as a sign of goodwill or demonstration of command and control. Internal Thai intelligence documents obtained by the author state that PULO has only thirty members in the southern provinces and roughly two hundred members in Malaysia. As General Sonthi acknowledged in May 2007, "The Pattani United Liberation Organisation . . . had weakened and become more symbolic."[21]

Even so, the government blamed PULO for trying to discredit it by spreading rumors of impending violence in southern Thailand in 2006, which led 131 Muslims to flee into Malaysia claiming persecution from Thai security forces. Thai government officials said that PULO even established a front organization called the Pattani Malay Human Rights Organization (PMHRO) that sought to call attention to the refugees and further discredit the government by publicizing trumped-up human rights abuses. "PULO's move was aimed at tarnishing the country's image," asserted a government spokesman at the time. PULO denied the allegation and asserted that PMHRO was an independent humanitarian organization.[22]

Although former PULO members are very clearly involved in the insurgency, it is not clear whether they are fighting in PULO's name or whether they have joined forces with newer and more radical organizations. Clearly their experience in cross-border operations and their control or ownership of land that can be used for training has been important for the younger insurgents. Perhaps PULO's most important role in the insurgency has been as an Internet-based advocate. Most Web sites dedicated to the Pattani cause are run by PULO's old Web site, www.pulo.org, which was shut down in 2005 and replaced by www.puloinfo.net, which is the Web site today most accessed by the media. This site is registered in Malaysia and run by Samir Adnan in Kelantan State (infopulo@gmail.com), but the funding and technical side is run out of Sweden, which is not surprising because much of the leadership is based there.[23] Another PULO Web site, www.patanimeredeka.com, was created in August 2005. It is administered by Desa Permai in

21. "Top Separatist Goes Unnoticed," *Bangkok Post*, May 17, 2007.
22. Don Pathan, "'Refugee' Incident: PULO Denies Role in Muslim Exodus," *Nation*, September 12, 2005.
23. Web site registration and administration date were found at www.betterwhois.com.

Narathiwat, Thailand, who provides the same e-mail address as Adnan and is paid for out of Sweden.[24]

The Insurgent Groups

But if PULO is only playing a limited role in the insurgency and no other group has taken credit for the attacks or publicly stated its goals or platform, who is behind the insurgency? On the basis of interviews and analysis of the range and styles of attacks, two Thai separatist organizations appear to be most responsible for the violence: the GMIP and the larger BRN-C. As a senior government official put it in December 2006: "I dare say the BRN is behind the unrest in the region. Don't divert public attention by saying that violent attacks are the work of drug traffickers or other groups."[25] Kasturi even went so far as to acknowledge in an interview with *Jane's Intelligence Review* that the insurgency is "being spearheaded by the Barisan Revolusi Nasional–Coordinate (BRN-C)."[26] Two smaller groups, Jemaah Salafi and the splinter organization New PULO, are also involved to a degree. This comports with Davis's conclusion that there are at least four groups actively involved in the insurgency. Based on an analysis of the types of bombs used and their composition, he found that there are at least four different bomb-making facilities supplying bombs to the south, with each facility having its own "signature" and with each being used by a different group.[27]

GMIP

The GMIP is a rural-based organization founded in 1986 by Vae-Hama Vae-Yuso. Following a period of internal squabbling,[28] Nasori Saesaeng (Awae Kaelae), Jehku Mae Kuteh (Doromae Kuteh), Nasae Saning,[29] and a handful of other veterans of the Afghan-Soviet war consolidated power in 1995. For most of the 1990s, the GMIP was more of a crimi-

24. Ibid.

25. "South 'Could Be Independent in Three Years,'" *Bangkok Post*, December 7, 2007.

26. Davis, "Interview: Kasturi Mahkota."

27. Davis, "Thai Militants Adopt New Bombing Tactics."

28. Chalk, "Separatism and Southeast Asia," 260.

29. Nasori disappeared in 2001. Warrants for his arrest were issued in 2000, 2001, and 2002. "Militants Face Treason Charge," *Nation*, January 5, 2004.

nal gang than a group of freedom fighters. It was thought to have run guns for other Muslim insurgent groups, in particular the MILF in Mindanao, Philippines, and the Free Aceh Movement (GAM) in Aceh, Indonesia. The GMIP also engaged in kidnapping and extortion and earned an estimated Bt10 million (US$220,000) per year in contract killings and "enforcement."[30] Thai military officials, albeit biased, assert that the GMIP had very close ties with the Wadah faction of Thaksin's TRT and often did its dirty work.[31] As one senior Thai intelligence official said, "The Gerakan Mujiheddin had a poor record in the past. It was really a criminal gang. But they purged their leadership."[32] Another Thai intelligence officer added, "After January [2004], they tried to improve their image."[33] Even so, the GMIP's longstanding ties to transnational criminal groups are unlikely to be completely severed, regardless of how its image or goals may have changed. Thai authorities seemed to take the GMIP more seriously beginning in August 2003, when security forces gunned down two senior members in Pattani—its Afghan-trained operations chief, Nasae Saning, and Mahma Maeroh.[34]

Although the government has not said much about the GMIP, a steady stream of arrest warrants and a handful of actual arrests of GMIP leaders suggest that this is one of the most important organizations behind the insurgency. In January 2004, the government announced that it was searching for Doromae Kuteh, "the mastermind of many evil attacks on the south." On January 26, Thai authorities announced that the Malaysian government had arrested him. Although he likely remains detained under the Malaysian Internal Security Act (ISA), unconfirmed reports suggest that Malaysia deported Kuteh to Indonesia and that he now lives in Bandung. Thai officials believe that GMIP head Nasori

30. "Muslim Group Linked to Attacks in Thailand," *Straits Times*, March 25, 2002.

31. Author interview, Bangkok, February 9, 2007.

32. Author interview, Bangkok, March 16, 2005.

33. Author interview, Bangkok, March 16, 2005.

34. Nasae Saning was arrested by Malaysian authorities and turned over to Thai officials. It is believed that the Thais staged his breakout and gunned him down. This infuriated the Malaysians; since then, Malaysian authorities have been reluctant to turn anyone over to their Thai counterparts. "Battle Is on for the Hearts and Minds in the South," *Nation*, January 12, 2004.

Saesaeng is based in Kelantan, Malaysia.[35] In January 2005, the Malaysians arrested Mareepeng Maha, a leading member of the GMIP, and turned him over to their Thai counterparts. Police have linked Mareepeng to a number of crimes since 1997 involving narcotics, robbery, and murder and previously had requested that the Malaysians turn him over.[36] Thai authorities arrested three other GMIP suspects in early 2005: Mahamaropee Yasi, Hasbulloh Dueramae, and Hama Pohtae.[37] Other Afghanistan-trained members of the GMIP include Wae Ali Copter Waeji,[38] who is believed to be one of the top military commanders of the GMIP, with two key lieutenants, Ni-asae Domae and Manu Mama. The Thai press has recently labeled Wae Ali Copter Waeji a leader of the Runda Kumpulan Kecil (RKK), although this label is probably inaccurate. Karim Karubang (Doromae Lohmae) is thought to be the GMIP chief in Yala,[39] and the leader of the January 4, 2004, raid that restarted the insurgency.[40]

JI approached the GMIP in 1999–2000 as part of the Rabitatul Mujahideen (RM), but it is unknown how deep or strong a relationship was forged between the two groups. Following the 9/11 attacks on the United States, the GMIP distributed leaflets in Yala calling for a jihad and support for Osama bin Laden.[41] It had a stated goal of turning Pattani Raya (Greater Pattani) into an Islamic state by 2008, and it shares al-Qaeda's vision of establishing a caliphate.[42]

---

35. "Militants Face Treason Charge," *Nation*, January 15, 2005.

36. Police said the bounty on Mareepeng was Bt500,000 (US$12,500), but in official documents submitted to Kuala Lumpur, the bounty was listed as only Bt100,000 (US$2,500). "Key Suspect Arrested in Narathiwat," *Nation*, January 6, 2005.

37. Ibid.

38. Davis, "Thai Militants Adopt New Bombing Tactics."

39. Anthony Davis, "Southern Thai Insurgency Gains Fresh Momentum," *Jane's Intelligence Review*, August 1, 2004.

40. The first warrant for Karubang's arrest came in 1996.

41. Anthony Davis, "Thailand Faces up to Southern Extremist Threat," *Jane's Intelligence Review*, October 2003.

42. Jason Gagliardi, "Behind the News—Fear and Fervour," *South China Morning Post*, February 5, 2004; Rob Fanney, "Gerakan Mujahideen Islam Pattani (GMIP—Pattani Islamic Mujahideen Movement)," *Jane's Terrorism and Insurgency Centre*, October 31, 2002.

The GMIP probably maintains a more important relationship with the Kumpulan Mujahideen Malaysia (Malaysian Mujahideen Group, KMM) in Malaysia.[43] The KMM was founded on October 12, 1995, by a veteran of the Afghan mujahideen, Zainon Ismail, at approximately the same time as the "new" GMIP.[44] Afghanistan experience was the common factor in both organizations. Nik Adli Nik Aziz, a leader of the KMM, trained with Nasori Saesaeng in Afghanistan, and the two became close friends.[45] In total, forty-five members of the KMM, nearly half of its membership, either fought against the Soviets or trained in al-Qaeda camps in Afghanistan in the 1990s.[46] Members of the KMM made frequent trips to southern Thailand, where they procured weapons and likely engaged in training.[47] In 1999, for example, Nik Adli Nik Aziz purchased a large cache of weapons there, including twenty-four pounds of explosives. In turn, many of the Thai secessionists were able to seek sanctuary in parts of Malaysia where the KMM had influence or government officials were sympathetic to their cause.

The GMIP tried to raise its profile in 2002 by staging a number of raids on police and army outposts to steal weapons in the three southernmost provinces of Yala, Narathiwat, and Pattani. In March alone, eight policemen and a teacher were killed in GMIP raids. In June, a raid on a remote (military/police/border) outpost netted seventeen assault

---

43. A number of analysts do not believe that the KMM is a separate organization from JI; they think it is an artificial construct of Malaysian security forces who were willing to acknowledge a homegrown militant organization but did not want to admit that it was part of a transnational terrorist organization.

44. Patrick Sennyah, Ainon Mohd, and Hayati Hayatudin, "KMM's Opposition Link," *New Straits Times*, October 12, 2001.

45. Nik Adli Nik Aziz is the son of Malaysia's fundamentalist Parti Islam Se-Malaysia (PAS) leader and Kelantan State chief minister Nik Aziz Nik Mat; for that reason, many critics have charged that his arrest was politically motivated. He is still being detained by Malaysian authorities. His arrest and possible connection to southern Thai separatism has raised suspicions about possible connections between the southern Thai insurgency and the larger institutions of Malaysian fundamentalist Muslim politics, leading many to wonder if Malaysian money and organizational expertise are assisting terrorist Thai Muslims.

46. Nelson Fernandez, "Police Have Videos, Pictures, Info on Afghan-Trained Students," *New Straits Times*, September 30, 2001.

47. Andrew Perrin, "Thailand's Terror," *Time—Asian Edition*, November 25, 2002.

rifles and sixteen shotguns.[48] In July, Ma Daeng, the top aide to Nasori Saesaeng, led a raid on an army outpost in Narathiwat. By the end of the year, GMIP rebels had killed twenty-one police officers. In April 2003, they attacked two marine units, killing five marines and seizing thirty M-16s. Between 2002 and 2004, the group was responsible for the deaths of forty police officers.[49]

The GMIP's operations reflect the group's rural origins. Indeed, Thai officials have not linked any of the urban bombings to the GMIP, although they acknowledge that the GMIP has the most sophisticated bomb-making skills of any of the separatist organizations. The primary tactics of the GMIP include attacks on military convoys using roadside IEDs and raids on rural police and military outposts. Thai intelligence documents estimate that the organization has forty well-trained cell leaders in the south.

Although the GMIP is not an ustadz- or pondok-based movement and many question the organization's Islamist credentials, pointing to its criminal past and its members' tattoos, its mission has fundamentally changed. The consolidation of power by the group's Afghanistan veterans has given the GMIP a radical Islamist agenda and a goal of transforming the south into an Islamic state. As a result, today's GMIP members are hardened terrorists and ruthless insurgents. That said, the religious core and the much larger component of the insurgency rests with the BRN-C.

BRN-C

The Thai National Security Council acknowledges that there is "a new Islamic group [that] through increasing contacts with extremists and fundamentalists in Middle Eastern countries, Indonesia, Malaysia, and the Philippines [has] metamorphosed into a political entity of significance."[50] Thai intelligence now speaks of the insurgency as being a "pondok-based" movement.[51] Stated Gen. Pisarn Wattana

---

48. Arul John, "South Thailand Attacks: Did Raiders Have JI Links?" *New Paper*, January 13, 2004.

49. Ibid.

50. National Security Council member quoted in Crispin, "Strife down South."

51. The Thai Ministry of Education has registered 214 Islamic schools but acknowledges that there are hundreds of small, unregistered, privately owned pondoks. "Muslim Teachers Extend Cautious Welcome to Aree," *Nation*, September 18, 2004.

wongkeeree, the former commander of Thai armed forces in the south, "There is no doubt that the basis for this new insurgency are the ustadz. This is something that has been in the making for a long time."[52] A police official similarly noted following a series of attacks, "We suspect some [Islamic] schools might have played a significant role in these shootouts. We think that they might have been used as training grounds for militants, or teachers might have indoctrinated their pupils with fundamentalist ideologies."[53] Col. Charin Amorn-kaeo, intelligence director of the Fourth Army, explained, "They are religious teachers and students. They are 25 to 40 years old. Older people who used to be key figures now play advisory roles."[54] By October 2004, even Thaksin was forced to concede that the insurgency was a student-based movement supported by radical clerics: "This is a domestic problem with the fashion of [an Islamic] brotherhood. Some religious teachers are recruiting students to stage violence. This has gained momentum since 9/11."[55]

Many of these radical clerics are quite young and are recent graduates of Middle Eastern and South Asian madrassas.[56] It is estimated that 160 Thai Muslims are currently studying in Saudi Arabia, 900 in Sudan, and some 1,500 in Egypt.[57] Further, some 2,500 graduates of Middle Eastern institutions have returned to the south. Most of these graduates are ineligible for government jobs, as the government does not recognize their degrees.[58] An even larger number of graduates of Malaysian and Indonesian schools are also thought to be in the region. The National

---

52. Elegant, "Southern Front."

53. Nopporn Wang-Anan, "Thai Muslim Schools Deny Militant Links," Reuters, May 7, 2004.

54. Wassana Nanuam and Anucha Charoenpo, "Militants 'Likely to Stay Hidden,'" *Bangkok Post*, September 19, 2005.

55. Prime Minister Thaksin, quoted in Elegant, "Southern Front."

56. Thai officials estimate that some two hundred clerics attended South Asian madrassas in the past decade, although it is unknown how many went to Afghanistan.

57. John R. Bradley, "Waking up to the Terror Threat," *Straits Times*, May 27, 2004.

58. Kavi Chongkittavorn, "Thailand: International Terrorism and the Muslim South," paper presented, March 18, 2004, Singapore.

Intelligence Agency (NIA) has revealed "about 200,000 Muslim men aged about 15 to 20 are under close watch by the authorities."[59]

The evidence that has emerged to date suggests that these pondoks, ustadz, and more militant students derive from the old, fractious BRN organization and networks established in the 1970s. In 1980, the BRN's two leaders, Abdul Karim Hassan and "Haji M" fell out.[60] Abdul Karim Hassan established the BRN-Uran (sometimes called the BRN-Ulama), which was distinctly Islamist and opposed the nationalist agenda of PULO, and Haji M formed the BRN-C, which pursued a more political struggle. Another faction, the BRN-Congress, under the leadership of Jehku Peng (Rosa Bursao), pursued a military struggle. Throughout the 1990s, the three factions of the BRN network developed and became far more religiously oriented. Thai intelligence officials note that the BRN network has traditionally changed its leadership often, which has allowed the organization to change its ideological orientation.[61] The BRN-C emerged as the largest and best organized of the three groups— and of all other separatist groups.[62] Indeed, the BRN-C, which was able to tap into the old BNPP and BIPP networks after both organizations became defunct in the 1980s and 1990s, has become the umbrella group for the various BRN splinters and is a more urban-based organization than the GMIP.

Another interesting shift in the BRN-C's focus is in its desire to become a mass organization. The number of members in the BRN-C and its larger youth wing Permuda (Youth) is not known, but Thai officials estimate that there are approximately 1,000 to 2,000 members and state that the group has considerable sympathy and support in the community.[63] Through Permuda, the BRN-C recruits from a large pool of pondok students. In a BRN-C document that was found in Narathiwat's Joh I Rong (Cho Irong) District, the authors outlined a plan to increase the group's popular support to between 200,000 and 300,000 people, 10

---

59. "Army Admits Southern Killings," *Bangkok Post*, April 11, 2007.
60. ICG, *Southern Thailand: Insurgency, Not Jihad*, 12.
61. Author interview, Bangkok, March 17, 2005.
62. ICG, *Southern Thailand: Insurgency, Not Jihad*.
63. Author interview, Bangkok, March 16, 2005.

percent of whom would then be recruited into the paramilitary wing.[64] According to the International Crisis Group (ICG), the BRN-C established Permuda as part of a strategy of expansion that began in 1992.[65] In 2005, the Thai government "blacklisted" some 4,000 youths for involvement in Permuda.[66] According to a police source, "They're brainwashed little by little and taught to believe in the independent state of Pattani. After a while, they are sent out to conduct a 'simple' operation, such as cutting down trees (to block a road) or planting spikes (to disable vehicles)."[67] One of the militants shot and killed by the army during the July 14, 2005, rampage in Yala was a member of Permuda.[68] Although its members are generally the cream of the crop from the pondoks, the very best are sent abroad for military training.[69]

The BRN-C's current leaders are, for the most part, schoolteachers and ustadz. Thai security officials suggest that the preachers and teachers from eighteen different schools are the central figures in the BRN-C and that they have tried to establish a network throughout three hundred schools.[70] The most important of these schools is the Thammawittaya Foundation School in Yala, but other suspected schools include the Samphan Wittaya School, the Jihad Wittaya School, and the Pattana Islam Wittaya School. The Thammawittaya Foundation School is one of the largest Islamic schools in Thailand. Founded in 1951 by Haji Muhammad Tohe Sulong, it has some 6,000 students spread across four separate campuses and 196 ustadz.[71]

The arrests of BRN-C members bear this out. On December 14, 2004, members of the Ministry of Justice's Special Investigations

---

64. Author interview, Bangkok, April 20, 2005.

65. ICG, *Southern Thailand: Insurgency, Not Jihad*.

66. "Muslim Religious Teacher, Gunman Arrested," Thai News Agency, January 13, 2005.

67. Wassayos Ngamkham, "4,000 Teenagers Blacklisted," *Bangkok Post*, October 11, 2005.

68. Nirmal Ghosh, "Fear Factor Takes Root in Thai South," *Straits Times*, August 2, 2005.

69. Author interview, Bangkok, January 12, 2006.

70. "Fugitive Headmaster May Be Top Insurgent," *Nation*, December 17, 2004.

71. The school's main campus is located in the Joh I Rong District of Narathiwat. The curriculum is mixed, and only four hundred students study only Islam. For more on the school, see "Top Islamic School Denies That It Is a Breeding Ground for Extremists," *Nation*, December 18, 2004.

Department launched a raid on five pondoks,[72] arresting four Islamic teachers from the Thammawittaya Foundation School: Yusuf Waeduramae, Muhammad Hanafi Doleh, Ahama Buleh, and Abdul Roseh Hayidoloh.[73] A fifth individual, Sapaeng Basoe, the principal of the school, escaped. In January 2005, another teacher from the Thammawittaya Foundation School, Hama Jehter (Sawmad Luepae), was arrested. Other Thammawittaya teachers identified the thirty-seven-year-old cleric as the mastermind of the insurgency.[74] Security forces also raided a school in Pattani's Yaring District, the Jihad Wittaya School, where Yusuf Rayalong (Ustadz Ismae-ae) actively recruited from the student body. They arrested a teacher and three students for possession of bomb-making components and manuals and other documents.[75] Security forces raided it again in May 2005. Authorities recovered military-training video compact discs (VCDs), al-Qaeda manuals, and bomb-making plans downloaded from the Internet. A shooting range was found on the school grounds. Four teachers were arrested, but the founder, Dulloh Waeman (Ustadz Loh), fled. Some twenty people from the Jihad Wittaya School have either been arrested or killed, or are wanted in connection with the April 2004 attacks.[76] The school has

---

72. The raid was made after a confession by another of the school's teachers, Usma Malakoe, who had earlier been arrested in connection with several armed robberies and violent attacks. Piyanart Srivalo, "PM Buoyed by Arrest of Key Suspects," *Nation*, December 16, 2004; "Breakthrough in the South: Hunting Down the Masterminds," *Nation*, December 17, 2004; Amy Kazmin, "Teacher Arrests Spark Thai Separatist Hunt," *Financial Times*, December 17, 2004; "Fugitive Headmaster May Be Top Insurgent," *Nation*, December 17, 2004.

73. According to Sirichai Thanyasiri, the director of the Southern Border Provinces Peace Building Command, Yusuf Waeduramae was believed to be the man who planned the January 4, 2004, raid on the army camp that netted more than four hundred weapons. Sombat Amornwiwat, the director-general of the Special Investigations Department, stated that documents found in Yusuf's house strongly linked him to the separatists. Thai officials believe that Abdul Roseh was the financial chief for the cell and that he solicited and disbursed foreign funds. See "Breakthrough in the South," *Nation*, December 17, 2004, and "Evidence against 'Masterminds' behind Insurgent Attacks Is Strong, Says SID," *Nation*, December 24, 2004.

74. "Muslim Religious Teacher, Gunman Arrested," Thai News Agency, January 13, 2005.

75. "Students Say Weapons Training Held at School," *Bangkok Post*, May 20, 2005; "Raids Lead to Valuable Haul," *Nation*, May 20, 2005.

76. "Suspect Sought over Thai Attacks," BBC, May 5, 2004.

been permanently closed.[77] Twelve other suspects (eight students, three alumni, and a former teacher) in the attacks were affiliated with an Egyptian-funded school.[78]

In October 2005, eight Islamic schoolteachers—Waeyusoh Waedu-eramae, Muhammad Kanafi Doloh, Abdulrohseh Hayidoloh, and Ahama Buleh, former teachers and administrators at the Thammawit-taya school; Masukri Hari, the manager of the Pattana Islam Wittaya School; and Salae Deng, Hama Jehteh, and Torleh Disa-eh—went on trial for helping to foment the insurgency. Prosecutors accused the men—all in their forties or fifties—of being members of the BRN-C.[79] Defense lawyers argued that prosecutors did not have evidence of a credible chain of command within the BRN-C and therefore could not link them directly to the organization.[80] In January 2006, police arrested a teacher at the Islamic Tadika School, Ibroheng Gasae, who admitted to recruiting and indoctrinating youth for the BRN-C.[81]

The BRN-C is led by Masae Useng and Sapaeng Basoe (sometimes spelled Basor). Masae Useng is believed to be the BRN-C's head of military training and its chief military tactician.[82] A teacher at both the Thammawittaya and Samphan Wittaya schools, he is believed to have been trained in Afghanistan. After attending a madrassa, he was con-scripted into the Royal Thai Army in 1980–82. After being discharged, he became a district officer in Joh I Rong and ran a madrassa. By all accounts, he was a well-respected member of the community. At some point, he joined the BRN. In 2003, he was arrested, but he disappeared when he was released. Thai officials are perplexed by how someone who was so well respected and willing to work within the system became so

---

77. "Students Say Weapons Training Held at School," *Bangkok Post*, May 20, 2005; "Ponoh School's Fate Sealed," *Bangkok Post*, June 13, 2005.
78. Wang-Anan, "Thai Muslim Schools Deny Militant Links."
79. "Thai Islamic Teachers Go on Trial for Insurgency," Reuters, October 11, 2005.
80. "Teachers 'Terror Masterminds,'" *Nation*, October 12, 2005.
81. Wassayos Ngamkham, "Muslim Teacher Admits Brainwashing Youths," *Bangkok Post*, January 25, 2006.
82. "Thailand Alleges Terror Campaign," Associated Press, December 23, 2004; "Reward for the Arrest of Two Islamic Leaders," Thai News Agency, December 19, 2004; "Police Say Mastermind Identified," *Nation*, April 8, 2005; author interviews, Bangkok, March 17 and 18, 2005, and April 20, 2005; and the Department of Special Investigation's (DSI) Web site, www.dsi.go.th (accessed October 1, 2008).

disenchanted. "Why did he turn against us?" one military officer asked rhetorically, stating that he is "educated, powerful, and wily enough to cause trouble." Papers found in Masae Useng's house in 2005 suggest that the militants were planning to execute a series of attacks against soft targets, such as tourist venues.

Sapaeng Basoe (sometimes spelled Basor) is described as the political leader of the BRN-C.[83] Born on March 1, 1936, in the Yaring District of Pattani, he is the son-in-law of the schoolmaster at the Thammawittaya school and was himself the schoolmaster of the Thammawittaya Mulniti school. He later was identified as a mastermind of the April 4 triple bombing in Hat Yai. Basoe's name is highly sensitive, because he had close ties with a group of Thai Muslim legislators from the Wadah faction. Although reports surfaced in 2005 that he was negotiating his surrender and has a Bt1 million (US$25,000) bounty on his head,[84] he remains at large. According to one report, he slipped out of Thailand and is being protected by "high-level authorities in a foreign country."

Other BRN-C leaders include Abdullah Munir, Dulloh Waeman (Ustadz Loh), Abroseh Parehruepoh, Abdulkanin Kalupang, Isma-ae Toyalong, Arduenan Mama, Bororting Binbuerheng, Yusuf Rayalong (Ustadz Ismae-ae), Kariya Yalahpae (Yalapae), Heepanee Marea (Hiani Mareh), Rohmulee Neataeroh, Yagareeya Yuerapae,[85] Ammad Muri Latea, Mamu Borodorya, Ismail Kengmalapi, Ahmad Tue-gneng, and Abdulmuris Saleh.[86] In 2004, the police announced that they had iden-

83. See "PM Says Alleged Insurgent Leader Not Linked to Islamic MPs," Thai News Agency, December 21, 2004; "Police Say Mastermind Identified," Nation, April 8, 2005; author interviews, Bangkok, March 17 and 18, 2005, and April 20, 2005; Muhammad Ayub Pathan and Wassana Nanuam, "Intelligence Sources Warn of Major Strike Late This Month," Bangkok Post, July 13, 2006; and the DSI Web site, www.dsi.go.th.

84. "Top Insurgent Leader Arrested in Malaysia, Says PM," Thai News Agency, January 26, 2005; "Rebel 'Mastermind' Held," Star (Malaysia), January 27, 2005.

85. He was believed to have been behind the spate of bombings in June 2006. "Army Chief Given Full Power over Far South," Bangkok Post, June 20, 2006.

86. "Police Distribute 'Wanted' Posters for Southern Insurgents," Thai News Agency, November 24, 2004; "Suspected Militants Demand to See Lawyers," Thai News Agency, December 20, 2004.

tified 100 additional BRN-C members.[87] Named members included Isamal Kengmalapi, Deng Wae-aji, Muhammad Murismaleh, Mamu Borodaya, Madari Along, Ahmad Tue-nga, Mahama Romueli Sameh, Madaree Arong, and Royi Hanyi Jehwae.[88]

In late 2005, the Thai government began to acknowledge that a number of BRN-C militants had been trained in Indonesia, although it was not known by whom, and began to make reference to a group known as the RKK.[89] However, the RKK is not an independent group per se, but rather a name for BRN-C militants who had received some training in Indonesia—mostly, it seems, while studying there. The report identifies six Indonesian schools and universities with large numbers of Pattani students. Police believe that the head of this cell is Rorhing Ahsong (Ustaz Rorhing) and that it has some five hundred trained members.[90] In late November 2005, then deputy prime minister Chidchai Wannasathit announced that he would travel to Indonesia to discuss counterterrorism cooperation.[91] In December 2005, General Sonthi traveled to Indonesia, where the two sides agreed to further cooperation in counterterrorism and counterinsurgency activities. The Indonesians agreed to monitor links between the southern Thais and the GAM.[92]

The seventeen suspects arrested in connection with the October 16, 2005, killing of a monk all claimed to be part of the RKK. Likewise, three men suspected of participating in an ambush on a commando unit in Yala's Banang Sata District on January 2, 2006, said that they had received training in guerrilla tactics from the RKK in Indonesia.[93] "These men were trained in this form of combat. We have been cooperating with the Indonesian authorities to see if those behind the attacks

87. Kimina Lyall, "Thailand Links Terror to Neighbors," *Australian*, December 20, 2004.

88. "Police Say Mastermind Identified," *Nation*, April 8, 2005.

89. "New Terror Group Active in the South," *Bangkok Post*, November 24, 2005.

90. Waedao Harai, "Five Killed on Patrol Guarding Teachers," *Bangkok Post*, June 28, 2006; "Six Arrested after New Wave of Blasts," *Bangkok Post*, June 17, 2006.

91. "Government Rejects Amnesty for Southern Insurgents," *Bangkok Post*, November 29, 2005.

92. "Indonesia Pledges Intelligence Sharing," *Bangkok Post*, December 17, 2005.

93. "Two Dead, One Hurt in Yala Attacks," *Nation*, January 10, 2006.

are linked to militant groups there," said Chidchai Wannasathit.[94] In late July 2006, police detained twenty-one-year olds Udeeman Samoh, who investigators maintain is a very skillful bomb maker, and Sapee-aree Jehkor, who is reportedly one of the cell's top members.[95] Police asserted that they were trained in Bandung, Indonesia. Stated Chidchai, "We cannot conclude whether Indonesian soldiers were involved, but we are certain they were trained in Indonesia."[96]

Recruitment into the BRN-C/Permuda network takes place in schools by pondok teachers and outside of schools in da'wah and religious study sessions. Within the schools, teachers look for youngsters who are pious, impressionable, and mentally agile.[97] Once identified, the students are invited to extracurricular sessions for more specialized religious training, where indoctrination and recruitment take place. Many da'wah preachers are foreigners, including Saudis, Yemenis, Cambodians, Malaysians, Egyptians, Kuwaitis, and Moroccans. The Tabliqhi Jemaat and other missionary groups have been involved in this process. In such sessions, the students are encouraged to move beyond propagation of Islamic values by word (da'wah) to propagation by deed (jihad). The actual process of recruitment begins with a respected imam who can call together three to six village-level imams; each is charged with recruiting five missionaries, and each missionary is responsible for running a study session for five to eight congregants after Friday prayers. In schools, each recruit is expected to form his own cell. The NIA's Veerasak Thipmonthien said that informants and local authorities "told us that insurgency leaders have been sending their members to meet Muslim youths in every village in the three provinces of Yala, Pattani and Narathiwat, as they want these people to be their youth allies."[98]

---

94. "Three More Die as Monk's Murderer Confesses Crime," *Thai Day*, January 10, 2006.

95. "Village Raid Nets 2 Men Linked to Blast Targeting Peace Team," *Bangkok Post*, July 29, 2006.

96. Wassana Nanuam, "RKK Insurgents Admit They Trained in Indonesia, Says Army," *Bangkok Post*, November 28, 2005.

97. ICG, *Southern Thailand: Insurgency, Not Jihad*, 26.

98. "Army Admits Southern Killings," *Bangkok Post*, April 11, 2007.

While the BRN-C was originally less militaristic than the GMIP and groups such as PULO and New PULO, it is now in the forefront of bomb making. As one Thai officer told Anthony Davis, "Before it was New PULO and GMIP that had the skills. But some BRN people have been trained in the past two years."[99] Moreover, BRN-C members have been implicated in a number of the grisly beheadings in the south,[100] and they murdered two marines in the Tanyong Limo stand-off after patiently infiltrating the village.[101]

The BRN-C is structured along strict cellular lines. Each *kawasan* (province) is composed of three to four *wilaiyeh* (areas); each wilaiyeh is composed of two to three tambon (districts); and each tambon is composed of at least four to five *ayoh* (villages). Each ayoh generally has about ten people in leadership positions, including an imam, a Permuda representative, and a logistician. The leader of an ayoh has forty to fifty men under his control. "These insurgents work as independent cells," said one security official. "There is no big boss, but there are several key members."[102] Despite being cellular, there is clear command and control; operations can be delegated to rank-and-file members. In April 2007, one BRN-C member claimed that there was at least one militant cell in 80 percent of southern villages. Many villages have two or more cells. In addition to cells, the militants also rely on trusted locals and have given "official ranks" to their supporters to systematize their duties. Under the ayoh system, "The rebel group would select some reliable people in each village who are ranked *tura-ngae* with responsibilities to

99. Davis, "Thai Militants Adopt New Bombing Tactics."

100. For example, on July 29, 2005, police arrested six suspected BRN-C members in connection with the decapitation of a policeman. On August 18, police arrested seven more suspected BRN-C members. The police are searching for one more member of this cell: Mahama Bahae, a teacher at the Thammawittaya Foundation School. "One Man Killed, 3 Wounded in the Deep South," *Bangkok Post*, July 31, 2005; Muhammad Ayub Pathan, "Seven Nabbed over Officer's Decapitation," *Bangkok Post*, August 19, 2005.

101. A Narathiwat court issued arrest warrants for three core members of BRN-C for the murder of the marines in Tanyong Limo. An-ensan Nikaji was arrested and Niasae Domae and Ni-Amran Nikaji are still at large. Twelve of the thirty suspects in the killings have been caught. Wassayos Ngamkham, "Three BRN Men Wanted for Killings," *Bangkok Post*, September 30, 2005; "BRN Group Infiltrating Key Villages," *Bangkok Post*, September 28, 2005.

102. "Violence Is on the Decline: Chidchai," *Nation*, January 2, 2006.

gather information about the geography of the village and the number of villagers, and also to take care of the militants' weapons."[103]

Most of the cells have a fixed geographical area of responsibility, and they are given a target list, sometimes specific, sometimes very general—such as police or soldiers. Although these cells are coordinated at the district level, there are also roving cells that perform operations across the four provinces and that are from the district-level leadership.[104] This allows the cells to demonstrate remarkable operational intelligence and innovation. "Insurgents have fantastic human intelligence; a superb network. They demonstrate learning and learn how to work around [our] countermeasures."[105] BRN-C leaders have admitted that they engage in regular assassinations of fellow Muslims to eliminate collaborators and to ensure discipline in the movement.[106] As a result, the BRN-C has become a power in the villages.

The BRN-C's siblings—the BRN-Congress, the BRN-Ulama, and the BIPP—still exist, but they are little more than very small splinter groups. Undated internal Thai intelligence documents name a handful of leaders from these groups, most of whom are living in exile in Malaysia.[107] They control few militants in Thailand. According to Thai intelligence, the BRN-Congress has seventy to a hundred members in Malaysia and ten to fifteen men operating in the southern provinces. This seems like a woeful underestimate; the government publicly gives higher figures.

Jemaah Salafi and New PULO

Although the GMIP and the BRN-C perpetrate most of the violence and radicalization, evidence suggests that two smaller fringe groups are also involved in the insurgency: Jemaah Salafi and New PULO.

Muhammad Haji Jaeming (Abdul Fatah) founded Jemaah Salafi in the late 1990s after training in the Sadda Camp in Afghanistan in 1989 and returning to southern Thailand, where he established the Hutae

---

103. "Rebel Group Gives Villagers 'Ranks,'" *Bangkok Post*, October 23, 2006.
104. Author interviews, Bangkok, December 19 and 20, 2006.
105. Author interview, Bangkok, February 9, 2007.
106. Author interview, Pattani, January 15, 2006.
107. The author acquired these documents in February 2006.

Tua madrassa in Narathiwat. He represented Jemaah Salafi at the three RM meetings in Malaysia in 1999–2000. While some intelligence officials denigrate him as being uneducated (apparently, he went only through high school), he served as a liaison to Hambali and seems to be one of the few Thais who favors the pan–Southeast Asia agenda of JI.[108] Some observers argue that Abdul Fatah and colleagues such as Ismail Lutfi Japagiya created Jemaah Salafi to avoid being subsumed into the greater JI organization and to keep the JI leaders at arm's length.[109] Although Jemaah Salafi has assisted JI, the group maintains its own identity and has held back on launching major terrorist attacks in Thailand, partly because Abdul Fatah is under intense scrutiny by Thai security forces and is in no position to get deeply involved in the current unrest. That noted, the group has played a role in the violence, but their involvement is so small that the role is likely very limited. Although the relationship between Jemaah Salafi and the BRN-C is unknown, the BRN-C likely sees the group as a security threat and a liability because of the scrutiny it is under from the intelligence community.

Two members of PULO—Ar-rong Moo-reng and Hayi Abdul Rohman Bazo—founded New PULO in 1995. New PULO's goal was greater autonomy rather than independence. Bazo and his deputy, Hadji Mae Yala, were two of the four Thai Muslim leaders arrested by Malaysian authorities in 1998 and turned over to Thai authorities.[110] After that, Saarli Taloh-Meyaw headed New PULO until his death in February 2000.

The current leadership of New PULO is unknown, but the organization has been most active in Yala and may be under the control of Kamae Yusof. Many of New PULO's leaders and original members were trained in Libya and Syria and have considerable technical bomb-making skills. A handful of arrests in 2006–07 suggest that New PULO's members are involved in the unrest. Two members of the group— Marudee Piya, who is the head of the group's Narathiwat operations,

---

108. Abdul Fatah took care of Hambali's wife, Noralwizah, in December 2001, and helped Hambali cross illegally into Malaysia.
109. The author would like to thank John Dacey for making this point.
110. "Separatists Arrested in Malaysia," *Bangkok Post*, January 20, 1998.

and Paosee Yi-ngor, a top demolitions expert—are on the Thai government's most-wanted list.[111]

The extent to which New PULO is cooperating with and coordinating its actions with the GMIP and the BRN-C is unknown. It is quite
possible that technology transfer from New PULO to the BRN-C
enabled the BRN-C to wage its urban terrorism campaign, as it did not
possess the needed skills in the past.

Bersatu

Although it has denied responsibility for the violence, Bersatu (a Malay
word for "united") claims to be the umbrella organization for all the
Thai insurgent groups and factions. Founded in 1989 and banned by
the Thai government, Bersatu is headed by a Thai national, Wan Abdul
Kadir Che Man, a former academic at the International Islamic University. He has lived in exile in Malaysia since the early 1980s and authored
the definitive history of Pattani separatism.[112]

If there is a coordinating body for the groups responsible for the
violence, Bersatu is an unlikely candidate. Wan Kadir has repeatedly
asserted that he has no formal control over the militants and has denied
responsibility for the violence.[113] Bersatu is a very loose coalition
thought to include New PULO, the BRN, the BNPP, the remnants of
PULO, and now the GMIP. At most, he is a go-between—and not the
head of the insurgent forces. Bersatu is known to have held only one
major meeting (in Kuala Lumpur, July 4–5, 1995) to promote a common platform among the groups and to search for nonviolent means to
promote their mutual agenda. A common flag was agreed on, but there
is little evidence of a consensus having been reached on anything else.
In August 1997, Bersatu managed to organize Operation Falling Leaves,
in which thirty-three state officials were targeted for assassination. But
for the most part this was a PULO and New PULO operation, with
limited involvement by the GMIP and the BRN-C.[114]

---

111. Davis, "Thai Militants Adopt New Bombing Tactics."

112. See Wan Kadir, *Muslim Separatism.*

113. "Thai Separatist Leader Reaches Out for Talks with Government," Xinhuanet,
May 22, 2004.

114. Chalk, "Separatism and Southeast Asia," 244.

Thai intelligence documents obtained by the author portray the group as the center of the insurgents' efforts, coordinating the activities of the BRN-C, BRN-Congress, BRN-Ulama, GMIP, BIPP, and PULO and serving as the focal point of a broad united front that includes both domestic and foreign actors. On the domestic side, the front is said to include the Wahhabis (and Ismail Lutfi Japagiya by name), religious teachers, Pattani academics, Muslim government officials and civil servants, the children of former Pattani mujahideen, ustadz, and youth organizations such as Permuda. On the international side, it is said to include the OIC, the MWL, the Parti Islam Se-Malaysia (PAS, the Islamist opposition party in Malaysia), and three separate diaspora associations: the Pattani Association in Malaysia, the Pattani Association in Indonesia, and the Pattani Association in the Middle East. Despite the statements made in the intelligence documents, there is little evidence to suggest that a coherent front actually exists or that Wan Kadir is actually in charge of the insurgency.

Wan Kadir offered to meet with Thai government officials in 2004.[115] Defense Minister Chetta Thanajaro initially expressed a willingness to meet with Wan Kadir but at the same time accused him of leading the attacks. The talks were canceled. Leaflets found later in southern Thailand and signed by Farday Jehman, a Bersatu leader, denied that the group played a role in the violence and asked the National Reconciliation Commission (NRC) to enter into negotiations.[116] A few days later, the Thai government hinted that it might allow Wan Kadir to return from exile. Any movement toward reconciliation with Bersatu seemed to come to a halt in April 2004, when the government arrested three suspected members of Bersatu for treason, all of whom claimed they were forced to make confessions and were later acquitted for lack of evidence.[117] In a politically sensitive move, in 2005 authorities issued arrest warrants for seven men—including Romli Utrasin, the elder brother of a leading member of the Wadah faction

---

115. "Thai Separatist Leader Reaches out for Talks with Government," Xinhuanet, May 22, 2004.

116. "Big Change from End of Month, Says PM," *Bangkok Post*, May 19, 2005.

117. "Three Acquitted of Treason Charges," *Nation*, October 26, 2005.

and, according to Thai officials, the BRN-C, and Ariphen Uttarasin—for conspiring with Hariff Soko, a member of Bersatu.[118]

Despite such arrests, a debate swirled within the government about what to do with Bersatu and Wan Kadir. In May 2005, Gen. Kitti Rat tanachaya, commander of the Fourth Army, suggested that "the government should set up a working group to conduct secret talks with Dr. Wan Kadir and other separatist warrants." The police believed he could play a positive role in national reconciliation, and the NRC was desperate to find someone—anyone—with whom to reconcile. As one political analyst put it, "It allows the government the conceit of actually reconciling with someone," while at the same time giving moderate Thai Muslims "someone whom to rally around."[119] Yet many people, especially in the military, questioned the utility of allowing Wan Kadir to return, as he had no control over the insurgents. And it was not just the government that was holding Bersatu at arm's length. Unwilling to countenance any degree of accommodation, BRN-C leaders threatened Wan Kadir's life if he attempted to return from exile to Pattani.

At one point Thai officials hinted that talks had been initiated, but little was expected. For its part, the Thai government likely expressed a willingness to talk with Kadir to signal to the international community that it was working toward national reconciliation. And for Kadir's part, he was likely trying to raise Bersatu's profile and to increase the organization's legitimacy in the eyes of the international community. Indeed, Wan Kadir even lobbied the OIC for observer status and sought international support for the southern Thai cause.[120] Most observers agree

---

118. The Wadah faction believed that the arrest warrant was politically motivated, but the supreme commander of Thai forces, Gen. Chaisti Shinawatra, said, "This action would not have been taken without strong evidence." Waedao Harai, "Bombers Detained/Civil Groups, Politics," *Bangkok Post*, August 22, 2005; "Ideas for Peace: Opposition to Decree Grows," *Nation*, August 23, 2005; "Wadah Group May Review Role in TRT," *Bangkok Post*, August 19, 2005; author interview, Bangkok, January 20, 2005.

119. A Muslim human rights activist also agreed that the "local communities may support Bersatu." Author interviews, Bangkok, June 23 and 24, 2005.

120. In a March 16, 2005, article in the *Star* (Malaysia), Wan Kadir stated, "I myself am preparing a letter to ask the OIC to attend the coming meeting as an observer. . . . In the past, as I understand it, no official status was given by the OIC to any Pattani liberation organization, although there were many occasions in which different fronts submitted requests for observer status." Currently, Thailand is an observer in the OIC.

that if Bersatu were to receive observer status, it would represent an important diplomatic step and would help improve relations between southern Thai groups and the states of the OIC, which the Thai government has lobbied intensely since the OIC's May 2005 fact-finding mission about the insurgency.[121]

"Bersatu" and the DPP

An unprecedented degree of cooperation and coordination exists among the present insurgent groups. In the past, Thai insurgent groups—such as the pan-Arab socialist groups and the Malayan Communist Party, the secular ethnonationalist PULO, and the Islamist splinter groups—were divided by their respective goals and ideologies. As a result, they proved absolutely incapable of working with one another, which is a major reason why the insurgency dissipated in the 1990s. But much has changed. For one thing, the groups that were active from the 1970s to the 1990s are now defunct. For another, the GMIP and BRN-C are not at ideological war with each other; indeed, they share an Islamist vision. No organization is trying to build up its power base at the expense of other organizations. Further, no group has claimed responsibility for the attacks or outlined a political platform that could serve as a basis for negotiations. This is particularly troubling because it suggests that the insurgents' demands are absolute.

Thai militants speak of *bersatu*, not in reference to the organization Bersatu but in reference to their "unity." Indeed, on the basis of interviews, it seems that there is some degree of coordination among the groups and that the leaders are on the same page, with a shared commitment to both means and ends. Although the centers of these organizations have little monetary or other resources to offer their cells apart from guidance, this is what allows them to execute mass attacks—between forty to sixty bombings across four provinces in a matter of days—and provides for some tactical coordination. But the attacks

---

Wan Kadir, however, seemed to be hoping that current OIC dissatisfaction with the kingdom would open the door for Bersatu. OIC secretary-general, Ekmeleddin Ihsanoglu, has expressed "serious dissatisfaction at the persistent bloody acts of violence perpetrated against Muslims in southern Thailand." For more OIC statements regarding Thailand, see www.oic-oci.org (accessed October 1, 2008).

121. Prayut Sivayavirote, "Wan Kadir May Return," *Nation*, May 20, 2005.

themselves can also appear disjointed precisely because the cells are so compartmentalized and removed from the leadership.

That said, there is also nascent evidence that the militants are trying to put together a larger political front. Based on documents captured in raids, Thai intelligence believes that Sapaeng Basoe has been made the chairman of a new and very secretive body, the Dewan Pimpinan Party (DPP), which serves as an umbrella organization for the insurgents. The DPP is itself divided into various sections, including foreign affairs, youth recruitment and training, psychological operations, and economic affairs.[122] One senior Thai army commander described the DPP as "an assembly."[123]

The Role of Religion

The conflict in the south is more religious in nature than it ever has been and the leaders of the movement—headmasters, ustadz, and clerics in the large private Islamic schools—are clearly religiously grounded. As one former BRN-C member told *Slate* correspondent Eliza Griswold, "The new generation of leaders uses religion as motivation. They turn to events around the world to show how America is treating Muslims, and they use this to motivate people."[124] Further, the militants are trying to impose a very austere and intolerant form of Islam on their society, and they countenance no opposition. They are going after not just collaborators and people who receive a government salary but also Muslim clerics who perform funeral rites for *murtad* (apostates) and Islamic teachers who work in schools that have mixed curricula and receive state funds.

One militant told his army captors that even the mid-level leadership was composed of ustadz who use their religious authority to compel people to join the movement. Low-level insurgents who have been caught have made similar revelations: they are not paid and are often treated as though they are expendable. They are given orders by religious authorities and do not believe that they can question or contradict

122. "PM Cancels Rebel Boss Bounties," *Bangkok Post*, April 7, 2007.
123. "PM Insists on Talks for the South," *Bangkok Post*, May 22, 2007.
124. Eliza Griswold, "Dispatches from Southern Thailand," *Slate*, September 27, 2005.

them. As one senior military officer recounted, "They are told what to do by their imams whom they feel they cannot go against or disobey their authority."[125]

It is also important to note that Islam in southern Thailand has grown more conservative and that 60 percent of the population self-identifies primarily as Muslim, not as Thai or Malay. Of the Malay-speaking Muslims in Robert Albritton's polling, two-thirds identify themselves primarily as Muslims.[126] Of those who identified themselves as Muslim, 24.2 percent supported separatism.[127] Of those who identified themselves as Malay, 29.6 percent supported separatism. These are not insignificant figures.

The insurgents are not fighting a Maoist struggle and trying to win hearts and minds; they seem to have little concern about garnering popular support. They have a clear radical Islamist social agenda that they are slowly implementing. Women have been ordered to stop going to state hospitals to give birth and are told ludicrous things about what "infidel" Buddhist doctors and nurses will do to newborn Muslim babies. As a result, births are not being registered, which means children cannot attend state schools and are not eligible for the national healthcare plan.[128] Additionally, people now turn to local sharia courts run by the insurgents, and insurgents are forcing people to send their children to private Islamic schools rather than free state primary schools. To wit, in one instance, a warning was left by two hoax bombs at a state school in Yala's Raman District: "Do not send your children to school for their safety." In effect, people are opting out (often out of fear) of the state and turning to a parallel set of rudimentary social institutions that the insurgents are gradually establishing, often referred to as *hijrah*. As one human rights activist explained, "[The insurgents] cannot coexist with non-Muslims. They are absolutely intolerant."[129]

Why are the insurgents doing this? Among radical Islamists, there is a belief that Islam can never triumph over its enemies as long as the

---

125. Author interview, Bangkok, December 19, 2006.

126. Albritton, "The Muslim South in the Context of the Thai Nation," 15.

127. Ibid., 17.

128. "Childbirth Deaths at Crisis Level in South," *Nation*, December 20, 2006.

129. Author interview, Bangkok, December 20, 2006.

religion is corrupted by impurities and incorrect interpretations of Islam, which include belief in secular rule. This is the heart of Salafism: to remove all innovations ("impurities") that have entered the religion since the death of the Prophet Muhammad. The goal is to Islamicize society and to inculcate it with Salafi values and norms that will strengthen the movement, regardless of whether these values and norms are popular. The militants have adopted the Wahhabite practice of takfir—that is, labeling fellow Muslims non-Muslims if they do not subscribe to Salafi values and practices. They have systematically targeted moderate Muslims, Sufis, and others whom they find to be too secular or too connected to the state.

Indeed, 55 percent of their victims are fellow Muslims. As Sunai Phasuk of Human Rights Watch noted, "Separatism used to be the priority, and religion followed after that, but with these new groups it's in reverse order: the new fighters seem to want to purify the area."[130] The militants seek not only to control the political movement but also to fundamentally alter the nature of Islam in southern Thailand by imposing a hard-line Salafist vision of society. The recent spate of flyers that militants have scattered in the south and the personal threats that they have made demonstrate the direction in which the militants seek to move the south. Messages in the flyers have included the following:

- warnings to people to not work on Friday and to observe it as a day of prayer, or risk death or the amputation of their ears;
- warnings to imams to not conduct funeral rites for Muslim security officers, guards at state schools, government employees, or "anyone who receives a salary from the state";
- warnings to people to not send their children to state-run schools;
- warnings to not become members of the village self-defense forces;
- warnings to anyone caught destroying the leaflets.[131]

These threats are being made from a perceived position of strength. The militants seem undeterred by the fact that their threats are broadly

---

130. Quoted in Tony Cheng, "Behind the Bombs."
131. "Ex-School Chief, Policeman's Son Killed," *Nation*, July 26, 2005; "Ongoing Mayhem," *Bangkok Post*, July 27, 2005.

unpopular among the Muslim community. The militants are not trying to create a popular government but rather are trying to impose a strict interpretation of Islam on society, which they believe will ultimately strengthen the community.

Not everyone agrees with this assessment. Liow still sees the conflict as more criminal and ethnonationalist than religious in nature,[132] although he now sees that "for the first time in recent history, the traditionally ethno-nationalist struggle assumed a patently discernable religious undertone."[133] Francesca Lawe-Davies of ICG sees far more religious identification in the south than ever before, but she sees it as being wrapped up in national identification.[134] Similarly, S.P. Harish of IDSS believes that the conflict is not religious in nature but that the militants use religion to "deepen the Thai-Malay divide." Harish argues that the "frequent portrayal of the conflict as religious nourishes the Buddhist-Muslim cleavage. Minority elites, who include separatist leaders, play a significant role in sustaining these subaltern identities."[135] Yet, these analyses fail to explain what is happening in the villages, such as the establishment of religiously based structures and the growing authority of religious leaders there.

Veteran journalists such as Don Pathan of the *Nation* see the rising influence of Wahhabism on the new generation of militants. As the old insurgency was dying out, the current militants were being raised in the roughly five hundred private pondoks, where the new insurgency incubated for the better part of a decade. In addition, there are several thousand Pattani studying across the Middle East.[136]

Although the Wahhabis are still a distinct minority in the region, their influence and numbers are growing steadily. Other strict

---

132. See, for example, Joseph Chinyong Liow, *Over-reading the Islamist Factor in Thailand's Southern Troubles*, IDSS Commentaries (Singapore: Institute of Defence and Strategic Studies, March 10, 2005).

133. Joseph Chinyong Liow, "International Jihad and Muslim Radicalism in Thailand? Toward an Alternative Interpretation," *Asia Policy* no. 2 (July 2006): 99.

134. Francesca Lawe-Davies, talk at the Foreign Correspondents' Club of Thailand, Bangkok, January 11, 2006.

135. S.P. Harish, *Insurgency in Southern Thailand: Ethnic or Religious Conflict?* IDSS Commentaries (Singapore: Institute of Defence and Strategic Studies, April 14, 2005).

136. "About 800 Thai Students in Egypt 'Reluctant to Return Home to South,'" *Bangkok Post*, August 20, 2006.

fundamentalist organizations, such as the Tabliqhi Jamaat, are rapidly growing their ranks in southern Thailand as well.[137] The Tabliqhi is exceptionally active in southern Thailand, erecting numerous madrassas and some of the largest mosques in the region. While the Tabliqhi claims to be an apolitical da'wah organization, there is considerable debate whether the Tabliqhi is involved in militant activities. Most analysts agree that the organization is an important ideological conveyor that at the very least gets people committed to living their lives in total accordance with the sharia. It is also exclusionary and intolerant of non-Muslims.[138]

While it is not clear whether Tabliqhi leaders select members for jihad or whether members are simply predisposed toward jihad and join on their own, it is clear that the Tabliqhi plays an essential role in the ideological indoctrination of new recruits. Tabliqhi members have also been involved in internationalizing the insurgency by bringing in foreign students to Thai madrassas.[139] Thailand's traditional Sha'afi community, the most common school of Islamic jurisprudence in Southeast Asia, is also becoming more theologically and ideologically conservative and pious.

Despite these trends, the south remains a very diverse region theologically. Many moderate Sha'afis and Sufis reject Wahhabite approaches and offers of money because of the conditions attached. As one Sha'afi told a reporter, "They came here to offer money to complete the school on the condition that we permit Wahhabite teachers."[140]

---

137. The author has spent time with Tabliqhis in southern Thailand and visited many of their mosques and madrassas. An enormous mosque for 4,000 to 5,000 people is being constructed outside of Sungai Golok, Narathiwat.

138. Alex Alexiev, "Tabliqhi Jamaat: Jihad's Stealthy Legions," *Middle East Quarterly* 12, no. 2 (Spring 2005).

139. For example, in October 2003, a Thai Tabliqhi missionary, Ustadz Abdullah, traveled to Marawi, Philippines. With the support of three Philippine Tabliqhis—Omar Madali, Jabar Palamuri, and Achmad Lucman—he recruited two batches of students (fifty-one in all) to study at the madrassa Tahfisul Quran Markaz in Yala. The school had students from across Southeast Asia, including thirty Cambodians, fifty Malaysians, fifteen Filipinos, forty Indonesians, and one Frenchman.

140. Don Pathan, "Planning for a Peaceful Future in the South," *Nation*, August 28, 2005.

The debates over the religious nature of the insurgency are further complicated by a booklet captured by Thai security forces and leaked to the press titled *Ber Jihad Di Pattani* (Waging Jihad in Pattani).[141] Divided into two distinct parts, the booklet—in the English translation—is twenty-two pages long. The main body of the booklet is structured in the form of a seven-day series of sermons that cajole people to support and sacrifice themselves for the Pattani nation.[142] The second part includes an introduction, commentary, and epilogue by a Malaysian cleric from Kelantan, Assuluk Ismuljaminah. Although the booklet itself is undated, the preface is dated August 10, 2002. There has been considerable debate about this booklet and what it means. Some analysts see the document as proof that the jihadists are not Salafis. They point to Sufi references and note that Salafis constantly try to purge their religion of Sufi heresy. They also point to two other facts: (1) the book refers to supporting the Sha'afi school of jurisprudence, which the Salafis tend not to support, and (2) it calls for the restoration of the Pattani sultanate, not a pan-Islamic caliphate.

However, others point out that this document advocates martyrdom and implores the reader to become a shaheed (martyr). Indeed, the book uses the same language as many Salafi jihadist tracts—focusing on the idea that Islam is under attack, that there is a global conspiracy against Islam, and that it must be defended at all costs. From the first sermon, the congregation is referred to as "shaheed warriors." Each day, the sermons become longer and fiercer, calling on the shaheed warriors to make greater sacrifices. The author chastises them for their complacency and goads them into action: "We should be ashamed of ourselves for sitting idly by and doing nothing while our brothers and sisters are trampled on by our conquerors. Our wealth that belongs to us and the wealth of our country are stolen. Our properties have been confiscated and our assets stolen from us. Our rights and freedoms have been curbed and our religion and culture have been sullied." He then reminds them of their highest religious obligation: "It is clarified that fighting to protect various rights is a responsibility that everyone must fulfill."

---

141. As noted in Chapter 3, a radical cleric named Poohsu Ismael is believed to be the author of this booklet.

142. Liow, "International Jihad and Muslim Radicalism in Thailand?" 101.

While there are many references to the Prophet Muhammad, who tends to be downplayed in the writings and oratory of Salafism, the booklet gives the theological justification and instruction for followers to kill both non-Muslims and Muslims who are not cooperating with the jihadists—not just those who are collaborating with the Thai government. This is the core of the Salafi approach—attacking *munafik*s (Muslims who do not live in accordance with sharia) and murtads (apostates). The author is unequivocal in his assertions that the greatest threat to "our honorable Islam"—that is, Salafism—comes from fellow Muslims:

> It is certain among the group of munafiks that they are the most dangerous enemies of God and ours for they are together within the Muslim circle. Sometimes you may see them fulfilling responsibility before God, such as praying, fasting, giving alms, etc. In reality, all their actions or practices are a disguise, for their hearts are filled with hatred and anger against Islam. And they have fear against the laws and orders of Islam.

These munafiks are believed to undermine their faith in two ways: (1) by not living in accordance with sharia and (2) by thereby collaborating with the Thai state.

One other point should be made about this document: its importance might be highly overrated. Although it has received a lot of attention because it is one of the only such documents that has been uncovered, it is simply one document. It does not necessarily reveal what is taught in da'wah sessions, where most of the indoctrination takes place. Regardless, the insurgents are clearly more religiously motivated than they have been in the past and previously secular groups are now dominated by religious leaders who are trying to impose an Islamic state.

Today's insurgent groups are all motivated by Islam and committed to establishing sharia law, which is incompatible with a secular state. Although the NRC reported in June 2006 that the insurgents were not separatists, insurgents do not want to live as a minority in a Buddhist state, in which the ideological pillars are religion and the monarchy (a Buddhist god-king). They may not have yet come out and publicly stated that they are separatists, but their beliefs make them separatists by default. Further, although the insurgents have been unwilling to speak to members of the press and do not use modern means of communication to outline their goals and agenda—for example, the BRN-C and GMIP do not have Web sites—as noted, the insurgents do communicate about their goals through fairly basic means: leaflets.[143]

The leaflets fall into several broad categories. They include threats to the Buddhist community, calling on them to leave the region—either collectively or individually; "beware of harm" warnings addressed to the Muslim community, outlining what Muslims have to do to not get killed or in trouble with the militants; directives to village headmen; reportage of facts, particularly of violence toward the Muslim community by security forces that goes unreported in the Buddhist-centric national media; statements of goals and ideology; and editorial cartoons (see Appendix A for examples of these leaflets). These leaflets routinely state the militants' goal of establishing an independent Islamic state (Pattani Darulislam), outline their vehemently sectarian agenda, and describe their desire to establish Islamic institutions.

Although few bother to collect or analyze these leaflets, and few Thai officials have taken them seriously, the government is now beginning to come to terms with the true face of the insurgency. As Watanachai Chaimuanwong, the top security adviser to army-installed prime minister Surayud Chulanont, stated in 2007, "This is a group of young turk militants who want to challenge the old groups. Their operations are more gruesome and more violent because they have imported those techniques from al-Qaeda and the Taliban, with the goal of creating a pure Islamic state. There are up to 20,000 of these militants active in the three southern provinces."[144]

The Goals of the Insurgents

The short- and medium-term goals of the insurgents are threefold: to make the region ungovernable, to provoke heavy-handed government responses that will further alienate the Muslim community, and to consolidate their authority and impose their values on the local community. Regarding the first goal, they not only seek to make the region ungovernable but they also want people to lose all faith in civic institutions and

143. The author has been collecting these pamphlets for the past few years and now has more than eighty in his possession that have been translated and analyzed.
144. Boonradom Chitradon, "Southern Extremists Learning from Bin Laden," Agence France-Presse, March 22, 2007.

the ability of the Thai state to offer them a degree of protection. They clearly would like to provoke more crackdowns so that the local population might come to believe their rhetoric that the Thai state is abusive and patently anti-Muslim. They also aim to establish a parallel set of institutions in which they can exert their authority and eliminate other contenders for power.

An important BRN-C document recovered by Thai soldiers in late 2006 details a seven-step plan to achieve these goals and makes clear that the insurgents are only in the very beginning stages of their struggle. As outlined in the document, the first step is "raising the consciousness of the people." In this phase the document argues that the insurgents should inculcate Muslim values and stress their common Malay and Pattani identity. It also states that their propaganda should emphasize that Pattani is an occupied territory and that the only way to end the occupation is through fighting.

The second step is "setting the mass of people." Once a general political and religious consciousness of Islam is inculcated, the insurgents hope to broaden that ethnoreligious identification through mass mobilization of religious schools, insurgent committees in the villages, village cooperatives, associations, and sports leagues. The third step entails greater institutionalization of the insurgents' political and military organization in order to lead Pattani through the following steps.

The fourth step, "developing manpower," focuses on developing those youth who are already being trained and those who are fighting now as future trainers. It also focuses on attracting skilled government officials to the cause and increasing military- and religious-training opportunities in Malaysia. The stated goal is to have a cadre of three thousand trained militarized operatives and three hundred trained experts. The fifth step is the further inculcation of the "ideal of nationalism," followed by "preparation" for an all-out "revolution," the sixth step. In the revolutionary step, the insurgents speak of their desire to acquire full political power, power over the masses, economic power, and self-sufficiency in their quest to establish an Islamic state (the seventh step).

It is clear that in the insurgents' own thinking, they are still in the very early stages of development and operations. Again, the immediate goals of the insurgents are to begin to inculcate Islamic values, create parallel networks, eliminate political rivals, and begin the mass social-ization of their values and goals.

The Sources of Funding

One of the key questions dogging Thai security services relates to the financial support for the insurgency. Specifically, from where is the money coming? There is no consensus, which may indicate that it is coming from multiple channels and that the insurgents are not depen-dent on any one source. Most of the evidence to date points to internal sources of funding.

To be sure, the insurgents' operations require little in the way of funding. Captured insurgents have said that they are not paid and that they often have to procure their own weapons and ammunition, hence the constant raids on police and volunteer village defense posts. Most people are killed in drive-by pillion motorcycle attacks. The majority of bombs are composed of readily available fertilizers, such as ammonium nitrate and potassium chlorate, packed in metal canisters (often fire extinguishers). These can be easily stolen. For example, militants stole 1.6 tons of ammonium nitrate from a quarry on March 30, 2004. Thai military commanders estimate that the insurgents have up to two years' worth of matériel at the current rate of bombing.[145] In short, this is a very cost-effective insurgency that does not require vast sums of money.

Reuters quoted a PULO member as saying that his group had tens of thousands of members inside Thailand and abroad who are "involved in the struggle" and who donate funds as often and as much as they can.[146] Thai intelligence officials believe that most of these donations are coming from Malaysia, although they have not offered any hard evidence of this. In fact, a diplomatic row followed Thai government assertions that a network of Thai restaurants operating in Malaysia, known locally as Tom Yam Kung, was supporting the insurgency, both through voluntary donations and protection money.[147] The Malaysian

---

145. Davis, "Thai Militants Adopt New Bombing Tactics."
146. Cropley, "Exclusive: Malay Separatists Say behind Southern Thai Unrest."
147. "Restaurants in Malaysia Aiding Rebels," *Bangkok Post*, November 22, 2006.

government angrily denied the allegations, calling them "baseless."[148] Some analysts have pointed to the affluent network of Pattani business-men across the Middle East, conservatively estimated to number from 30,000 to 50,000, as possible donors. In 2006, one Thai intelligence official estimated that the insurgents had received up to Bt6 million (US$183,000) in Ramadan donations from Muslims in Egypt, Libya, Sweden, Indonesia, and Malaysia.[149] There are also some three thousand Pattani students in Egypt alone, who are thought to be active in fund-raising. Funding also comes from the greater Muslim community. One regional intelligence official said that French intelligence officials had briefed their Thai counterparts on how some North Africans living in Asia were directing their donations to the Asian region rather than to movements in their homelands or in Europe. A detained member of the BRN-C, Ussaman Useng, told authorities that the insurgents use zakat (local donations) to fund the insurgency.[150]

The Thai government increasingly believes that the large community of Pattani students in Indonesia serves both as a base of support and pool of recruits for the insurgency. According to documents recovered by Thai security officials, Persatuan Mahasiswa Islam Pattani (Selatan Thailand) Di Pattani, an association of Thai students in Indonesia, has been active in fund-raising.[151]

Insurgent leaflets and strategy documents also speak about diversifying sources of funding. Plans include increasing the presence of Malay lottery dealers in every subdistrict and every village—"We are the only Malay lottery dealers. If any area has Thai dealers for the Malay lottery, kill them. . . . We will be able to dominate the three provinces because the prizes are higher than the government lottery"; occupying all financial organizations—"Having money is having power. All Muslims have to remember this. The Muslims have to try to work for the treasury, all government and private financial organizations, all ministries and tele-

148. "Malaysia Denies Restaurants Fund Thai Separatists: Report," *Nation*, November 22, 2006.

149. "Separatists Divided on Peace Offer," *Bangkok Post*, November 20, 2006.

150. "Thaksin down South This Evening," *Nation*, November 6, 2005; Nanuam and Charoenpo, "Militants 'Likely to Stay Hidden.'"

151. "PM Cancels Rebel Boss Bounties," *Bangkok Post*, April 7, 2007.

communication. They have to be in the high positions in every district and subdistrict"; and collecting as much money as possible from rich Muslims—"We will sequentially send other Muslim kids who are not our kids to study in old Afghanistan. This can give good result."[152]

There is also considerable evidence that the insurgents engage in extortion (see Appendix C for two examples of extortion documents). One Thai Muslim academic said that up to "70 to 80 percent of the owners of shops and construction companies paid for protection by the insurgents."[153] Beyond extortion of businesses, insurgents are now also engaging in the Islamic practice of dhimmi, in which non-Muslims have to pay a tax to their Muslim "rulers." In Yala Province, Buddhists have received letters threatening harm if they do not publicly pay a monthly tax of Bt500 (US$30) at the mosques. In return they receive a piece of green cloth to be displayed at their door.[154] The insurgents mail letters or leave them at the target's house, company, or shop. Insurgents also sell "protection" to Muslims who support the insurgency.

And, of course, insurgents often simply steal money. For example, in Songkhla's Saba Yoi District, two suspected militants shot dead a rubber merchant and stole Bt100,000 (US$2,738).[155] Money also comes from a variety of quasilegal sources, including government funds for villages that are skimmed by sympathizers, and donations from companies or shops owned by insurgents and their supporters. Much of the money also seems to be coming through Sururiyah networks based in Europe.

Financial support to the BRN-C and its network of schools has come from foreign sources through the Pusaka Foundation. Ostensibly a non-governmental organization (NGO) that promotes Islamic education and Malay culture, it is believed to be an important clearinghouse for Saudi and Gulf funds. According to Panitan Wattanayagorn, a leading security specialist at Chulalongkorn University, "About 20,000 students have studied under the umbrella of Pusaka, of which about 500 to 1,000

---

152. Leaflets and documents are in author's possession.
153. Author interview, Pattani, January 16, 2006.
154. "Extremists Kill 2, Warn Buddhists," *Bangkok Post*, December 13, 2006.
155. "Friend of a former MP Gunned down in South, Southerners Who Fled to Malaysia Planning to Return," *Bangkok Post*, November 5, 2006.

radicals have emerged, dividing themselves [into cells] in the south."[156] The Thammawittaya Foundation School, for example, received significant funding from the Pusaka Foundation.[157] In 2004, one of Pusaka's leaders, Najmudin Omar, a member of parliament from Narathiwat and a member of Wadah, was arrested and charged along with another codefendant with twelve criminal offenses, including allegations linking them to the January 4, 2004, raid on the army depot.[158] He was ultimately acquitted because of insufficient evidence; it is likely that the government overplayed its hand and levied charges against him that were too broad.[159]

The Pattani groups have always received Saudi and Gulf funding. Wan Kadir writes that the prominent Saudi sheikh Abdul Aziz Ibn Baz issued a fatwa that allowed the BNPP to establish a charitable arm and to receive zakat. The BNPP also received funds from the Al-Auqaf (Welfare Department) and Islamic Call Society in Kuwait.[160] While less money is today coming from prominent Saudi and Gulf charities such as the MWL, Al Haramain, and the International Islamic Relief Organization, U.S. and regional intelligence officials believe that the Gulf remains an important source of funds. Most of it goes through smaller, less well-known charities, such as the OAQ, or directly to individuals in Thailand via personal courier. Warned a U.S. intelligence official, "We've found that some terrorist groups donated money in the guise of charity to Islamic communities and Islamic schools which are linked to the insurgents who have bombed the south of Thailand."[161] One Western analyst contends that the imposition of Salafi values such

---

156. Quoted in "Thailand Fears More Attacks as Muslim Separatists Blamed for Violence," Agence France-Press, April 30, 2004.

157. Documents recovered by Thai authorities in 2004 in Joh I Rong, Narathiwat, confirmed Pusaka's role in funding organizations such as the Thammawittaya Foundation. Author interview, Kuala Lumpur, April 19, 2005.

158. Author interview, Bangkok, March 16, 2005; "Former Thai Rak Thai MP Acquitted of Insurgency," Thai News Agency, December 15, 2005.

159. Omar's deputy at the Pusaka Foundation was Masae Useng.

160. Wan Kadir, *Muslim Separatism*, 104–105.

161. Celina Realuyo, quoted in Wassana Nanuam, "US Tracing JI Links with South Rebels," *Bangkok Post*, February 16, 2005.

as veils and the closing of shops on Fridays, as opposed to the violence, has been the key to winning financial support from the Gulf.[162]

There is increasing evidence that money is coming from South Asia, namely HUJI-Bangladesh, via the large network of Rohingas and Bangladeshis in Malaysia and Thailand, and Thai officials often assert that the insurgents have become connected to drug-smuggling rings. In 2007, for example, the government announced that it had uncovered a drug ring that is believed to be an important source of militant funding. Police raided twenty-one locations in six districts of Narathiwat and seized Bt115 million (US$2.875 million) in funds from bank accounts. A senior government official said, "We will simultaneously launch a war on drug traffickers, influential figures and separatists. Suppression operations against drug gangs must be continuous and in all regions from the north to the south, since the southern region is a key transit route for drugs."[163]

A second large drug raid led to the arrest of three individuals in Sungai Golok, including drug kingpin Kittisak Dorkorheng. Government officials seized vehicles, land, and Bt1.2 million (US$30,000), telling the press that the suspects had colluded with the militants and used drugs to "lure youngsters into the insurgency."[164] Police arrested an important drug dealer, Paosi Nisare, in mid-June 2006, stating that he was behind some of the unrest, including that month's spate of bombings.[165] His arrest led to the arrests of three additional suspected drug dealers who were accused of indirect involvement in the insurgency. Police said they seized Bt5 million (US$136,900) worth of items—including 25 kg (55 lb.) of cannabis, five pistols, 460 cartridges, and 4 kg (8.8 lb.) of urea-rich fertilizer.[166]

---

162. The author would like to thank Paul Quaglia for making this point.

163. Yuwadee Tunyasiri and Waedao Harai, "Traffickers Financing Separatists," *Bangkok Post*, November 15, 2005.

164. Waedao Harai, "Assets Worth B10m Seized in Drug Raids," *Bangkok Post*, November 26, 2005.

165. Police recovered two pistols and Bt220,000 (US$5,700) in cash. "Drug Dealer behind Southern Bomb Blasts," *Bangkok Post*, June 18, 2006; "Six Arrested in Thailand for Series of Bomb Attacks," *Gulf Times*, June 17, 2006.

166. The three were Chom Thongnamdam from Pattani, Phaitoon Phothiwan from Trat, and Phothi Chairat from Songkhla. "More Southern Drug Suspects Held," *Bangkok Post*, June 19, 2006.

Despite these arrests and assertions by the Thai government, one U.S. law enforcement adviser based in Thailand strongly stated, "There is no evidence that [the insurgency] is being funded by drug money. The Thai police insist that it is, but there is no evidence this is the case. For one, the Malaysians wouldn't tolerate it."[167] Indeed, Malaysia has extremely harsh antinarcotics legislation and would not tolerate insurgent activities on its soil, especially if it involved drug trafficking. But as one security analyst argued, "The [drug dealers'] alliance with the insurgents is not clear. But what is clear is that the drug smuggling networks [were] disrupted by Thaksin's [crackdown] and they are angry. So they might very well contribute to the militants simply to create instability."[168]

A Whole New Ball Game

Many diplomats in Bangkok continue to view this insurgency through the prism of the insurgency that raged in the 1970s and 1980s. One Southeast Asian diplomat even used the Maoist term "fish in ponds" to refer to the insurgents. Many see the violence simply as a result of criminal gangs fighting to control lucrative smuggling networks and other sectors of the underground economy. Others see it as an extension of elite politics in Bangkok. But the current insurgency is fundamentally different from past ones in a number of distinctive ways.

First, the scope and rate of violence have never been higher. More people died in the forty months since January 2004 than in the previous twenty-five years. In 2004, much of the violence occurred at night, so villagers were free to live their lives during the day. Now violence occurs at all hours, creating an intense climate of fear. By May 2007, there had been more than six thousand violent incidents, nearly two hundred a month, compared with twenty per month in January 2004. By early 2007, on average four people were being killed per day. Since Tak Bai, there have been more than six hundred bombings or attempted bombings and more than thirty beheadings, many of them

---

167. Author interview, Bangkok, January 2, 2007.
168. Author interview, Bangkok, December 30, 2005.

in broad daylight before stunned onlookers. Further, brutal attacks, such as the hacking deaths of monks, have sent fear through communities. Execution-style killings have demonstrated a ruthlessness that has never before been seen in southern Thailand. Women, children, monks, and clergy, who in previous iterations of the insurgency would never have been routinely targeted, are now dying in appalling numbers. "It's a new movement," observed an army unit commander in Narathiwat. "The old separatists were in the jungle, and the fighting was there. It didn't affect the daily lives of the Buddhists and Muslims."[169]

Second, there is an unprecedented degree of coordination among the insurgents—a conspiracy of silence. No group has taken credit for any attack, tried to discredit its rivals, or stated its platform. Their silence is intentional and does not indicate, as many in Bangkok believe, that they are a bunch of nihilist teenagers bent on destruction. They have demonstrated command and control in their attacks and have a very effective political and social program that they are implementing in the villages.

Third, the discourse has been transformed from one of ethnonational liberation to one of international jihadism. As one official told me, in the 1980s people spoke of "Pattani liberation" and "Siamese hegemonism." Now they speak of "Islamist jihadism."[170] As a militant stated after his capture in April 2004, "All of us were sacrificing ourselves for God."[171] Thai officials noted that the funerals of eighteen militants killed in the raids of the Krue Se mosque were "conducted in a manner accorded only to Muslims who die as martyrs, and whose corpses do not need to be washed because they are cleansed by their actions."[172] As a local academic put it, "Those who died must have believed they were dying for their religion. They must have an ideology beyond separatism; otherwise, why would they attack with their bare

---

169. Simon Montlake, "Tension Grows between Thai Security Forces and Muslim Locales," *Christian Science Monitor*, July 12, 2005.

170. Author interview, Bangkok, March 20, 2004.

171. Quoted in "Thailand Fears More Attacks as Muslim Separatists Blamed for Violence," Agence France-Presse, April 30, 2004.

172. Ibid.

hands and swords?"[173] In *Ber Jihad Di Pattani*, the author repeatedly exhorts his congregation to "sacrifice your flesh to the last drop of blood . . . blood that will trickle down the warriors' bodies and flood the soil in red, reflecting a red radiance across the sky at dawn and dusk, the East and West calling on warriors to declare jihad."[174] Observed journalist Simon Elegant, "What is so noteworthy is the paucity of references to the liberation of the [Thai] south."[175]

Fourth, the militants currently do not have the numbers to control physical space (although this is changing), so they are trying to control mental space. They have a clear political and social agenda that they are implementing in the villages. They have established parallel social structures and have forced people to opt out of the state's legal, medical, and educational systems. They have been ruthless toward moderate Muslims who preach accommodation with the Thai state and coexistence with the Buddhist community. Not all moderate Muslims who have been killed could possibly have been collaborators with the Thai security services.

Fifth, popular support for the movement is growing rapidly. General Sonthi recently claimed that the army has been successful in getting "99 percent" of the Muslim population to support the government.[176] But this claim is utterly delusional. Maj. Gen. Chamlong Khunsong, the army chief of staff in the south, has made comments reminiscent of U.S. vice president Dick Cheney's May 2005 assertion that the insurgency in Iraq was "in its final throes": "Militants are stepping up violence because more and more villagers are supporting and cooperating with the government."[177] Other Thai security officials and independent analysts are less sanguine. Defense Minister Boonrawd Somtas contradicted his boss General Sonthi in a hearing at the National Legislative Assembly, where he admitted that support for insurgent groups had grown dramatically.

---

173. Quoted in Nopporn Wong-Anan, "Over 100 Dead in Muslim Battle in Thailand," Reuters, April 28,2004.

174. *Ber Jihad Di Pattani* [Waging Jihad in Pattani], 5.

175. Elegant, "Southern Front."

176. "Sonthi: Insurgency Intensified after Coup," *Bangkok Post*, March 28, 2007.

177. "Two Soldiers Killed in Pattani," Agence France-Presse, April 24, 2007.

He also acknowledged the scope of the government's intelligence failure: "We do not know them. We do not know who is working against us," he said. "As long as they mingle with ordinary people, it's difficult to tell them apart."[178] It was initially thought that only 2 percent of the population was actively supporting the militants. But by 2007, this figure was conservatively estimated at 5 percent. Anantachai Thaiprathan, a member of the now dissolved NRC, further estimated that about 30 percent of the population had become "sympathizers" and that a full 2 percent of the population could be counted as insurgents—close to 60,000 people.[179] Although this figure seems slightly high, the insurgents are certainly benefiting from a bandwagon effect. Anantachai also estimated that roughly half of the population in the south was "neutral," supporting neither the insurgents nor the Thai government. With the insurgency having passed its fourth year and the government getting no closer to stemming the bloodshed, the local population is increasingly casting its lot in with the insurgents. Some of this shift stems from coercion and the recognition that the state is unable to provide any degree of security. As long as the insurgency rages, a parallel infrastructure will continue to spring forth and Buddhists and moderate Muslims will be increasingly cowed into submission or compelled to vote with their feet.

The Thai government has always played down the role of the jihadists. It argues that their numbers are very small and that their doctrinaire Salafism/Wahhabism makes them ill-suited to the Malay community. A similar refrain was heard in Indonesia, when officials did not want to confront the growing specter of JI. In reality, Thai security forces are unwilling to acknowledge the role of groups with more international aspirations and contacts. A homegrown, localized insurgency that does not threaten the tourism industry or the national economy is somewhat tolerable. A group with ties to al-Qaeda—a group that cares little about equity or social justice and a lot about eliminating the enemies of Islam

178. "Minister: Support for Thai Rebels Growing," United Press International, February 24, 2007.
179. Vasana Chinvarakorn, "Tak Bai Sits Heavy on the Conscience," *Bangkok Post*, October 27, 2007.

(especially allies of the United States) through indiscriminate violence—is altogether a different thing: it is dangerous and threatening.

Indeed, the insurgency also has a very different feel to it now than in
past decades because of the influx of foreign ideas, which has been made
possible by globalization, the Internet, and increased educational
opportunities. It has also been made possible because of changes in the
country's physical infrastructure, which have allowed greater freedom
of movement. The growing network of roads facilitates travel within
the region and farther afield, creating a different reality from past eras,
when people never left their villages.

But why did the insurgency break out when it did? The simplest
answer is that the leaders were ready. Sources have said that the turning
point came in a 1995 meeting in Malaysia, when a group came together
to discuss the former insurgency's demise, the laying down of weapons,
and mass surrenders. Increasingly disgusted with the perceived social
ills brought about by the Thais, these leaders focused on da'wah,
patiently doing their political work. They recruited and indoctrinated
young Thai Muslims, especially in the mosques pondoks, building new
cells. Because the leaders had no connections to the previous insurgency and were seen as religious figures, not militants, Thai security
forces were ill-equipped to recognize and counter them. Indeed, the
Thai government—first under Prime Minister Thaksin and then under
General Sonthi and the ensuing rapid succession of democratic admin-
istrations—has been in utter denial over the goals and nature of the
insurgency. By asking the wrong questions, it has been unable to come
up with any effective solutions. It has likewise tended to flatly deny the
possibility of foreign involvement in the insurgency.

5

Is Transnational Terrorism Involved?

T here is tremendous concern that the insurgent groups operating in southern Thailand might have links to international
terrorist organizations.[1] For years, the Thai government has
denied that any such links exist. Stated NRC chief Anand Panyarachun in 2005, "I have looked into every place and there is no convincing
evidence that insurgent attacks are related to al-Qaeda or JI. There's
no financial support. There's no military training outside the country.
The killings are domestic problems that can be resolved at the government level."[2] For the most part, this statement echoed the view of the
international community. For example, a 2002 white paper from the
Singapore Ministry of Home Affairs stated that "there is as yet no
evidence that supporters of Jemaah Islamiyah have formed a formal
structured network in Thailand,"[3] and the CIA asserted in 2003 that
it had no evidence that any al-Qaeda fighters had fled Afghanistan for
southern Thailand.[4] There is considerable evidence to suggest that
Thais who once fought with the Taliban have returned home, however.[5] Thai intelligence officials estimate that between 120 and 150
Thais passed through Afghanistan over the two decades beginning

1. For more on Jemaah Islamiyah, see Abuza, *Militant Islam in Southeast Asia*; Abuza,
"Terrorism: The War on Terror in Southeast Asia," in *Strategic Asia: Fragility and Crisis*,
eds. Richard Ellings, Aaron Friedberg, and Michael Wills (Seattle: National Bureau of
Asian Research, 2003), 321–364; ICG, *How the Jemaah Islamiyah Terrorist Network
Operates*, Asia Report No. 43 (Singapore/Brussels: ICG, December 11, 2002); ICG,
Jemaah Islamiyah in Southeast Asia: Damaged but Still Dangerous (Singapore/Brussels:
ICG, August 26, 2003); Maria Ressa, *Seeds of Terror* (New York: Free Press, 2003).

2. Ampa Santimatanedol, "No Proof of outside Terror Input," *Bangkok Post*, July 7, 2005.

3. *The Jemaah Islamiyah Arrests and the Threat of Terrorism*, white paper (Singapore:
Republic of Singapore, Ministry of Home Affairs, 2003), 10.

4. CIA, "Unclassified Responses to the Worldwide Threat," 159.

5. Bradley, "Waking Up to the Terror Threat."

in 1982—particularly in 1988–89, when the mujahideen structure there became more organized.[6]

With the growing specter of a broader sectarian conflict in the south, there is some concern that the insurgency will begin to attract foreign elements. As a Thai Foreign Ministry spokesman said, "The causes of the situation [are] domestic. It's not part of any international terrorist network but of course we are concerned about the introduction of extremist ideologies among the youths. We are concerned about the possibility of extremist groups in the region connecting together, and this could become a serious problem." Summing up the general concerns of the international community, Malaysian foreign minister Syed Hamid Albar expressed similar sentiments: "We must not allow any breeding ground for terrorism to exist or to be nurtured. We hope that they [Thailand] will find a way that will not allow for any terrorist groups to take advantage of the instability or unhappiness. In anywhere there is always a danger if people are not happy, some terrorist groups may take advantage of it."[7]

For the most part, however, Thai officials seem unconcerned that transnational Islamist groups may punish the Thai government for its repression of Muslims in the south. For example, Prime Minister Thaksin lashed out at suggestions that it was a matter of time before Bangkok was targeted: "Until now there's been no trace of a possibility of terrorism spreading to Bangkok as suggested."[8] One Thai academic noted that the NSC is blithely indifferent to the potential for a major terrorist attack and thinks that Thailand is "just a way station for JI."[9] Despite such views, it must be remembered that while Hambali noted the reluctance of Thai Muslims to help with an al-Qaeda and JI terror plot in Bangkok, reportedly telling his captors that Thai Muslims "did not agree with the targets,"[10] he admitted that Khalid Sheikh Muhammad

6. Author interview, Kuala Lumpur, April 19, 2005.

7. "Malaysia Warns against Thai South Becoming Terrorist Hotbed," *Nation*, February 8, 2007.

8. Ismail Wolff, "Thaksin Dismissed Threat of Terrorist Attack in Bangkok," *Thai Day*, January 7, 2006.

9. Author interview, Bangkok, August 13, 2005.

10. Quoted in Andrew Perrin, "Targeting Thailand," *Time—Asian Edition*, January 11, 2004.

wanted to target tourist spots there despite the objections of local muja-hideen. It also must be remembered that Hezbollah came very close to blowing up the Israeli Embassy in Bangkok in 1994. The operation was aborted due to a traffic accident—and not to good police work.

In January 2008, Thai military officials announced—for the first time—that JI and al-Qaeda were involved in the south.[11] They provided no substantive evidence to support their claim, however, and other Thai government officials quickly denied it. Although there is absolutely no evidence to suggest that JI is directing the insurgency, the Thai militants have clearly been inspired by JI and it is dangerously naive to think there are no connections between them. Indeed, informal and institutional ties date back to the mid-1990s, and new links continue to be uncovered. When they categorically state that the insurgents have no ties to al-Qaeda and JI, Thai authorities overlook four important facts.

First, al-Qaeda and JI traditionally have injected themselves into situations where fellow Muslims are being persecuted, whether they are invited or not. As Michael Scheuer, the former head of the CIA's Bin Laden unit, noted, "When they [al-Qaeda operatives] arrive, they're not there to tell the local boys what to do. They ask 'What do you need?' "[12]

Second, Hambali was referring to a reality in 2002–03, before the current insurgency had begun. Much has changed on the ground, and it remains to be seen what course of action the southern Thai militants will take if they become desperate in their struggle.

Third, JI is preoccupied with its own survival, regrouping in Mindanao and launching attacks in Indonesia, its primary country of operation. Thailand will never be of primary interest to JI, but neither will JI sit by if a nearby government brutally represses its coreligionists or if a broader sectarian conflict explodes.

Fourth, JI is not an organization but a network based on shared ideological beliefs. From its point of view, it would have nothing to add to the southern insurgency other than a bit more training and support. JI

11. Nirmal Ghosh, "Thailand Claims Al-Qaeda Funding Muslim Separatists," *Straits Times*, January 18, 2008.

12. Quoted in Corrine Hegland, "Counter Terrorism at the Cross Roads," *National Journal*, July 15, 2005.

shares similar goals and values with the Thai militants, but it would have little to gain by becoming more involved in the insurgency. The technological proficiency of the militants' bomb makers is such that they do not need JI. In short, JI does not have to be involved.

To date, the insurgency in Thailand has had a very small impact on the global media and consciousness, and it is covered surprisingly infrequently on jihadist Web sites. Perhaps the only silver lining of the war in Iraq is that it has attracted most of the itinerant jihadists and the attention of the multitudes of angry Muslims in the world. So far, the situation in southern Thailand ranks low on the list of grievances toward the West and apostate regimes, well behind Iraq, Palestine, Pakistan, Afghanistan, North Africa, Kashmir, Chechnya, Mindanao, and Indonesia. The principal focus of ire remains those places where the United States is leading what is perceived as the Zionist-crusader charge: Iraq and Afghanistan.

Although the American presence in Thailand and its support for the Thai government is minimal—even when compared to the small presence of U.S. forces in Mindanao—there are already some signs that the jihadists' focus is changing. The veteran Middle East journalist Amir Taheri wrote in a March 2006 article in the pan-Arab *Asharq al-Awsat* newspaper that "international jihadist circles" on the Internet and across the Muslim world had begun discussing the possibility of waging a broader jihad in southern Thailand: "The buzz in Islamist circles is that well-funded jihadist organizations may be preparing a takeover bid for the southern Thailand insurgency."[13] As the insurgency drags on, southern Thailand's profile will only be raised higher in the consciousness of Muslims around the world, and the insurgency will inevitably attract more attention and funding.

Known JI Links to Thai Militants

JI approached several small Thai groups, asking them to become a *wakalah* (regional cell) of the organization, at the JI-sponsored RM meetings in Malaysia in 1999–2000. Attended by a group of JI offi-

---

13. Quoted in Ismail Wolff, "Jihadist Threat to South Insurgency," *Thai Day*, March 13, 2006.

cials—including Tamsil Linrung, Agus Dwikarna, Faiz bin Abu Bakar Bafana, Al Chaedar, and Omar al-Faruq—and representatives of regional separatist and activist Islamic organizations from Aceh, Thailand, the Philippines, Burma, and Bangladesh, the RM meetings were held with the intent of establishing a new networking organization that would bring together militant Islamist groups of all stripes from across Southeast Asia. JI preferred to bring all these militant groups into the JI family and coordinate jihad activities throughout Asia. If that was not possible, JI wanted to at least support these groups in their struggles. It met only three times—in late 1999, in August 2000, and November 2000. After the United States declared its war on terror, several of the principals were either arrested or forced underground.[14] No one really knows how successful the RM was in establishing a network, but Faiz bin Abu Bakar Bafana, a senior JI operative arrested in Singapore in late 2001, told his interrogators that Hubungan Antarabangsa (Indonesian for "international relations"), one of JI's functional committees headed by Hambali, "handles the liaison works with other militant organizations like . . . Islamic militant groups in Pattani, Thailand."[15] Further, both Bafana and al-Faruq specifically mentioned the GMIP in their interrogations.[16]

One organization that certainly maintains some sort of link to JI is Jemaah Salafi, headed by Abdul Fatah. Although this organization is very small, Abdul Fatah has been linked to JI members since the 1980s, when he and two other Thais—Abu Hafiz of PULO and Furqon—trained in Abdul Rasul Sayyaf's camps in Afghanistan along with JI's chief of military operations, Zulkarnaen.[17] Abdul Fatah and Abu Hafiz are both known to have attended the RM meetings.[18] Additionally, ICG reports that in September 2000, Mukhlas, a top JI leader, dispatched a Kelantanese JI member, Mochamad Azmi, to Narathiwat to request

---

14. *The Jemaah Islamiyah Arrests and the Threat of Terrorism*, 7.

15. Philippine National Police, "Debriefing Report: Faiz bin Abu Bakar Bafana," March 31, 2002, 4.

16. BIN, "Interrogation Report of Omar al-Faruq," June 2002.

17. ICG, *Southern Thailand: Insurgency, Not Jihad*, 37.

18. ICG, *How the Jemaah Islamiyah Terrorist Network Operates*.

Abdul Fatah's assistance in acquiring weapons. Azmi reportedly returned with thirteen weapons.[19]

More important than these ties was the trust Hambali himself placed in Abdul Fatah. For example, Hambali left US$25,000, which had been given to him by Khalid Sheikh Muhammad for operations, in the care of Abdul Fatah and his lieutenant Johon, who served as JI's "emergency banker." Mukhlas later used US$15,500 from these funds to help bankroll the Bali bombings.[20] Further, Abdul Fatah and Ismail Lutfi Japaigiya provided JI with local operatives and assistance in 2000–01, including caring for Hambali's wife, finding refuge for top JI operatives, and procuring travel documents. Abdul Fatah also helped Hambali to plot attacks and arranged a meeting in Bangkok between Hambali and a Jemaah Salafi member, Zakaria Ibuhama (Maliq), the brother-in-law of the Cambodian JI member Sman Ismail.

Although JI's connections with Abdul Fatah and the Jemaah Salafi were the exception rather than the rule, there have been other examples of cooperation between JI and southern Thai militants. For example, Hambali's lieutenants—Zubair Muhammad (M. Farik bin Amin), Bashir bin Lap (Lillie), and Arifin bin Ali—recruited several local Thai Muslims to help them execute attacks against Western embassies and in Bangkok's backpacker quarter.[21] These Muslims were tied to a Thai-Cambodian cell that had financial and operational links to al-Qaeda. Although the plotters were ultimately foiled, the four Thai JI suspects were acquitted of terrorism charges in May 2005 on a technicality.

Another notable point of connection between international jihadist organizations and Thailand involves a senior British al-Qaeda operative, Abu Issa al-Hindi (also known as Eisa ak-Britani or Dhiren Barot), who moved to southern Thailand in 1988 after several years of fighting

---

19. Mochamad Azmi is currently detained in Malaysia under the Internal Security Act. ICG, *Southern Thailand: Insurgency, Not Jihad*, 37.

20. Abuza, *Funding Terrorism in Southeast Asia*, 55.

21. Minister of the Interior Wan Muhammad Noor Matha announced that the plan entailed "high-powered explosives to be concealed in vehicles at the targeted place" for simultaneous attacks. Quoted in Dan Murphy, "Southeast Asia's 'Mini-Al-Qaeda' Nests in Thailand," *Christian Science Monitor*, June 13, 2003.

in Kashmir.[22] An ethnic Indian who married a local Thai Muslim woman, he posed as a businessman. It is unknown when he left Thailand, but by 1998 he had become a lead instructor at an al-Qaeda camp in Afghanistan. In early 2001, he was dispatched by Khalid Sheikh Muhammad to the United States "to case potential economic and 'Jewish' targets in New York City." Later, Khalid Sheikh Muhammed sent him to Kuala Lumpur "to learn about the jihad in Southeast Asia."[23] He was arrested in England on August 3, 2004. Additionally, Imam Samudra, the mastermind of the Bali attack, shared a room at an al-Qaeda camp in Afghanistan with a Pattani Muslim who later returned to southern Thailand. It is not clear which organization dispatched this individual to the camp.

Many JI suspects also have personal ties to secessionists and to leading Wahhabis in southern Thailand. Hambali, Wan Min Wan Mat, Mukhlas, Mas Salamat Kastari, and others have all spent extended and frequent periods of time lying low in Thailand. While Hambali's capture in Ayudhhya in August 2003 is well known, what is less known is that Hambali spent time living at the Thammawittaya Foundation School in Yala, the same school run by BRN-C leader Masae Useng.[24] How well developed are these personal networks? Prime Minister Thaksin (without mentioning JI) warned in 2005 that the radicals were influenced by "extremists in Indonesia."[25] He continued, without elaborating, "They got radical ideas from studying in Indonesia, or from friends in Indonesia, and then [they] trained in Indonesia and Malaysia."[26] What do we make of these assertions? Thaksin is notorious for speaking off the cuff without knowing all the facts, and he fre-

---

22. He recounts this in his memoir, *The Army of Medinah in Kashmir* (Birmingham, UK: Maktabah al Ansaar, 1999). No further details about al-Hindi's time in southern Thailand have emerged in the open-source literature. For more, see Patrick E. Tyler, "Officials Investigate al-Qaeda Suspect's Shadowy Life," *New York Times*, August 13, 2004 (note: this article inaccurately dates his time in Thailand as 1998). See also www.newsean.in.th/english/london8.html (accessed October 1, 2008).

23. *9/11 Commission Report*, 150.

24. Author interview, Bangkok, March 3, 2007.

25. Quoted in Kimina Lyall, "Thailand Links Terror to Neighbor."

26. "Thai Premier Links Indonesia to Southern Unrest," Channel News Asia, December 19, 2004.

quently deflected criticism of Thai policies by blaming exogenous causes. These statements are clearly hyperbolic. While there is no specific evidence of students having trained in Indonesia, the influence he mentions is likely; his comments can also be seen as an attempt to shy away from criticism of Malaysia.

Close ties—often forged in Afghanistan—exist among members of the southern Thai and Malaysian groups, especially Nasori Saesaeng's GMIP and Nik Adli Nik Aziz's JI-linked KMM. Their relationship includes weapons procurement, training, and the provision of safe havens. Many contend that the KMM is actually one of JI's wakalah—not a separate and distinct institution committed to establishing an Islamic state. Even if the KMM is a distinct organization from JI, there is a good deal of overlap between them, particularly in ideology and membership, and a shared experience in the training camps of Afghanistan. The GMIP's ties to the KMM are so close that the two groups might be considered codependent. Again, the ties from Afghanistan are the key. The ICG reports that an Indonesian known as Mukhtar was operating with the GMIP in late 2003.[27]

Other foreign nationals have also been involved with the insurgency. In the April 2004 attacks, for example, a man believed to be a Bangladeshi was killed in the fighting. In November 2004, an Indonesian man originally described by officials as a member of JI was arrested, although they later backtracked and announced that he was simply an employee of the Saudi-financed Medical Emergency Relief Charity (MERC). MERC has been very active in the Malukus and Poso (Central Sulawesi), Indonesia, which from 1998 through 2001 were afflicted by sectarian conflict and remain unstable.[28] JI was also very active in the

---

27. ICG, *Southern Thailand: Insurgency, Not Jihad*, 37.

28. MERC was established on August 14, 1999, as a result of sectarian fighting. It now has twelve offices in Indonesia, concentrated in the regions most directly affected by sectarian violence (Sulawesi, Malukus, and Kalimantan). While MERC members were not implicated in directly supporting Laskar Jundullah and Laskar Mujahideen paramilitary operations in the Malukus and Central Sulawesi to the extent that KOMPAK (another Indonesian charity) was, its one-sided approach to the Malukus conflict and the actions of some individual members raised suspicions. For example, when Omar al-Faruq (the senior al-Qaeda official in the region after Hambali) was first detained by Indonesian security officials for immigration violations, a MERC official in Central Sulawesi, Pak Hafiz, bailed him out. MERC's operations abroad—in particular, in Iraq, Palestine, and Afghanistan—have also raised some concerns. Indeed, the MERC

unrest there, and JI members established two paramilitary arms—the Laskar Mujahideen and the Laskar Jundullah—to combat Christian elements. MERC and another Saudi charity, Al Haramain, worked closely with JI-linked charities Pertubuhan al Ehasan (Malaysia) and KOMPAK (Indonesia) to finance these paramilitaries. MERC created several jihadist videos that were used for fund-raising and recruitment purposes.[29] Thai officials have not commented on this MERC employee's specific duties.

While radical groups in Indonesia—such as Habib Rizieq's Islamic Defender's Front (Front Pembela Islam, FPI)—have threatened to support their coreligionists in southern Thailand, for the most part this is grandstanding. Other lesser-known groups of Indonesian Islamic students have come to Thailand to show common cause, as has the Ulama Council of Indonesia. The Fourth Army commander, Gen. Kitti Rattanachaya, revealed that seven Indonesian militants had conducted indoctrination and training for a hundred Thai militants in Yala's Yaha District.[30]

Indeed, Thai officials have expressed concern that Indonesians are becoming more involved in the insurgency. Thai police have identified an Indonesian man known as Mudeh, who has been working with the BRN-C's Sapaeng Basoe, as someone who allegedly runs a cell called the South Warriors of Valaya,[31] and they arrested an Indonesian national named Sabri Amiruddin (aka Zablee Hamaeruding) on June 16, 2006, following a four-day wave of bombings. A native of Sumatra, he was caught in Narathiwat Province with 10 kg (22 lb.) of urea fertilizer and 3 kg (6.6 lb.) of nails and spikes in his possession.[32] It is unclear whether Sabri Amiruddin has connections with Acehnese

---

Web site stated that the organization operates in the tribal areas of Pakistan with the support and permission of the Taliban. MERC was very involved in relief efforts in Aceh, Indonesia, following the December 26, 2004, tsunami. The Laskar Mujahideen also dispatched members to Aceh. See www.mer-c.org (accessed October 1, 2008); Abuza, *Funding Terrorism in Southeast Asia*, 31.

29. Abuza, *Funding Terrorism in Southeast Asia*, 31.

30. Wassana Nanuam, "End to Unrest Sought," *Bangkok Post*, August 11, 2005.

31. Wassana Nanuam, "Newest Rebel Group Headed by an Indonesian," *Bangkok Post*, September 20, 2005.

32. "Narathiwat Police Nabs Indonesian Bomb Suspect," *Nation*, June 19, 2006.

militants or JI—or, indeed, whether he and Mudeh are the same man. In May 2007, another Indonesian man, Sulaiman Abdulganee, and his Thai wife were arrested in Yala for firearms possession and drug trafficking. He was suspected of being a trainer for the militants and was at least the sixth Indonesian arrested in southern Thailand since the insurgency began. Two senior Thai military officers asserted in 2007 that extremists from Indonesia and Cambodia were training insurgents in the south, although they did not provide any hard evidence to support their assertion.[33] As noted in Chapter 4, Persatuan Mahasiswa Islam Patani (Selatan Thailand) Di Patani, an association of Thai students in Indonesia, has been active in fund-raising,[34] and GMIP leader Doromae Kuteh is believed to be in Bandung, home of the largest concentration of Pattani students in Indonesia.

The Thai government has arrested an undisclosed number of foreigners, mainly Indonesian, in conjunction with the insurgency, but it has offered few details on the arrests. Military intelligence officials suspect that there are Middle Eastern trainers involved in the insurgency, particularly given how quickly IED technology improved in the south. They tend to be dismissive of conjecture that such technology simply came across the Internet.

There is also growing concern about connections between Thai militants and the MILF and JI cells in Mindanao in the southern Philippines.[35] In March and April 2006, Malaysian authorities arrested a twelve-man logistical cell that was responsible for getting jihadists in and out of Mindanao, where they were being trained in MILF camps. The group was composed of Indonesians, Malaysians, and two Filipinos. The Filipinos told the Philippine National Police who were sent to question them that they were bringing in Pattani militants for training.[36] This revelation aligns with reports about a Pattani Muslim named Ruli (aka Ahmed) who studied at the State Institute of Islamic Studies (IAIN) in Jakarta, Indonesia, before joining the MILF. Identi-

---

33. "Former Aceh Rebel Arrested in Yala," *Bangkok Post*, May 20, 2007.
34. "PM Cancels Rebel Boss Bounties," *Bangkok Post*, April 7, 2007.
35. Author interview, Bangkok, February 9, 2007.
36. Philippine National Police, "Debriefing Report: Binsali bin Omar/Kiram Hadji Harun," July 1, 2006.

fied by name in an undated Thai intelligence document, he went to Afghanistan in 1998 and later returned to Indonesia, where he engaged in the sectarian fighting in Ambon and the Malukus following the fall of Suharto. He is now believed to be running the training for Pattani militants in the camps.

Beyond JI: The Role of Pakistani and Bangladeshi Organizations

While much attention has been focused on the relationship between Saudi organizations and international terrorism, much less attention has been focused on the role of Pakistani NGOs and terrorist organizations. More Southeast Asians are educated and radicalized in Pakistani madrassas than in Saudi institutes. Saudi Arabia provides funding; Pakistan provides experience. Further, the Pakistan-funded MWC, which has links to al-Qaeda, has played a long-standing role in both southern Thailand and Mindanao. Informal ties also existed between the nineteen-member JI cell in Karachi, Pakistan, known as Al Ghuraba, and Thai students studying at the Lashkar e-Toiba madrassa. The JI cell included Hambali's brother Gunawan and the brothers and sons of other senior JI leaders.

Sabrina Chua, formerly of Singapore's International Center for Political Violence and Terrorism Research, notes that there are deep, long-standing ties between Thai Muslims and very hard-line militant Pakistani madrassas. "Examples include the Darul Uloom Islamia Binori Town and Jamia Khalid Bin Waleed seminaries in Karachi," which she says are "two of the most influential centers of hard-line Deobandi Sunni Muslim ideology in the world. Many top-ranking leaders of the former Taliban regime in Afghanistan and the Harakat ul Jemaat Islamiyah (HUJI) are alumni of these schools."[37] Currently, some 350 Thai students are studying in Pakistani schools, with the vast majority (280) studying in madrassas. Roughly 160 of these

---

37. The school was established in 1947 and is known as the "cradle of the Taliban." Two of the suicide bombers in the 2005 London terrorist attacks attended the school, bringing greater attention to it. It is actually located in Akora Khatak, outside of Peshawar. Chua, "Political Islam in Southern Thailand—A Radicalisation?" 13. For more, see Zahid Hussain, "University of Jihad Teaches Hate and Bigotry," *Times of London*, July 15, 2005.

students are in noncertified schools or schools that resist certification by the Pakistani government.[38]

The Thai government is also concerned about Thai militants forming links with the Bangladesh-based Rohinga Solidarity Organization (RSO), which was founded in the mid-1980s. The Rohingas are a stateless Muslim minority from Burma. More than a hundred thousand Rohingas live as refugees or illegal immigrants in Bangladesh,[39] and an estimated forty thousand of them have settled or work as illegal immigrants in southwestern Thailand and Malaysia.[40]

One Bangkok-based analyst estimated that roughly a hundred Thais are receiving military training in the Chittagong (Bangladesh) region, and an official confirmed that "the RSO and HUJI-B played a role in training."[41] The head of the Thai Muslim Youth Organization was arrested in Bangladesh in 2005, although he was later released.[42] Thai officials estimated in May 2007 that roughly one thousand Rohingas had entered Thailand illegally through the coastal provinces of Ranong, Satun, and Phuket since late 2006, with most coming in search of jobs.[43]

Regional security services have expressed specific concern about the RSO for three reasons. First, it is closely affiliated with a number of

38. Following the 2005 terrorist attacks in London, General Musharraf announced that all foreign students would be expelled from Pakistan, although he soon backslid on this promise. Technically, Thai students must now receive "nonobjection certification" from both the Thai and Pakistani governments to study there. Many of Pakistan's madrassas have refused certification, prompting concerns among Thai Muslims that the Thai students would be deported. See Sopaporn Saeung, "Students to Remain in Pakistan," *Nation*, August 4, 2005; Sopaporn Saeung, "Wait, Students Advised," *Nation*, August 22, 2005; Zaffur Abbas, "Madrassas Resist Regulation Drive," BBC, August 24, 2005.

39. The Burmese government refuses to give them citizenship. For more on the Rohingas, see Imtiaz Ahmed, "Globalization, Low-Intensity Conflict and Protracted Statelessness/Refugeehood: The Plight of the Rohingyas," *Global Security and Cooperation Quarterly* 13 (Summer/Fall 2004).

40. Ahmed, "Globalization, Low-Intensity Conflict and Protracted Statelessness/Refugeehood," 16.

41. Author interview, Kuala Lumpur, April 18, 2005.

42. Author interview, Bangkok, April 21, 2005. For a differing view, see John Funston, "Troubles in the Deep South: Importance of External Linkages?" (paper presented at the Ninth International Conference on Thai Studies, DeKalb, Ill., April 3–6, 2005). See also, Liow, "International Jihad and Muslim Radicalism in Thailand?" 94.

43. "Top Separatist Goes Unnoticed," *Bangkok Post*, May 17, 2007.

militant organizations, including HUJI (originally a Pakistani jihadist organization) and its Bangladeshi affiliate, HUJI-B; both organizations have been linked to bin Laden and al-Qaeda.[44] Further, Bertil Lintner, a veteran correspondent and analyst of Burmese affairs, found that the RSO had maintained close links and received material support from the Hizb-e-Islami in Afghanistan, the Hizb-ul-Mujahideen in Kashmir, and the Jamaat-e-Islami in Bangladesh.[45] More than a hundred RSO fighters trained with the Hizb-e-Islami in Afghanistan, and Afghan trainers have visited RSO camps.[46] Additionally, in the 1980s, the RSO sent volunteers to Afghanistan to fight the Soviets.

Second, like several of the Thai militant groups, the RSO was approached by JI and was present at the RM meetings in 1999–2000.

---

44. The radical HUJI-B was founded in 1992 and is led by Shawkat Osman (Sheikh Farid). Its general secretary is Imtiaz Quddus. HUJI-B has recruited from Bangladesh's 60,000 madrassas and is now believed to have more than 15,000 followers and several thousand cadres. HUJI-B operates at least six training camps throughout the country and was listed by the U.S. Department of State as a foreign terrorist organization on May 21, 2002. Of greater concern is that HUJI-B is the leading member of a group called the Jihad Movement of Bangladesh (JMB). As Bertil Lintner has written, "This is not believed to be a separate organization but a common name for several Islamist groups in Bangladesh, of which HUJI is considered the biggest and most important." Founded in 1998, the JMB was led by Fazlul Abdur Rahman, an Afghan veteran and an associate of Osama bin Laden who, before going underground, signed bin Laden's February 23, 1998, declaration of holy war on the United States. Abdur Rahman was arrested in early March 2006. Bangladeshi police believe that Rahman financed the roughly 400 to 500 bombs that were detonated across the country on August 17, 2005. Soon after, Bangladeshi authorities arrested Bangla Bhai, the leader of the Jagrata Muslim Janata Bangladesh (JMJB), an affiliate of the JMB. For more, see U.S. Department of State, "Patterns of Global Terrorism 2002," http://www.state.gov/s/ct/rls/crt/2002/ (accessed October 1, 2008); Bertil Lintner, "A Recipe for Trouble," *Far Eastern Economic Review*, April 4, 2002; Bertil Lintner, "A Cocoon of Terror," *Far Eastern Economic Review*, April 4, 2002; Kanchan Lakshman, "Islamist Extremist Mobilization in Bangladesh," *Terrorism Monitor* 3, no. 12 (June 17, 2005); David Montero, "Quiet Bangladesh Woken by Bombs," *Christian Science Monitor*, August 18, 2005. For a more thorough analysis, see Bertil Lintner, "Bangladesh Extremist Islamist Consolidation," *Faultlines* 14 (July 2003), www.asiapacificms.com/papers/pdf/faultlines_bangladesh.pdf (accessed October 1, 2008).

45. Bertil Lintner "Championing Islamist Extremism," *South Asia Intelligence Review* 1, no. 9 (September 16, 2002).

46. According to Lintner, Rohinga recruits who were sent to fight with the Taliban were well paid by Bangladeshi standards: they received 30,000 Bangladeshi taka (US$525) upon joining and 10,000 taka (US$175) per month. See Lintner, "Championing Islamist Extremism."

Although the extent to which the RSO-JI relationship developed is not known, some reports suggest that a number of JI leaders are hiding in Bangladesh.

Third, the RSO is based in the Chittagong region of Bangladesh—which is known for its lawlessness and arms smuggling.[47] Thai security officials are quite concerned about this because arms smuggling along the porous Thai coast has become a real security issue.[48] Bangladeshi authorities, meanwhile, are concerned that Rohinga youth are becoming increasingly involved in militant activities. For example, twenty-five Rohingas were arrested in connection with the August 17, 2005, bombings in Bangladesh, and the government has taken steps to deport them to Burma.[49]

The biggest problem with trying to analyze the role of South Asian organizations in southern Thailand is that little hard evidence is available. Thai security forces have not disclosed much regarding these connections.

Still No Resolution

Although Thai intelligence officials acknowledge that social links exist between JI members and their southern Thai counterparts, there is little current evidence to suggest that JI is behind the attacks in southern Thailand. Indeed, the attacks themselves, which have not been aimed at Western targets or been suicide-based, do not reflect JI's trademark strategy. In fact, only one Westerner has been killed in the insurgency to date. For the most part, Thai officials see the relationship as one-sided. They state that although Thai militants might occasionally assist JI and provide passive support to it—for example, through the provision of safe havens—JI does not assist the Thai militants. They further insist that JI is on the run and cannot afford to help the Thai militants at present. Even so, they have arrested a handful of Indonesians and are

---

47. The RSO had a large training camp in Ukhia, southeast of Cox's Bazaar; in the 1990s, the camp was taken over by Fazlul Rahman's HUJI-B and staffed with Afghan veterans.

48. Wassana Nanuam, "Army Camp on Alert for Fresh Raid," *Bangkok Post*, January 5, 2006.

49. "Rohingas Involved in Militant Activities, Home Ministry Instructs Close Monitoring," *Prothom Alo*/BBC World Monitoring, October 18, 2005.

increasingly concerned about the radicalization and training of Thai Muslim students in Indonesia. Other observers suggest that the Thai militants do not need JI's technical expertise—that their technical proficiency has already improved dramatically and that their insurgency is already going well without JI involvement.

The likely reality is that the Thai groups rely on JI for propaganda, legitimacy, and some training, while JI benefits from the safe havens accorded by the Thai militants and the country's well-known transit routes, document forgers, and human-trafficking networks. But perhaps the real reason that JI and the Thai groups have not formally linked up is that they operate at cross-purposes. Specifically, JI believes in waging war against the "far enemy," defined by bin Laden as the supporters of apostate and anti-Muslim regimes (the United States, Israel, the United Kingdom, Australia, etc.), while the Thai groups believe in focusing on the "near enemy"—the greater Thai-Buddhist culture and society—and have decried the nihilistic violence of al-Qaeda.

However, there is concern in all quarters that JI will eventually attempt to make itself central to the conflict. Sectarian conflict is one of JI's key tools in terms of recruitment, fund-raising, and propagandizing. Lateral violence creates a sense of victimization, a sense that one's religion is under attack and that the secular state is not doing anything to defend fellow Muslims. Such conflict enables JI to indoctrinate new members and to give them a taste of jihad. One need only to look at the role played by JI in the Malukus and Poso between 1998 and 2001 as proof of this. In neither case did JI start the unrest, which was based on local causes, but JI was quick to take advantage of the conflicts. It not only sent operatives and established paramilitary groups but also assisted in the movement of a number of Arabs and Afghans to the areas, escalating the violence. More important, the jihads in the Malukus and Poso proved to be a formative experience for the participants, psychologically conditioning the young men to the idea of jihad in defense of their religion. Al-Qaeda has always supported such conflicts to give new generations of recruits their own "Afghanistan."

Like southern Thailand, Indonesia's troubled regions of Mamasa, Poso, and Ambon (Maluku) saw a dramatic upsurge in community violence between 2004 and early 2006.[50] Although there is no evidence to suggest that the outbreaks of sectarian violence in Thailand and Indonesia are connected or are being coordinated by JI, JI is a much-weakened organization. Sectarian conflict is essential to its regeneration, so it would not be surprising if JI leaders focused their efforts on escalating it. Indeed, evidence from JI and Abu Sayyaf suspects in the southern Philippines suggests that the groups are considering heightening lateral conflicts as a strategy.[51]

Are the Thai militants themselves becoming more predisposed to the targeting and radicalism that Hambali said they previously eschewed? Many in Thailand's security forces think so. While insurgents have not attacked soft targets out of area, it is on the table; they know where the Thai economy is vulnerable. General Kitti said in 2005 that security officials had seized documents proving that the militants were planning to attack tourist venues, including in Phuket and Pattaya.[52] Teams were later caught in Bangkok in November 2005 and in Phuket in September 2006. Even so, one Thai security official contended in 2007 that the militants would not attack such soft targets as a new tactic because "they are winning with their old tactics."[53] Indeed, do the Thai insurgents have the will to escalate the violence or engage in large-scale terrorism that would target the heart of the Thai economy? Will their strategy change if they become desperate? If history serves as a guide, it remains a distinct possibility. After all, insurgents did attack Don Muang Airport and other soft targets outside the south-

---

50. ICG, *Indonesia Backgrounder: Jihad in Central Sulawesi*, Asia Report No. 73 (Singapore/Brussels: ICG, February 3, 2004); "Interview: Jakarta Peacemaker Says Worst of Violence Is Over," Reuters, August 6, 2002; "Police, Troops Regain Control after Muslim-Christian Violence Kills 23," Agence France-Presse, April 26, 2004; "Hundreds of Police Rush to Maluku," *Age*, April 26, 2004; "Tension in Sulawesi After 2 People Die in Clashes," October 17, 2004; M. Azis Tunny, "Police Raid in Ambon Nets Bombs, Ammo," *Jakarta Post*, March 29, 2005; "Three Suspects Arrested in Indonesia," *Age*, May 3, 2005; "Six Killed in Attack on Police Post in Maluku Islands," Associated Press, May 16, 2005; "Reports Say Muslim Radicals Likely Responsible for Attack in Maluku," Associated Press, May 20, 2005.

51. Zachary Abuza, *Balik Islam: The Return of the Abu Sayyaf* (Carlisle, Pa: Army War College, Security Studies Institute, 2005).

52. The documents were seized in early 2004 from the house of Masae Useng. "Thailand Alleges Terror Campaign," Associated Press, December 23, 2004.

53. Author interview, Bangkok, February 22, 2007.

ern provinces in the 1970s and 1980s. Further, circumstances have changed a lot since Thai Islamists spurned Hambali's entreaties, and Islamists have an obligation to come to the defense of their coreligionists anywhere Islam is under attack. Southern Thailand is of secondary importance to JI; most of the organization's resources and manpower will remain focused on Indonesia. But JI and al-Qaeda never sit by idly while their coreligionists are persecuted.

Although Iraq is the epicenter for international jihadism, at some point the insurgency there will ebb, and there will be a "bleed out" of fighters from Iraq to other conflict zones. Unlike Afghanistan, where the mujahideen were primarily involved in guerrilla combat, the jihadists in Iraq are getting intensified training in urban warfare and terrorism. They will take that experience to the next jihad. It is only a matter of time before Thailand attracts the interest of the broader jihadist community. To be sure, Bangkok is already a legitimate target in their eyes. From the situation in the south and the video footage of Tak Bai, to the country's role in the war on terror and its alleged willingness to serve as an American "salt pit"—or covert interrogation site for high-ranking al-Qaeda captives—Thailand is fair game. It is also one of the only countries in the region with a visible Israeli presence. As Prime Minister Abhisit Vejjajiva, leader of Thailand's Democrat Party, warns, "Given other conflicts going on in the world, if we let the situation [in the south] deteriorate further, obviously it could spread out and there could be complications in terms of interference from outside forces."[54]

Unfortunately, the failure of Thai security forces to correctly identify the perpetrators of the violence—both the primary domestic actors and even the limited number of foreign actors—has hampered the development and implementation of an effective counterinsurgency program. Indeed, the government's half measures and misguided policies have only served to fuel the crisis.

---

54. Ismail Wolff, "Abhisit Warns of Foreign Infiltration in the South," *Thai Day*, August 16, 2006.

6

The One Baht COIN: Thai Counterinsurgency Efforts

The Thaksin administration vacillated wildly in its policies toward the south, from pursuing an unapologetically hard-line military approach to downplaying the seriousness of the situation. Consider the contrasts: on one hand, the government imposed martial law; on the other, it offered limited amnesties, staged an airdrop of 1 million origami "peace cranes,"[1] and installed television sets so disaffected youth could watch English football matches.[2] Thaksin also vacillated on troop levels. For example, he ordered the withdrawal of some of the forty thousand police and army troops from the south only to redeploy them following a spike in violence. And after his reelection in February 2005, he both announced punitive measures for villages that supported the militants and expressed hopes for reconciliation through the formation of the NRC.

Although the administration's surprisingly inept and inconsistent policies exacerbated the insurgency, Thaksin only understood two things: power and money. Thus, government policies fell into two categories: repressive/punitive and remunerative. The former category included the implementation of martial law and the Emergency Decree, and reliance on extrajudicial killings, arrests, and blacklists. The latter category included the formation of the NRC and offers of amnesty and development assistance. As a result, government policies were ill-equipped to deal with a hard-line ideological movement. On top of this, Thailand suffered from chain-of-command problems and bureaucratic

---

1. This was very offensive to the Muslim community, which saw it as a declaration of war. According to Sura 105 of the Quran, God sends "birds in flocks" upon his enemies.

2. In August 2005, Minister of the Interior Kongsak Wantana announced plans to install some five hundred television sets in teahouses around the south that would air British football matches. This, he said, would reduce violence, because youth who would otherwise be predisposed to violence would be "glued to the matches." "Government Hopes English Football Can Curb Southern Violence," *Nation*, August 16, 2005.

competition. Given such conditions of personnel and organizational flux, even the best of policies could not be properly implemented.

Under the Sonthi-Surayud regime, established following Thaksin's ouster in September 2006, the government applied a policy of saman-chan—or reconciliation—that included public apologies, less reliance on military force, a halting of death squads, and an attempt to negotiate with insurgents. However, this policy failed. By mid-2007, with the violence hitting record levels, the government was forced to escalate troop levels in the south and to be more aggressive in rounding up suspected insurgents.

What is clear is that the Thai security forces—under both the Thaksin administration and the Sonthi-Surayud regime—have failed dismally. Their intelligence networks are abysmal, and the police are unable to make cases against insurgents. Even after force levels hit forty thousand in 2007, military patrols were never seen in the countryside or red zones. Indeed, the leaders of the security forces, mirroring the political elites, have had little interest in the south and have been more preoccupied with elite machinations in Bangkok than with resolving the conflict.

In short, the Thai counterinsurgency has been an abject failure. But it has also been a victim of political interference, rapid transitions in the military leadership, unclear lines of authority, and a state of political denial.

Who's in Charge?

The policy vacillations of the Thaksin administration were, in part, the result of repeated cabinet reshuffles and turnovers in the leadership of the security agencies.[3] The southern crisis was first exacerbated in 2002, when Thaksin shut down the institutions responsible for the south and purged all officials with experience there because of their long-standing relationship with the Democrat Party. Later, when the insurgency broke out in January 2004, Thaksin consulted no one with long-standing

---

3. For example, in March 2004, weeks before the Krue Se mosque incident, Thaksin reshuffled his cabinet, including the ministries of Defense and Interior, the two government bodies with greatest responsibility for the south.

Figure 6.1 Thai Government Restructuring, 2002

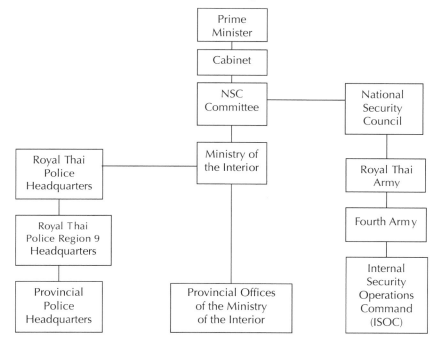

experience in the south when drawing up his response, simply because too many of them had ties with the political opposition.[4]

The "CEO" nature of Thaksin's leadership style—which included a demand for instant results and a take-charge attitude—led to the appointment of a succession of ineffective policymakers and officials responsible for the south. For example, in four years, there were six Fourth Army commanders. As a result, there was no policy continuity in the south.[5] Moreover, the chain of command under the SBPPC and the CPM-43, while not perfect, was infinitely more manageable and understandable than in subsequent organizational charts, such as after Thaksin's restructuring in 2002 (see Figure 6.1). As one Thai academic complained, there has been "a lot of confusion and competition" and a

4. Author interviews.

5. In January 2006, it was announced that Lt. Gen. Ongkorn Thongprasom would replace Gen. Kwanchart Klaharn as commander of the Fourth Army. Ismail Wolff, "The Government Is Listening, Says Anand," *Thai Day*, January 2, 2006.

"constant changing of units, agencies and policies."[6] In 2005, for example, it was announced that governors would be responsible for approving security budgets in their provinces, although the SBPPC would continue to handle security budgets for matters that went beyond provincial jurisdiction. Additionally, it was announced that authority to command forces would still lie with the Fourth Army.[7] But would the SBPPC, headed by the Fourth Army commander, have operational control over the police, rangers, or DSI?

Chain-of-command problems have been further exacerbated by the sheer number of government agencies working in the south:

- Fourth Army
- Royal Thai Army Internal Security Operations Command
- Armed Forces Security Centre (military intelligence unit run by the headquarters of the Royal Thai Army)
- Royal Thai Police Region 9 Command (and its new forward-operating headquarters in Yala)
- Royal Thai Police Special Branch (responsible to the RTP headquarters in Bangkok)
- Ministry of the Interior
- Ministry of Justice
- Rangers (an army-trained paramilitary force of roughly twenty companies engaged in guerrilla-warfare operations)[8]
- Border Patrol Police
- Ministry of Justice Department of Special Investigations
- National Intelligence Agency
- National Security Council
- Southern Border Provinces Peace-Building Command

In all, there are 65,000 to 80,000 government personnel in the south, including 15,000 to 20,000 troops and 20,000 police.[9] By mid-2007, the

6. Panitan Wattanyagorn, presentation at the Asia Foundation, Washington, D.C., April 7, 2005.

7. "Governors to Handle Budget," *Nation*, November 8, 2005.

8. Wassana Nanuam and Waedao Harai, "Rangers to Adopt Guerrilla Warfare," *Bangkok Post*, November 5, 2005.

9. Author interview, Bangkok, December 30, 2005.

number of army soldiers there reached 40,000. Coordination is all but impossible. One analyst contends that the Emergency Decree further muddles the chain of command, as it gives too much power to the Bangkok-appointed governors.[10] Nonetheless, even with this large presence of security forces, the police have claimed that they were too short of manpower to investigate and arrest hundreds of suspected insurgents.[11] In fact, the police seem unwilling to countenance inter-agency cooperation.

In addition to the thirteen government bureaucracies, the royal family is also active in the south, both directly through visits and indirectly through the Privy Council, which has begun to take on a much more prominent role there, many say as a repudiation of the government's policies. For example, in January 2006, Lt. Gen. Ongkorn Thongprasom, the Fourth Army commander and director of the SBPPC, ordered all units to report daily incidents and remedial measures to the president of the Privy Council, his patron Gen. Prem Tinsulanond.[12] Duncan McCargo contends that the Privy Council's foray into the south was meant to check the growing powers of Thaksin, noting that three individuals who had been newly elevated to the Privy Council were critics of the government. Indeed, two of them—Palakorn Suwannarat, former director of the SBPPC, and Surayud Chulanont, former supreme commander of the Thai forces—were not only elevated to the Privy Council but were also charged by Prem to take responsibility for the south.[13]

Such organizational confusion and conflict has had serious consequences. Four of the most highly publicized incidents that got out of control—Krue Se Mosque, Tak Bai, Tanyong Limo, and a school hostage situation in 2006—all escalated because there was no clear command and control. The Tak Bai video shows representatives from an alphabet soup of agencies all shouting orders. In the case of the Tanyong Limo hostage standoff, the situation got out of control because, in the absence of a command structure, the various agencies were unwilling to

---

10. Author interview, Bangkok, January 12, 2006.

11. "Police 'Lack Manpower to Go after Suspects,'" *Bangkok Post*, August 5, 2006.

12. "Solving the Conflict: Army, SBPPC to Report to Prem," *Bangkok Post*, January 9, 2006.

13. McCargo, "Network Monarchy," 516; Author interview, Bangkok, January 4, 2005.

take the initiative. As one security analyst explained, "Tanyong Limo should never have happened, but it did because the standard operating procedure of bureaucracy is to do nothing until there is a clear chain of command. In a situation like Tanyong Limo, you get chaos."[14] In short, no one wanted to take command for fear that the situation would get out of control. In the case of the school hostage situation, a group of Muslim women held two Buddhist teachers hostage after police arrested two suspected militants. Although the teachers were being beaten—one went into a coma—the security forces, facing a mob of mainly unarmed women, were hampered by clear lines of authority.[15] The Fourth Army's commander tendered his resignation over the handling of the situation, but as the third commander in two years, the acting prime minister rejected it.[16] As a *Bangkok Post* editorial summed up: "The Fourth Army continues to be weighed down by weak leadership, incompetence, poor morale and lack of preparedness to deal with emergencies like hostage situations, let alone the readiness or the will to engage insurgents."[17] The army now controls ten of the thirty-three districts in the three provinces that the government describes as plagued by violence, while police control the "pacified" zones.[18]

Competition among the various agencies is widespread. In one notorious incident, the police raided the NIA headquarters after learning that the NIA was reporting on police culpability in a number of extrajudicial killings.[19] The police and military still refuse to share informa-

---

14. Author interview, Bangkok, December 30, 2005.

15. The incident began after police arrested Muhammad Sapae-ing Mueri and Abdulgarim Matae. Mueri's wife was later arrested for inciting the crowd to hold the teachers hostage. In all, some twenty-five warrants were issued. For accounts of the hostage situation, see Wassana Nanuam and Waedao Harai, "Hostage Drama," *Bangkok Post*, May 20, 2006. For more on the implications, see "Teachers in South May Shut Schools," *Bangkok Post*, May 21, 2006; "Some 100 Schools in Narathiwat to Be Closed 'Indefinitely,'" *Nation*, May 21, 2006. For more on criticism of the Fourth Army's handling of the situation, see "Army Vows Rapid Rescue for Hostages, More Suspects Held in Assault on Teachers," *Bangkok Post*, May 23, 2006; Martin Petty, "Forces Told to Act Now, Ponder Later," *Thai Day*, May 25, 2006.

16. "Ongkorn: I'm Ready to be Replaced," *Bangkok Post*, May 22, 2006.

17. "Editorial: No More Room for Incompetence," *Bangkok Post*, May 23, 2006.

18. "Army to Take Control of 10 Districts," *Nation*, June 28, 2005.

19. Author interview, Pattani, January 15, 2006.

tion; indeed, intelligence sharing is poor even among the police, such as between the Region 9 Command and the Special Branch. For example, even after two weeks, local police still had not received the debriefing of a militant whom the Malaysians had turned over on January 6, 2006.[20] Even more intense is the competition between the highly professional DSI and the police that has played out in the press. Specifically, the police see DSI's increased focus on forensic investigations as an attempt to usurp police authority.[21] The level of antagonism was raised further still in January 2006, when DSI announced that it would exhume three hundred unidentified bodies in Pattani for DNA tests in a search for people who had gone missing in the southern violence—a perceived double swipe at the police, which has employed death squads.[22]

The general level of bureaucratic competence has also been a problem. The Ministry of the Interior, the lead civilian agency in the south, all but imploded. Sen. Sophon Supapong, a member of the NRC, criticized the SBPPC and proposed that an administrative body similar to the then defunct SBPAC be reestablished, as the military-oriented SBPPC lacked a civilian structure like that of the SBPAC and thus would never have local legitimacy. In large part, the Ministry of the Interior's incompetence has been to blame for the government's handling of the insurgency.[23] Reporting directly to the Prime Minister's Office, the SBPPC was consistently at odds with the Fourth Army. In a May 2005 overhaul, Fourth Army head Gen. Kwanchart Klaharn was appointed to serve concurrently as SBPPC chief in an effort to bridge the gulf between the army and the SBPPC.[24] Thaksin then dispatched a close ally, Police Lt. Gen. Adul Saengsingkaew, to take over all police operations in the south.[25] The police became slightly better organized and shifted its headquarters from Hat Yai to Yala to

---

20. Ibid.

21. Author interview, Bangkok, December 30, 2005.

22. Khunying Porntip said that most of the bodies appeared to be slain migrant workers from neighboring Cambodia and Burma. "Porntip to Exhume 300 Bodies to Find 'Missing,'" *Bangkok Post*, January 18, 2006; "Porntip Urges Probe to Clear Air" *Bangkok Post*, May 29, 2006.

23. Author interview, Bangkok, December 29, 2005.

24. "Back to Square One on Security," *Bangkok Post*, May 26, 2005.

25. Ibid.; "PM Touts New Security Line-up," *Nation*, May 27, 2005.

better coordinate its activities.[26] It was not until January 2007 that the SBPAC was restored.

Even more damaging has been the hoarding of intelligence by various agencies. The insurgency caught the Thai security establishment by complete surprise, and intelligence has not improved substantially since it began. Only a handful of caches of explosives have been found, and not a single safe house has been raided. Despite the arrests of 190 insurgents by the end of 2007, only 12 of 57 suspected leaders had been arrested (and the authorities are surprisingly candid in admitting that they do not know how many leaders there really are).[27] In January 2008, several top leaders broke out of their holding cell immediately after being arrested, demonstrating the rampant corruption in the security services.[28]

Under the current organizational structure, there are a handful of separate intelligence bodies: the Fourth Army's Intelligence Office; the Intelligence Operation Centre (under the command of the NIA); the Joint Intelligence Centre (ostensibly under the Fourth Army's command), and the independent Armed Forces Security Centre (AFSC). The DSI has also been trying to increase its intelligence-gathering role. Technically, these bodies are supposed to report to the SBPPC; in actuality, there is little reporting, let alone intelligence sharing.

In May 2005, Chidchai Wannasathit announced an intelligence restructuring plan that called for the police's Special Branch to be responsible for intelligence gathering in Pattani, the army's Internal Security Operations Command to be responsible in Narathiwat, and the DSI to be responsible in Yala. Giving de facto acceptance to bureaucratic competition, this plan did not represent a real attempt to solve the problem and it came under attack from all quarters.[29] Although Chidchai argued that clear lines of authority would enable better coordination of intelligence gathering, detractors argued that giving each agency its own province was flawed. The NIA privately expressed

26. Author interview, Bangkok, June 25, 2005.

27. "South Beheadings Inspired by Iraq," *Nation*, July 5, 2005.

28. Author interview, Bangkok, January 19, 2008.

29. Sermsuk Kasitipradit and Wassana Nanuam, "Intelligence Units to be Restructured," *Bangkok Post*, May 7, 2005.

reservations about the plan and asked for a secret budget of approximately Bt21 million (US$525,000) to support "six operations" to help combat the southern insurgency.[30] Following 101 nearly simultaneous arson attacks across four provinces (28 attacks in Pattani, 47 in Yala, 17 in Narathiwat, and 9 in Songkhla) on January 18, 2006, Chidchai lashed out at the intelligence agencies' performance. Said Chidchai, "I would like to see how the intelligence operations have been being carried out there since over 100 arson attacks should involve a lot of people."[31]

After some seventy-four bombs were detonated across the south in a four-day period in June 2006, Thaksin announced on June 20 that he would give full authority to army chief Sonthi Boonyaratglin to bring the area under control.[32] Sonthi claimed that with sole army control, the insurgency could be quelled in a year.[33] Sonthi's appointment was criticized from all quarters. Human rights and peace activists saw absolute military control as a green light for abuses and military impunity. Others, such as Democrat Party leader Abhisit, questioned whether military control could stop the violence: "The southern insurgency is a political problem, and it's not possible for the army to solve it alone. It needs cooperation from all parties, both state and non-state organizations."[34] Some observers saw Sonthi's appointment as a rebuke to the deputy prime minister, who had previously been in charge.[35] But others saw the appointment as an opportunity to scapegoat Sonthi, with whom Thaksin had battled over a number of top appointments and personnel decisions. Indeed, as some noted, Chidchai, a close ally of Thaksin, remained in charge of southern policy even after the announcement. To wit, Sonthi's formal authorization was delayed until early August.[36]

---

30. Author interview, Bangkok, June 24, 2005; "NIA Seeks to Boost Intelligence on South," *Nation*, September 5, 2005.

31. "Chidchai Criticizes Intelligence Operations in Deep South," *Nation*, January 19, 2006.

32. "Fifty Bombs Kill Three in South," *Bangkok Post*, June 16, 2006.

33. "Army Chief Given Full Power over Far South," *Bangkok Post*, June 20, 2006.

34. "SIM Law Fails to Stop Bombings," *Bangkok Post*, July 18, 2006.

35. "Push for Sonthi to Boost His Role," *Nation*, June 20, 2006.

36. Waedao Harai and Muhammad Ayub Pathan, "General Still Doesn't Have Needed Powers," *Bangkok Post*, July 28, 2006; "Sonthi to Take over in South," *Nation*, August 2, 2006.

The issue of lack of government coordination became heated in August 2006, when Fourth Army commander Ongkorn Thongprasom criticized the "interference" of cabinet members in the southernmost provinces who "disrupted" the work of security officials: "A minister who comes down and takes things into their own hands, or gives orders involving budgets or other vested interests, causes considerable problems for local officials."[37] A week later, Chidchai asserted that the problem rested with a lack of coordination among officials on the ground, and the government announced that Ongkorn would be replaced, making way for the sixth commander of the Fourth Army in three years.[38]

Throughout the Thaksin administration, the lack of unity and direction for the security agencies and the inability to consistently understand the threat hamstrung both security officials and policymakers. There was no coherent or unified government response and a dearth of actionable intelligence on which to base effective policies. The few policies that the Thaksin administration adopted either did not address the root causes of the conflict or exacerbated the unrest. At the end of the day, the ultimate responsibility rested with the prime minister, but Thaksin accepted no responsibility or blame. He passed the buck and demanded resignations even when policies had not had time to be implemented.

Repressive and Punitive Measures

The government has primarily employed a security-oriented policy toward the south, one meant, above all else, to maintain economic stability in the rest of the country. Days after the January 4, 2004, raid, Thaksin declared martial law in the three provinces. In part, this was an off-the-shelf strategy for Thaksin, one that he used very effectively with no popular backlash (indeed, with electoral support) in his war on drugs, which was launched in February 2003 and led to the extrajudicial killings of more than three thousand drug dealers and addicts.[39] Some

---

37. Ismail Wolff, "Politicians Hobbling Peace Efforts," *Thai Day*, August 18, 2006; "Bombings Leave 19 Hurt in Deep South," *Bangkok Post*, August 18, 2006.

38. "Ongkorn Set to Be Replaced in Bid to Improve Peace-Keeping," *Bangkok Post*, August 24, 2006.

39. Human Rights Watch, "Not Enough Graves: Thailand's War on Drugs, HIV/ AIDS, and Violations of Human Rights," July 8, 2004, http://www.hrw.org/legacy/

twenty thousand additional security forces were deployed to bolster the twenty thousand already based in the region. And yet, Sonthi said the extra twenty thousand soldiers were still not enough to ensure access to all villages in the south, leaving a hundred villages "out of touch."[40]

While the government has tried to withdraw some troops during lulls in the violence, troop levels have actually trended up. For example, in January 2006, the government announced that five more companies of rangers, roughly 400 men, would be deployed, and the police announced that they were sending another 5,300 officers to the south.[41] In August 2006, Sonthi sent an additional 5,000 troops to the south, including twenty companies of infantrymen and thirty companies of paramilitary rangers.[42] The move was very conventional—heavy firepower coupled with relaxed rules of engagement—with little to show for it.

An insurgency is never easy to combat, and the strategy for successfully fighting one is counterintuitive for most militaries. It requires less firepower and fewer men, and rejects "force protection." It also requires a very low "tooth-tail" ratio of combatants and support troops. Most of all, effective counterinsurgency operations rely on good human intelligence that comes from the support of the local population. This support is unlikely to occur when the number of troops overwhelms the local population, creates suspicion and hostility, and leads to the martialization of society. Thai military forces, which were effective in counterinsurgency operations in the 1960s and 1970s, simply became too conventional a force in the 1980s and 1990s and are in desperate need of a new counterinsurgency doctrine and training program.[43] Thai forces have been largely on the defensive. Too often they have been in static defenses, vulnerable to attack, and have not been putting pressure on the insurgents. Neither the militants nor the security forces

campaigns/aids/2004/thai.htm (accessed October 1, 2008).

40. "Three Yala Schools to Remain Closed Today," *Bangkok Post*, June 2, 2006.

41. "Another 5,300 Police to Be Deployed to Restive South," *Nation*, January 1, 2006; Ismail Wolff, "Govt Assures It Can Restrain Militants," *Thai Day*, January 2, 2006; Wassana Nanuam and Waedao Harai, "Rangers to Adopt Guerrilla Warfare," *Bangkok Post*, November 5, 2005.

42. "Sonthi Sends Another 5,000 Troops," *Bangkok Post*, August 19, 2006.

43. Author interview, Bangkok, June 6, 2006.

have hesitated to use lethal force; indeed, they are operating under a "shoot-to-kill" order.

Journalists and human rights activists have long suspected that the military has established death squads and is actively involved in extrajudicial killings. In reviewing the daily death toll, it is clear that many of the insurgency-related deaths in the south can be attributed to the security forces. A perfect example of a death-squad operation occurred on June 21, 2005, when a group of armed men, equipped with silenced 9 mm and 11 mm pistols, shot three ustadz. One of the victims, Ridwan Waemanor, was the nephew of the owner of the Jihad Wittaya School, which security forces had shut down three days earlier.[44] Witnesses stated that the three Muslims had been lying low and that security forces had made no attempt to arrest them.[45] In another example, days after the January 4, 2004, raid on the army arsenals, Matorlapee Maesae, a Muslim cleric thought to have ties to the militants, died in very suspicious circumstances. According to the autopsy, his hands had been bound with wire, he had been beaten on the head, and then he had drowned.[46] Aside from those instances in which people have clearly died at the hands of security forces, there are also those instances in which individuals have simply "disappeared." As human rights activist Sunai Phasuk commented, "The issue of injustice obstructs everything in the south. No matter how hard the government tries, it's not going to win over the Muslim population . . . with this culture of impunity."[47] Indeed, from an intelligence-gathering perspective, it is hard to see how death squads improve the government's understanding of the situation.

In late 2005, the government began to assemble "blacklists" of suspected militants and their sympathizers. The existence of the lists was

44. "Relatives Suspect Police Involvement," Bangkok Post, June 22, 2005; Anucha Charoenpo, "NRC Deeply Concerned over Murders of Muslim Teachers," Bangkok Post, June 28, 2005.

45. The chief of police in Pattani, Pritoon Pattanasopon, denied that his officers were involved, labeling the deaths a "homicide case, not an extrajudicial killing." Wassana Nanuam, "Chaturon Urged to Spur Probe," Bangkok Post, July 31, 2005.

46. Asian Center for Human Rights, "Education and Conflicts in Southern Thailand," January 21, 2004, www.achrweb.org/Review/2004/0404.htm (accessed October 1, 2008).

47. Quoted in Montlake, "Tension Grows between Thai Security Forces and Muslim Locals."

later acknowledged by Sonthi, although he stopped short of admitting that any government agency used the lists to commit extrajudicial killings.[48] According to him, people on the lists are divided into four categories: suspects with arrest warrants, militant leaders, cell members, and militant sympathizers.[49] Although the *Nation*, which was provided with a list, reported that some three hundred individuals were identified, the blacklist held by Narathiwat governor Pracha Tehrat contained two thousand names. The governor admitted to the possibility that the lists themselves might not be completely accurate and might have been abused: "It's possible local politicians might have used their influence to manipulate the blacklist to get rid of their opponents."[50] He then added, "It's better if we had more people to help screen and check before putting any names on the list."[51] According to a 2007 report from Human Rights Watch, twenty-two people have "disappeared" in the south.[52]

One senior intelligence official explained that insurgents have taken advantage of the blacklists by targeting for recruitment those who are on it or otherwise under suspicion.[53] Although the insurgents offer those individuals who join them some degree of protection, they have threatened to kill those who show up at the government reeducation centers or otherwise provide information to the government, leading many individuals to be pressed by both the insurgents and the state. According to Human Rights Watch, soldiers often march into a village and threaten "serious consequences" to militants and sympathizers who do not voluntarily surrender for reeducation.[54] The reeducation program has been so badly mishandled that people who did not support the insurgency when they first report for reeducation are often committed

48. "Army Chief Admits Agencies Are Using 'Blacklists' in South," Nation, April 26, 2006; "Govt Must Probe Blacklist Fiasco," Nation, April 28, 2006.

49. "Local Chiefs to Scrutinise 'Militant' Blacklists," Nation, April 28, 2006.

50. "Blacklist Should Be Reviewed: SBPPC," Nation, April 26, 2006.

51. "Local Chiefs to Scrutinise 'Militant' Blacklists," Nation, April 28, 2006.

52. Human Rights Watch, "Thailand: Security Forces Responsible for 'Disappearances,'" March 20, 2007, http://hrw.org/english/docs/2007/03/20/thaila15499.htm (accessed October 1, 2008).

53. Author interview, Bangkok, January 10, 2006.

54. Human Rights Watch, "Thailand: Blacklists Create Climate of Fear," December 16, 2005, www.hrw.org/english/docs/20005/12/16/thaila12317_txt.htm (accessed October 1, 2008).

to it by the end of the program's thirty days.[55] Further, under the Emergency Decree, anyone who defies a summons to provide information can be imprisoned for up to two years and fined Bt40,000 (US$1,000). Even though those who are summoned for this purpose are not considered criminal suspects, they have no right to legal counsel and no right to remain silent.[56] One intelligence officer went so far as to complain that many of the people who volunteer for the reeducation program are militants who go along with it so they can "whitewash" themselves.[57] The government, meanwhile, has taken DNA records of men in the program in Narathiwat to create a database of suspected insurgents.[58]

Martial law and the Emergency Decree have been the most glaring examples of the excesses of the government's security approach. The NRC and other proponents of lifting martial law have contended that doing so would be a positive gesture of reconciliation on the government's part. Former Thai prime minister Anand Panyarachun, for one, has argued that martial law has a "threatening ring" to it.[59] Not surprisingly, the Ministry of Defense has resisted lifting martial law, which gives full authority to the army, arguing that the law provides an essential tool in allowing the military to arrest and detain suspects for up to seven days and to conduct searches without a warrant.[60]

After a week of active debate in May 2005, the government announced that it would end martial law and replace it with a sweeping new law that would give the government even more authority in emergencies.[61] The new law allows the prime minister, with the consent of the cabinet, to declare emergency zones nationwide. The proposed legislation shifted lead authority back to the police, although it gave the

---

55. Author interview, Pattani, January 18, 2006.

56. Human Rights Watch, "Thailand: Blacklists Create Climate of Fear."

57. "Army Plans to Take a Leaf out of Insurgents' Book," *Nation*, July 23, 2006.

58. "Militant 'Sympathisers' on Parade," *Nation*, February 24, 2006.

59. Yuwadee Tunyasiri, "Martial Law Could Go, Says PM," *Bangkok Post*, May 6, 2005.

60. Other aspects of martial law include the imposition of a curfew, the barring of civilians from public areas, and the use of civilian vehicles by security forces. Sermsuk Kasitipradit and Yuwadee Tunyasiri, "Muscle Could Depend on PM's Order," *Bangkok Post*, May 9, 2005. See also the Supreme Command's statement defending the use of martial law, "Martial Law Necessary," *Nation*, May 11, 2005.

61. "Law to Give Premier Sweeping Powers," *Nation*, May 12, 2005.

army a role in "abnormal situations."[62] A public outcry forced the government to backtrack on the proposal.[63] But the government redoubled its efforts in June 2005, when its case against the "JI four" collapsed as a result of "impracticalities in the legal code."[64] Shocking the government, the July 14, 2005, raid on Yala finally lead the Thaksin cabinet to declare an immediate "severe state of emergency," to revoke martial law, and to replace it with the Emergency Decree. Thaksin announced that national reconciliation was not enough: "We want to reconcile with the people causing the trouble, but they do not want to reconcile with us. They care only about causing problems, so we need to use the law. There is no one way to solve problems there. We have to do it both ways."[65] The rapidity with which the decree was implemented raised eyebrows, and cynics even suggested that the government had staged the raid in order to enact it.[66]

Human rights activists immediately pointed to the severe negative repercussions the decree would have, stating that the government had already proved itself unable or unwilling to respect fundamental human rights and the rule of law.[67] For example, the March 12, 2004, disappearance and murder of human rights lawyer Somchai Neelapaijit had already convinced most Muslims (and democracy and human rights

---

62. The debate has broadened to address the fact that Thailand does not have specific counterterrorism legislation. The government previously had looked at proposals to increase the power of the security services to conduct investigations. In particular, the Justice Ministry was instructed by the Office of the Prime Minister to review the constitutionality of a Singapore- or Malaysia-style Internal Security Act (ISA) that would permit the police to hold national-security suspects indefinitely without charge. See Penya Plewsangwang and Piyanart Srivalo, "Police Set to Get back Lead Role," *Nation*, May 6, 2005.

63. "Security Law: Deputy PM Warns of the Dangers of Legal Overkill," *Nation*, December 3, 2004.

64. "BK Bomb-Plot Trial: Acquittal of 4 Shows 'Need for Special Laws,'" *Nation*, June 3, 2005.

65. "Reconciliation Alone Can't Cure South," *Bangkok Post*, July 28, 2005.

66. Adding to this suspicion was a lame and unconvincing announcement by the government that it knew the Yala attack was coming but was "afraid to take action for fear of being sued." Quoted in Yuwadee Tunyasiri and Preeyanat Phanayanggoor, "Govt Knew Yala Attack Pending," *Bangkok Post*, July 17, 2005.

67. See "A Perilous Year Looms for Civil and Human Rights," *Nation*, December 20, 2004.

activists) that Thaksin was committed to circumventing the rule of law, or at least to turning a blind eye to police and military abuses. Indeed, before the Emergency Decree was even passed, the government had been detaining suspects without charge for longer than allowed under the existing law.[68] And the army's extralegal detention of several hundred protesters had led to the egregious human rights violation in Tak Bai.[69] Further, critics noted that the government already had five existing laws—including the Martial Law Act, the Administration in Emergency Situation Act, and the Special Investigation Act—to deal with the situation in the south.[70]

What is most glaring about the law is that it provides blanket immunity for the security forces in the line of duty, thus exacerbating the public's perception that the security forces operate in a culture of impunity. Additionally, the law undermined the decentralization that the 1997 constitution implemented to specifically give aggrieved communities, including the Malays in the south, a greater say in how they are governed. Although the blame for excesses by security forces falls on the government, much of the blame must also be placed on the insurgents themselves. For example, violence directed at state officials and the murder of a judge in Pattani on September 17, 2004, led half of the judiciary in the three provinces to seek transfers.[71] The resulting

---

68. The 1997 constitution allows Thai police to hold a suspect up to forty-eight hours before seeking court approval, after which they may hold the suspect an additional twelve days before they have to file charges. If no charges are filed, the suspect must be released. See "Suspected Militants Demand to See Lawyers," Thai News Agency, December 20, 2004; "Court Extends Custody over Key Militant Suspects," Thai News Agency, December 28, 2004.

69. See the report by the Thai Senate's Social Development and Human Security Committee that labeled the detention a "gross violation of the law." The report stated that "such operations violated Article 59 of the Penal Code." For more, see Supalak Ganjanakhundee, "Military Slammed: Senate: Tak Bai a Crime," *Nation*, December 25, 2004.

70. "Security Law: Deputy PM Warns of the Dangers of Legal Overkill," *Nation*, December 3, 2004.

71. The Thai government announced efforts to enhance security at courts but not for individual justices. See "Cabinet Endorses State-Run Pondoks," *Nation*, September 29, 2004.

lack of judicial oversight made excesses by security forces that much more likely.

While Thaksin's earlier policies had been heavily criticized for their excesses, the Emergency Decree is an affront to democracy and human rights that allows the prime minister to order a state of emergency in certain regions and grants the state sweeping powers. For example, it authorizes the following: the detention of suspects for up to thirty days, searches and seizures without warrants, bans on public assembly, restrictions on the sale of items that can be used for bomb making (though most bombs are made of readily available hardware and chemicals), the tapping of phones without court orders, limitations on freedom of movement, and press censorship if the government deems reporting to be counter to the national interest (see Appendix D for the text of the Emergency Decree's key points).[72] People feared that such sweeping powers would give the prime minister extra tools to crush dissent—without necessarily improving the security situation in the south. What angered people most was that the decree reinforced the state's culture of impunity. For instance, Section 16 offers protection to officials from prosecution for human rights violations, and Section 17 grants almost blanket immunity to security forces from criminal and civil prosecution. As a 2005 ICG report noted, "citizens are left with no redress for abuses of emergency powers."[73]

The NRC was infuriated by the Emergency Decree and worked with civil society to pressure the government to tone down its more egregious aspects. Anand Panyarachun warned, "The local community sees this decree as a license to kill."[74] The opposition Democrats also excoriated the decree, arguing that the government already had all the power and legal tools it needed and that this was simply an erosion of the constitution and a blatant power grab by the prime minister. The ruling TRT even had to deal with opposition to the decree from within its own

---

72. An unofficial translation of the decree can be found at www.geocities.com/changnoi2/stateofemergencydecree.pdf (accessed October 1, 2008).

73. ICG, *Thailand's Emergency Decree: No Solution*, Asia Report No. 105 (Singapore/Brussels: ICG, November 18, 2005), 3.

74. "Irreconcilable?" *Nation*, July 29, 2005. For more on Anand's position, see his letter to the cabinet dated July 19, 2005, published in the *Nation*, July 25, 2005.

ranks.[75] In the end, though, parliament passed the bill in September 2005 by a large majority.[76] One Senate critic of the new law summed it up this way: "The southern violence was spawned by bitterness of local residents who saw injustice inflicted by authorities, and the empowering of unjust local officials might worsen the situation."[77] Philip Alston, the UN special rapporteur on extrajudicial, summary, or arbitrary executions of the UN Human Rights Council, concurred with this assessment: "Impunity for violence committed by the security forces has been an ongoing problem in Thailand, but the emergency decree has gone even further and makes impunity look like the official policy."[78]

Following the decree, actionable intelligence improved slightly in late 2005 and early 2006 and security forces made some progress in seizing arms caches and recovering stolen weapons in 2006 and 2007, but overall the government's heavy-handed approach and broad sweeps had a negative effect on legal proceedings. For example, of the twenty-seven insurgents arrested between July 2005 (when the Emergency Decree went into effect) and September 2005, only six were charged with causing unrest; nine were released, and the rest were detained without charge.[79] Ten of the thirty-four persons arrested in connection with Tanyong Limo were released. In another case, officials arrested nineteen teachers at the Thammawittaya Foundation School in March 2006.[80] All were released by the end of the month.[81] In some instances, Thai prosecutors reached too far in bringing charges against detained militants or suspected insurgents. By 2007, more than 90 percent of

---

75. Thirty members of the TRT's Wang Nam Yen faction condemned the decree. "Abhisit Lashes out at Govt," *Nation*, August 25, 2005; "Anand Calls for Release of Students," *Nation*, August 16, 2005.

76. There was greater opposition in the Senate, where 121 voted in favor, 38 voted against, and 5 abstained.

77. Sen. Sophon Supapong, quoted in "Senate Passes Emergency Law," *Nation*, August 30, 2005.

78. Quoted in Ismail Wolff, "Amend Decree, Urges UN Official," *Thai Day*, July 20, 2006.

79. "27 Arrested Since Decree Enacted in the South," *Bangkok Post*, September 12, 2005.

80. "9 Islamic Teachers Rounded up in Yala," *Bangkok Post*, March 29, 2006.

81. "Yala Court Sets Four Islamic Teachers Free," *Nation*, April 8, 2006; "Police Released All but One Ustadz," *Nation*, April 8, 2006.

those who had been arrested in connection with the insurgency had been released due to a lack of evidence against them.

Although the Thai government is constantly searching for the "mastermind" behind the insurgency, the courts have had none of it. Indeed, by May 2007, only two individuals had been arrested, tried, and convicted in a court of law. As Francesca Lawe-Davies of the ICG commented, "The only impact of the [Emergency] decree has been the increase in arrests, but none of these have resulted in successful prosecutions. Many of these arrests have been on shaky ground, so people have been released or held beyond the length of time the decree mandates. This is only continuing to fuel the resentment."[82]

The limitations of such an aggressive security approach to the conflict are many. The enormous influx of security forces did little to quell the insurgency, which continued to escalate in scope and violence. And most of the nine thousand surveillance cameras that were set up across the south were poorly maintained, leading many of them to become inoperable. If anything, the government's use of "the stick" created a backlash. Broad sweeps and the alleged routine use of torture to coerce confessions from suspected insurgents only alienated the communities whose intelligence was essential.[83] "In police custody, people are beaten. They cannot come here and arrest our students and teachers without evidence," explained one Islamic schoolteacher, Abdul Karim, who claims he was tortured. "Because of emergency laws, we cannot fight back. There is no way for us to complain or appeal against this."[84] Popular discontent over the high troop levels was hardly surprising—this has been at the heart of the unrest. Both the government's repression and the militants' targeting of fellow Muslims have deterred many people from providing the government with useful intelligence. As the violence escalated and the government responded, the Muslim radicals' claims that the government is patently anti-Muslim and patently aggressive were only proved in the eyes of the public.

---

82. Quoted in Martin Petty, "Will Decree Lead to Peace?" *Thai Day*, April 19, 2006.

83. Ampa Santimatanedol, "Muslim Lawyers Say Police Still Using Torture," *Bangkok Post*, November 27, 2005.

84. Martin Petty, "Decree Must Be Revoked, Southern Muslims Say," *Thai Day*, May 16, 2006.

Rewards and Inducements

The government has not relied solely on a security approach in dealing with the south; it has also offered a handful of reward and inducement programs to encourage cooperation. However, these programs have been poorly implemented and have created a backlash, even those that were once implemented with great effect in the 1980s. The programs fall under one of four broad categories: (1) amnesty, (2) educational reform, (3) job creation, and (4) economic development.

While the NRC called for a general amnesty as a "most reconciliatory" gesture in 2005, the government rejected a blanket six-month amnesty program, offering amnesty only for those not responsible for "serious crimes."[85] The cabinet approved a plan to reduce the punishment for insurgents and their sympathizers who turned themselves in but insisted that this plea-bargain proposal was not an amnesty.[86] People were encouraged to surrender, but they had few legal safeguards. Explained Narathiwat governor Pracha Tehrat: "We will cross-check their names with our list of those wanted on criminal charges and only people with none against them will be accepted. Those who have committed serious crimes will face legal action."[87] Those who had not been found to have committed serious acts of violence were sent to reeducation camps.[88]

The government's plan had a number of problems. First, many alleged that the "surrenders" had not always been voluntary. For example, a Muslim member of the NRC, Amadsomboon Mualuang, asserted that ten Muslim students who had just returned home from university in Bangkok were forced to "surrender" before the cameras and that the same thing had happened to some low-level government employees.

85. "Government Rejects Amnesty for Southern Insurgents," *Bangkok Post*, November 29, 2005; Wassana Nanuam, "Thammarak Offers Trade: Amnesty for Total Surrender," *Bangkok Post*, August 16, 2005; "General Amnesty Hailed as 'Only Way,'" August 17, 2005; "Insurgents Surrender in Narathiwat; Killings Continue," *Nation*, August 31, 2005.

86. Wolff, "Govt Assures It Can Restrain Militants."

87. "Dozens of Fighters to Surrender," *Nation*, August 17, 2005.

88. For example, sixty-five admitted Muslim insurgents surrendered to Thai government authorities in Narathiwat on July 5, 2006; all were sent for reeducation in the region's so-called peacebuilding schools. "65 Insurgents Surrender in Deep South," *Bangkok Post*, July 6, 2006.

"They have nothing to do with the violence," he said.[89] Further, there was some evidence to suggest a "Potemkin village" at work, particularly if the author's estimate that there were 2,000 militants active in the south at the time is accurate; the numbers simply did not add up. In the first two months of the amnesty program, 111 rebels surrendered in return for amnesty; a few months later, 66 rebels or sympathizers turned themselves in; and 10 others surrendered in a one-week period in November.[90] The number of surrenders in such a short time seemed very high, especially considering that the back of the insurgency had not been bruised, let alone broken.

More important, not much thought was given to how to reintegrate these individuals into their respective communities. They were promised jobs and protection by the SBPPC after a brief reeducation, but the SBPPC had no money at its disposal to create jobs, and security forces had long since proved incapable of providing adequate protection to villagers. Without protection, village informants were killed at an alarming rate. Yet the government insisted that these individuals could effectively serve as "goodwill ambassadors" to their communities.

In August 2006, after he was given full authority to deal with the south, Sonthi announced a new amnesty to win over the insurgents.[91] It was not clear, however, how the new amnesty program would differ from the much-maligned one that was feebly implemented in 2005 or if any more militants would trust the government's offer.

A telling incident from earlier in the insurgency demonstrated well the government's overall attitude toward amnesty. In 2004, there was talk that the government would send former rebels to the south to appeal to the militants to lay down their arms. Four imprisoned PULO leaders—Haji Dato Sama-ae Thanam, Haji Sama-ae Thanam (Haji Ismail Ghaddafi), Abdurrahman bin Abdul Kadir, and Haji Buedo Betong—all serving life sentences for their role in the insurgency,

89. Ampa Santimatanedol, "Innocents 'Forced to Surrender,'" *Bangkok Post*, September 15, 2005.

90. Waedaoh Harai and Anucha Charoenpo, "Another 34 Suspected Rebels Give up," *Bangkok Post*, September 16, 2005.

91. Amornrat Khemkhao, "Three Killed in Shop Attack," *Nation*, August 14, 2006.

agreed to be taken to the south by the police to appeal for calm.[92] In the end, however, the government did not grant the men parole and an appeals court upheld their life sentences.[93]

The Thaksin administration also emphasized education as a cornerstone of its southern policy. Because it believed that the unrest was being fomented by Islamic teachers in a network of Saudi- and Middle East–funded madrassas, the cabinet endorsed a plan to establish fully funded, state-run Islamic schools, which would preclude the need for foreign assistance (and influence).[94] The government appointed Aree Wongsearaya, a Muslim, as deputy education minister in charge of reforming Islamic schools and set aside additional funding for vocational education in pondoks.[95] In mid-September 2004, Aree announced that the Ministry of Education would register all pondoks and would vet lists of instructors.[96] More than 50 percent of the schools (totaling some 7,000 to 10,000 students) refused to comply with the order.[97] As a result, only 214 of the pondoks are currently registered and roughly 400 remain unregistered.

This education program was problematic in several ways. First, a state-controlled, state-approved curriculum has never been accepted by Thailand's Muslim community. Indeed, it has historically seen state attempts to influence the curriculum as a component of the assimilation program. Second, mere state sponsorship would not make the schools less radical. For example, being a state employee has done nothing to temper the rhetoric of Yala State University rector Ismail Lutfi, a very radical cleric with ties to JI who is influential in Bangkok and across the

---

92. The four were turned over by Malaysian authorities in 1998 and sentenced in October 2002. "Jailed Insurgents Seen as New Hope in Peace Plan," Thai News Agency, November 24, 2004.

93. "PULO Four Lose Treason Appeals," *Nation*, November 16, 2005.

94. According to Thai government spokesman Jakrapob Penkair, "The government will consult with religious leaders and local leaders to build state-run pondoks that will have a high standard in both religious and secular subjects." See "Cabinet Endorses State-Run Pondoks," *Nation*, September 29, 2004.

95. "Muslim Teachers Extend Cautious Welcome to Aree," *Nation*, September 17, 2004.

96. Ibid.

97. Author interview, Pattani, January 16, 2006.

region. In addition, several observers have noted that a half-madrassa, half-secular curriculum would in itself be counterproductive, because the students' base of knowledge would be wider but certainly not deeper, and the schools would not be providing students with the tools to find gainful employment. Third, it is doubtful the state would be able to fund all the schools, which would continue to solicit aid from the Middle East. Fourth, central-government interference in Islamic education and placing military guards at the schools were among the things that antagonized the Muslim community in the first place. Fifth and finally, the new policies would do nothing to address the Muslims' complaint that the government did not accredit many Middle Eastern Islamic schools and universities or allow graduates of unregistered pondoks to sit for civil service or university exams.

In response to this complaint, the government announced in 2005 that it was changing policies slightly to allow Muslims who had studied in the Middle East to teach in state-run schools, although those individuals would still be required to have six additional months of training in Thailand.[98] In another important concession, the Ministry of Education also reversed its long-standing policy on the language of instruction, announcing that it was lifting the ban on Yawi in state schools and that a bilingual curriculum would be introduced.[99] The ministry later decided to teach in standard Bahasa Malayu using romanized script rather than Yawi.

On the job-creation and economic-development front, the government designed a plan through which it hoped to create 42,000 positions in the south. Ten thousand jobs would be in royal development projects and 20,000 in community peacebuilding projects.[100] The SBPPC itself planned to employ 4,500 peacebuilding volunteers.[101] This plan experienced problems on implementation, however, as locals complained that it favored the children of village chiefs and the politically con-

98. Pradit Ruangdit, "Islamic Degrees Will Be Recognized," *Bangkok Post*, September 20, 2005.
99. Sirikul Nunnag, "Ministry Takes Bilingual Route to Revoke Ban," *Bangkok Post*, September 28, 2005.
100. Author interview, Pattani, January 16, 2006.
101. "Security Job Scheme Causes Splits," Issara News Centre, November 21, 2005.

nected. Additionally, because the insurgents have threatened to kill anyone who worked for the government, many individuals were deterred from participating.

The Thaksin administration also offered direct financial assistance to the southern provinces. In 2004, Thaksin pledged US$300 million for economic development.[102] He later increased the figure to US$500 million. In 2005, the government announced a number of other funds to assist southern residents, including a US$22.5 million assistance program for government employees posted in the south and relief for businesses and farmers whose livelihood had been affected by the violence.

While such job-creation and economic-development programs have been important, they never had a chance of being a panacea for two principal reasons. First, they were not offered equally in all areas.[103] For example, Thaksin made clear that the 358 red zones (200 in Narathiwat alone) would not be receiving any funds: "We don't give money to those red villages, because we don't want them to spend the money on explosives, road spikes or assassins. If the money sanctions do not work, I will send soldiers to lay siege to the red zone villages and put more pressure on them."[104] Second, the militants have not been motivated by economic concerns but by their own ideological brand of Islam—and by resentment over government policy and the Emergency Decree. Indeed, the local population at large has even shown some hostility toward certain development projects that could jeopardize their environment and way of life. It is also acutely aware of the threats made by the militants against those who receive government funding.

The National Reconciliation Commission

Thaksin's realization that the security approach had failed to curb the insurgency was not driven home by the continued bombings but by the utterly dismal performance of his political party in the south. The TRT dominated the February 2005 national elections, winning 376 of 500 seats in parliament; this was the first time a single party had won the election outright. The Democrat Party won only 99 seats, but it swept

---

102. Andrew Perrin, "Hearts and Pockets," *Time—Asian Edition*, May 17, 2004.
103. "Thaksin Plan for South Criticized," BBC, February 18, 2005.
104. Don Pathan, "PM's Remedy for Crisis in South," *Nation*, February 17, 2005.

the south, winning 52 of the 54 seats, a gain of 4 seats from the 2001 elections.[105] Despite fielding eleven veteran and well-funded politicians, the TRT won only two southern races—in several cases, to political newcomers.[106] The Wadah faction of the TRT was expected to dent the Democrats' hold over the south, but the Democrat Party ran on what was known as the "Pattani Declaration," a road map for a southern peace process that explicitly rejected the "violent approach" of the government. Most constituents seemed to have voted for the Democrats as a rejection of the government's handling of the situation.

What was heartening for the government, despite the electoral defeat in the south, was the very high voter turnout of roughly 77 percent. As one senior Thai politician noted of the southerners, "They chose to be Thai citizens. If they wanted to back the separatist line, then they would have quit the political process."[107] This politician contended that only 6 percent to 7 percent of the population in the south actively supported the militants. Chaiwat Satha-Anand of Thammasat University concurred with this contention: "They are not separatists. They voted, so they want to remain in the Thai political society. They didn't have to vote. It put to rest concerns that they are separatists."[108] A senior Thai intelligence official similarly estimated that the elections demonstrated that "90 percent of the population is with us."[109] Although the polls gave the government something positive to present, the mood on the ground was turning decidedly against it.

Following the elections, Thaksin announced a number of new policies and initiatives, showing a dramatic shift in approach. He began by signaling a slight shift in the security approach, calling for one division (12,000 troops) to be moved into an economic-development unit.[110]

---

105. "Why They All Love Thaksin," *Economist*, February 12, 2005.

106. Pupalak Ganjanakhundee, "No Thai Rak Thai Fever in the Troubled South," *Nation*, February 8, 2005.

107. Author interview, Bangkok, February 19, 2005.

108. Chaiwat Satha-Anand, presentation at the Asia Foundation, Washington, D.C., April 7, 2005.

109. Author interview, Bangkok, March 16, 2005.

110. The Thai cabinet allocated Bt8.8 billion (US$225.6 million) for the unit, which would be broken off from the Sixteenth Infantry Division. "Govt to Set up New Development Force in Deep South," *Nation*, February 16, 2005.

He then announced that the respected former prime minister Anand Panyarachun would lead an independent, forty-eight-person commission on national reconciliation.[111] The fact that Thaksin gave in to demands to establish the NRC after winning the single largest landslide in Thai electoral history suggested that a deal was already in place before the election. Bangkok insiders theorized that the king, who repeatedly expressed his displeasure at Thaksin's militarized approach, demanded the formation of the NRC.

Not everyone agreed with this theory. In fact, Duncan McCargo believes that Thaksin established the NRC to undermine the king's authority: "Thaksin had created the NRC simply to neutralize his critics while using state power to regain the upper hand over a resurgent network monarchy."[112] But even McCargo acknowledges that Anand was very much part of the "network monarchy," dominated by Prem, that Thaksin hoped to curb. As he states, "The NRC came almost to symbolize an alternative government for Thailand, comprising the wise men of the network monarchy dedicated to keeping alive the spirit of the 1997 Constitution."[113]

Regardless of whether Thaksin or the monarchy was the force behind the NRC's establishment, the body was highly critical of the government's handling of the situation. Thaksin's turnaround came at a rare joint parliamentary debate on southern Thailand held March 30–31, 2005. At the session, Thaksin conceded, "I had a lot of free time to contemplate what was right or what was wrong in what I've done. Violence cannot be solved with violence."[114] He announced that some of the forty thousand security troops would be demobilized.[115] Most important, Thaksin finally seemed to understand that a pervasive sense of injustice rested at the heart of the problem, and he ordered the implementation of many of the policies outlined by Abhist Vejjajiva and Surin Pitsuwan and other Democrat Party leaders. These included:

111. It was expanded to forty-nine members in April 2005.
112. McCargo, "Network Monarchy," 115.
113. Ibid.
114. "Thai PM Indicates Switch on South," BBC, March 3, 2005.
115. "Troop Levels to Be Reduced," *Nation*, April 1, 2005.

- a review of force used by government agents, further investigation into the Tak Bai incident, and punishment of government officials implicated in abuses;
- an increase in the evidentiary standards needed to detain suspected militants;
- the release of detainees against whom there is limited evidence;
- financial compensation for the families of the eighty-five people killed and the seven missing at Tak Bai, as well as free education programs for their children and compensation for those injured by security forces.[116]

Many people considered Anand's NRC to be the "last hope." Only he, it was perceived, had enough political independence from Thaksin and the power of the TRT behind him. Anand commands loyalty and respect from the military, as well as from the palace. He has considerable personal moral and political authority. However, there was concern that the NRC would not have the independence and authority it needed, and NRC members believed that Thaksin wanted the insurgency resolved before it had a negative economic impact. Indeed, the NRC had limits, and it had clear dividing lines. The commission was composed of three distinct groups—politicians (including members of both the TRT and the Democrats), government agents, and civil society representatives—and quickly split along institutional lines, leading to suspicion that Thaksin agreed to its formation in the hopes that it would fail, thereby creating a scapegoat and giving him carte blanche to revert to his own policy agenda. As it was, the Thaksin government was very displeased with some of the NRC's initial findings and suggestions and even implemented policies that were inimical to the NRC's goals. In fact, Thaksin had every incentive to undermine the commission.

---

116. The relatives and victims of the Tak Bai incident filed lawsuits against five state agencies demanding Bt18 million (US$450,000) in restitution. Then, relatives of seventy-five protesters killed in Tak Bai filed a joint lawsuit of some Bt103 million (US$2,575,000), rejecting the government's proposed compensation program. "PM Vows Justice for South," *Nation*, April 3, 2005; "Govt Attorneys Vow to Fight Tak Bai Compensation Demands," *Bangkok Post*, October 25, 2005; "Tak Bai Relatives File 103 Million Baht Lawsuit," *Bangkok Post*, October 26, 2005; "Tak Bai Victims and Relatives File Law Suits," *Bangkok Post*, October 23, 2005.

The NRC's reports on Krue Se and Tak Bai, which found the military culpable, were very objective and well received. The NRC was also outspoken with regard to suspected military and police death squads,[117] and came out against the military's calls for more resources.[118] Members of the NRC made frequent tours of the south and held numerous consultations, although it was not lost on anyone that most members were from Bangkok. But the NRC's most important contribution was in its attempts to regain some of the trust of the Muslim community by focusing on issues of social justice. The NRC's point of view was that local Muslims would never cooperate with Thai security services unless trust was restored. As Anand stated, the culture of police-military impunity has to be overcome: "If they are not cooperating with the government, it's because they are in deep fear. They're afraid that the government cannot guarantee them safety. They're also afraid that they won't get justice."[119] To that end, the NRC took a number of important actions.

First, it raised the issue of the "disappeared" and pushed for investigations into ten confirmed cases of disappearance. As minister of education and NRC member Chaturon Chaisaeng said, "They [villagers] believe the police were involved with the disappearances. They think the police abducted those people."[120] Particular attention was focused on the border patrol police. Some twenty-one families ultimately filed complaints alleging that state officials had abducted one of their family members.[121] The NRC also pushed for the establishment of a special investigative panel in the Ministry of the Interior to investigate the disappearance of Somchai Neelaphaijit.

117. Anucha Charoenpo, "NRC Deeply Concerned over Murders of Muslim Teachers," *Bangkok Post*, June 28, 2005.

118. The Ministry of Defense submitted a budget request for an addition Bt2.78 billion (roughly US$70 million) for equipment to be used in the south, including 7 attack helicopters, 21,000 rifles, 2,500 machine guns, and signals-intelligence equipment. "Army Wants Bt2.8 Bn for Choppers, Weaponry," *Nation*, July 8, 2005.

119. Quoted in Sanitsuda Ekachai, "What's Lacking with the News? Truth," *Bangkok Post*, August 10, 2005.

120. Anucha Charoenpo and Ampa Santimatanedol, "NRC Touts Centre for 'the Missing,'" *Bangkok Post*, August 7, 2005.

121. "21 Families in Deep South Say Their Children Abducted by State Officials," *Nation*, July 5, 2006.

Second, interventions by the NRC led to the release of suspects, and the government agreed to review all insurgency-related cases since January 2004.[122] The NRC also pushed the government to drop the charges against the remaining detained Tak Bai demonstrators,[123] and it tried to force the government to extend legal counsel to detained suspects within forty-eight hours. A portion of the NRC's Bt63 million (US$1.58 million) economic relief fund was set aside to pay for defense lawyers.[124] The government also established a Bt100 million (US$2.5 million) legal assistance fund for suspected militants.[125]

Third, the NRC called for a general amnesty as a "most reconciliatory" gesture. As noted, the government refused to implement a blanket amnesty, offering amnesty only for those not responsible for "serious crimes."[126]

Despite these important actions, the NRC had significant limitations. For one, as a Thai Muslim complained, it was dominated by people from Bangkok and included few southerners.[127] More important, the commission did not fully understand the nature of the insurgents. As an example, NRC members came out with blithely naive statements, such as this one by Gothom Arya: "We should pursue a reconciliation approach with the insurgents. . . . They are essentially Thai nationals."[128] This perception is based on a faulty analysis—

---

122. Pradit Ruangdit, "Calls for a New Legal Body," *Bangkok Post*, July 27, 2005; Onnucha Hutasing, "New Panel to Close Legal Loopholes," *Bangkok Post*, August 25, 2005.

123. Thaksin agreed with the NRC and ordered the police to drop charges if there was not strong evidence against the demonstrators. Piyanart Srivalo, "Police Told to Drop Charges over Tak Bai," *Nation*, July 27, 2005.

124. Ampa Santimatanedol, "NRC Funds to Be Sped to Those in Need," *Bangkok Post*, August 7, 2005.

125. Yuwadee Tunyasiri and Bhanravee Tansubhapol, "South to Get Data Base of Those Missing," *Bangkok Post*, June 16, 2005.

126. By August 2005, thirty-five militants had turned themselves in. After a brief reeducation, they would be given jobs and protection by the SBPPC and would serve as "goodwill ambassadors" to their communities. For more, see Wassana Nanuam, "Thammarak Offers Trade: Amnesty for Total Surrender," *Bangkok Post*, August 16, 2005; "General Amnesty Hailed as 'Only Way,'" August 17, 2005; "Insurgents Surrender in Narathiwat; Killings Continue," *Nation*, August 31, 2005.

127. Author interview, Bangkok, June 23, 2005.

128. "Army Wants Bt2.8 Bn for Choppers, Weaponry," *Nation*, July 8, 2005.

that the insurgency is like all past ones, simply a conflict over poverty and social justice. But the militants had shown absolutely no indication that they were interested in any form of negotiation. Further, they had not stated any demands or platforms, so there was no set issue to negotiate about. Thus, the NRC advocated negotiations with Bersatu's Wan Kadir—someone with whom they could talk. The NRC contended that more power sharing in decision making—"not autonomy or self-rule"—was on the table. The government, with NRC backing, considered turning the three southern provinces into a special administrative area, like Bangkok, but the militants would be unlikely to accept such a solution.[129]

Although NRC officials stated that they would reconcile with the Muslim population, most of the Muslim population had been cowed into submission by the militants, who targeted those Muslims who did seek accommodation. As one leaflet warned, "A dog is still a dog, even if it is friends with a goat." Further, southerners never believed that the NRC could address the government's culture of impunity. For their part, the militants saw the NRC as a paper tiger that had no influence over the government.

Although the NRC could not stop the insurgency, and it had only a limited, short-term impact, it ultimately may leave an important legacy in the long term because of the issues to which it called attention. Its key recommendations—focusing on social justice, rule of law, democracy, local empowerment, accountability, and transparency—are all absolutely essential, not just for the south but for the entire country. As already made clear, the democratic and human rights gains Thailand made in the 1990s came under relentless assault during the Thaksin administration.

The NRC was due to issue its final report in March 2006, but its release was delayed due to the political stalemate caused by the surprise resignation of Thaksin and the political gridlock that ensued. On June 5, 2006, the NRC finally issued the report. The long-awaited report listed several reasons for the escalation in the south, including the Thaksin administration's heavy-handed policies and its misunderstanding of

---

129. Anuraj Manibhandu, "Power-Sharing, Not Self-Rule," *Bangkok Post*, August 10, 2005.

the cultural and historical context of the situation. The report had several policy recommendations, including the following:

- the establishment of a new regional administrative body—the Peaceful Strategic Administrative Center for Southern Border Provinces (PSAC)—that would administer the three provinces, mediate conflicts, and give residents greater voice in local government decisions;
- the decentralization of political power;
- the improvement of judicial systems;
- the strengthening of mechanisms that would allow public participation not only in policymaking but also in checking the use of state power;
- the introduction of Islamic law;
- the adoption of the Malay dialect and the written Yawi script as an official second language in the Muslim-dominated south.

Although the NRC's recommendations were clearly the result of many compromises and collectively would not be enough stop the insurgency, some of them were much needed. Thaksin's interim government ordered all "appropriate" proposals from the NRC to be implemented as soon as possible, but it stated that proposals requiring parliamentary legislation "would have to wait for the relevant approval procedures in the Parliament."[130] The government rejected the calls for greater autonomy. Moreover, both the government and the Privy Council rejected calls for establishing Bahasa Malayu as the official second language. Prem made this clear: "We cannot accept that (proposal) as we are Thai, the country is Thai, and the language is Thai, so we have to make efforts to learn Thai and command it as good as the rest of the kingdom. We have to be proud of being Thai and having the Thai language and the sole national language."[131] One prominent madrassa educator lamented this decision: "Rejecting this shows they are unwilling to accept the differences in the culture and language of the southern people. We want them to recognize Malayu. We feel we are treated like

---

130. Ismail Wolff, "South Awaits Approval of New Plan," *Thai Day*, June 7, 2006.
131. "Prem Disagrees with Proposed Use of Malay as Official Language," *Nation*, June 25, 2006.

second class citizens. We don't want to be different, we want to be accepted."[132] Because the government was being "inflexible and uncompromising," Surin Pitsuwan indicated that he was no longer confident that the NRC's work would be taken seriously: "I'm afraid the attitude and the mind-set will not be to explore the [NRC's] practical recommendations but to reject what is most sensitive."[133]

The NRC was officially disbanded with the issuing of the report, and Thaksin's caretaker administration went about ignoring the report, causing Anand to lash out at Thaksin for "having no clear national agenda, except for its own survival."[134] The *Bangkok Post* issued a scathing editorial of Thaksin's response to the NRC report: "The beleaguered leader showed his true colours—that he does not care about improving the situation in the strife-torn deep South. It is an open secret that he has exploited the conflict in the region to his own advantage all along."[135]

Post-Coup Policies

On September 19, 2006, Royal Thai Army commander Gen. Sonthi Boonyaratglin seized power from caretaker prime minister Thaksin Shinawatra in a bloodless coup d'état. It marked the country's eighteenth coup since 1932 and the first since 1991. Although the coup transpired less than a week after a series of bombings rocked the southern Thai commercial hub of Hat Yai, precipitating concerns that the violence was spreading beyond the three Muslim-dominated provinces, the insurgency was only one of many reasons for the military intervention. Elite politics, a political stalemate, and the specter of street violence also motivated the coup. For example, Thaksin often interfered with the annual military promotions, creating anger among many in the security establishment by promoting many of his former colleagues, friends, and relatives over better-qualified and more senior officers. Ironically, the man chosen by the coup leaders to be the interim prime minister was Gen. Surayud Chulanont, the former supreme com-

---

132. "Language Issue Dismays Muslims," *Thai Day*, June 27, 2006.
133. Ibid.
134. "Anand Slams PM," *Nation*, July 29, 2006.
135. "Editorial: NRC Report Needs a Govt Worthy of It," *Bangkok Post*, July 21, 2006.

mander of the Thai armed forces who had been responsible for depo-
liticizing the military. In fact, Thaksin had earlier forced him from
office in favor of one of Thaksin's cousins. There was particular disgust
among both the police and army officer corps over the amount of
political interference that they faced in their efforts to quell the southern insurgency, which by September 2006 had left some seventeen
hundred people dead. The generals also chafed at Thaksin's blatant
dismissal of the NRC's findings.

Thai citizens looked to coup leader Gen. Sonthi Boonyaratglin to
put a stop to the insurgency. He and his installed government, led by
Surayud, adopted a two-pronged strategy: improving capabilities to
defeat the insurgents and winning back the support of the moderate
Muslim community. The Council for National Security (CNS), as the
junta that staged the coup called itself, and caretaker prime minister
Surayud's government made many important gestures and scrapped the
most egregious programs of the Thaksin administration. They seemed
genuinely committed to tackling the insurgency and winning the support and trust of the Malay community. And although they were at least
cognizant of the gravity of the situation and pledged their commitment
and resources to resolving the underlying grievances, they remained
blithely naive about the real problems in the south.

With regard to the former strategy, they tried to improve the capability and coordination of the security services. For starters, Sonthi
scrapped the Thaksin-established, civilian-led SBPPC and reinstated
the army-led SBPAC and CPM-43 commands that Thaksin had dismantled in May 2001.[136] Additionally, the army's ISOC was given
greater prominence as a coordinating body. Moreover, Sonthi pledged
that there would be more consistency in personnel and policies. Not
surprisingly, the Ministry of Defense's 2007 budget jumped by almost
50 percent to Bt115 billion (US$3.5 billion). Even so, ISOC received
only Bt1 billion (US$29 million)—half of what was requested—for
operations in the restive south because it had already used up the existing budget of Bt5.9 billion (US$181 million).[137] For the 2008 budget,

---

136. "Thailand Revives Agency to Tackle Muslim Insurgency," Reuters, October 25,
2006.
137. "ISOC Granted Only Bt1 Bn for South," *Nation*, May 16, 2007.

the military received a staggering 24.3 percent budget increase to Bt143 billion (US$4.4 billion), as well as another Bt456 million (US$14 million) in a secret budget for the three armed forces. Despite these increases, the budget priorities showed no concern for combating the insurgency. The military announced major arms purchases of Swedish Gripen jet fighters, Ukrainian armored personnel carriers, Chinese surface-to-surface missiles, and submarines, but these are hardly the weapons systems needed to combat an insurgency.[138] In fact, the army requested only Bt17.6 billion (US$541 million) to fund counterinsurgency efforts in the south for the years 2008–11.[139]

Regarding the latter strategy, Surayud made several important overtures to the Muslim community. These included a public apology to the Muslim community for the previous government's policies and actions, the dropping of charges against some fifty-eight Tak Bai protesters, a renewed pledge to solve the disappearance of Somchai, which the government had by then labeled a "murder," and a larger quota for hajj pilgrims.[140] Significantly, Surayud announced that the practice of compiling blacklists would be abandoned and expressed a willingness to implement sharia law: "They should have the Islamic law in practice, sharia, because of the way they are dealing with normal practice in their life is completely different from us."[141] The government designed a plan to revamp Islamic education in the south and announced the hiring

---

138. "Cabinet Nod for B7.7bn to Buy Arms, Equipment," *Bangkok Post*, September 26, 2007.

139. Wassana Nanuam and Nattaya Chetchotiros, "Military Puts in B18bn Request," *Bangkok Post*, June 28, 2007; "Military Deserves No Budget Boost," *Nation*, July 5, 2007; "Queries about Military Budget," *Matichon*, July 5, 2007.

140. "I apologise on behalf of the former government for what happened. I want to extend my hand and say that I am wrong. . . . I sincerely apologise because most of the mistakes of the past were largely made by the state and we have to help each other correct them. . . . I tried to oppose several policies of the last government and am partly to blame for failing to get results. That is why they let me stay as an objector. That's why I have to apologise once again today," stated the prime minister. "PM Apologises to the South," *Bangkok Post*, November 3, 2006. See also "Tak Bai Charges Dropped," *Bangkok Post*, November 6, 2006; "Arrests of Top Police Discounted," *Nation*, November 5 ,2006; "Somchai's Wife Urges Brake on Warrants," *Bangkok Post*, November 5, 2006; "Extra Quota to Hajj under Negotiation," *Nation*, October 31, 2006.

141. Charlotte McDonald-Gibson, "Thai PM Supports Islamic Law in Restive South, Rules out Separation," Agence France-Presse, November 8, 2006; "No More Blacklist: Surayud," *Nation*, November 8, 2006.

of nine hundred more Islamic teachers.[142] Interestingly, there was, for the first time, an explicit acknowledgment by the government of the insurgents' Islamist agenda and demands.[143] The government also said that it would allow Malayu as the language of instruction in classrooms in the south and pledged a large budget increase in the south to make up for the period in which Thaksin had starved it of funds.[144]

As noted, the government also held a series of Malaysian-brokered peace talks with the "insurgents" in an attempt to reach a political settlement with them. Referred to as the "Langkawi process," the talks represented "an attempt to identify common ground between the two sides and . . . to reconcile differences."[145] A myriad of issues was discussed, including amnesty, language rights, social justice, education, and economic development. After the "insurgents" dropped their demand for an independent Islamic state, the two sides came up with the Joint Peace and Development Plan for South Thailand, but the plan was never made public.

Conducted by the military at the behest of the crown, the talks were an end run around Thaksin. Although there was great fanfare about the talks when they were announced in September 2006, the talks fell apart. For one thing, the "insurgents" with whom the government was talking consisted of members of PULO, Bersatu, and other like groups—that is, the last generation of insurgents and not those individuals responsible for the present violence. As Wan Kadir acknowledged to the press, "The government cannot find anyone willing to come to the negotiating table, because we cannot identify the real leaders."[146] Later, the government acknowledged this same fact. Said then defense minister Boonrawd Somtas, "In the past, we have had negotiations with insurgent groups, but we held talks with the wrong groups such as Bersatu and the Pattani United Liberation Organisation which did not launch attacks.

---

142. Sirikul Bunnag, "A New Face for Islamic Teaching: Interview with Prasert Kaewphet," *Bangkok Post*, July 12, 2007.

143. Ibid.

144. "Budget Distribution in South Is to Be Completed," Thai News Agency, May 19, 2007.

145. Don Pathan, "Talks Vital to Restore Peace in the South," *Nation*, November 27, 2007.

146. "No Headway in Talks with Separatists," *Nation*, November 23, 2006.

We need to talk with the BRN Coordinate, who are the real ones behind the bloody attacks. But it has refused negotiations so far as it is gaining the upper hand and winning greater support from local residents."[147]

The government initially demanded that the "insurgents" implement a one-month cease-fire as a show of goodwill and sign of command and control. The "insurgents" could not deliver a day of peace, even after the government reduced the time frame to two weeks. In fact, the violence dramatically escalated following the talks, and the daily rate of killing nearly tripled. The Thai government went to great lengths to describe the talks as a "dialogue," not as formal negotiations, and it has steadfastly refused to countenance any plan for regional autonomy. Both sides did outline a set of preconditions for further talks, but neither side was willing to even consider implementing them. For example, the government demanded the surrender of weapons and matériel, while the insurgents called for a blanket amnesty, the adoption of Malayu as an official working language, more development funds, and the scrapping of the Emergency Decree.

The Thai government asserted that there were growing rifts among the insurgents and that more of them were opting to negotiate, although it offered little proof of this. The divide between the old and new generations of insurgents is clear. As Wan Kadir told Al-Jazeera, "this new generation of people, they are very young and they are very determined. . . . This new generation seems to still want independence."[148] Indeed, there is little evidence to suggest that the actual operational cells want to negotiate. The insurgents have shown absolutely no interest in negotiations or in the possibilities accorded by the change in government. In fact, the number of violent incidents spiked to record highs after the coup, because the insurgents wanted to discredit the "insurgents" who had been trying to negotiate with the government. In fact, militants gunned down a former PULO leader just two days after the coup.[149]

---

147. "Two Reporters Injured in Bomb Blast Ambush," *Bangkok Post*, January 17, 2007.

148. "JI May Have Infiltrated S. Thailand," *Nation*, November 22, 2006.

149. Mahama Jehna, who had defected to the authorities in 2004, was found dead in Ban Dahong village in tambon Choeng Khiri. "Fourth Army Chief Believes Rebels Will Halt Major Attacks," *Bangkok Post*, September 22, 2006.

The violence also reflected the reality that the insurgents had no reason to negotiate: parties come to the table only when they feel that they have nothing more to gain from fighting.

Nonetheless, the government tried to put a positive spin on the spike in the violence, asserting that it was a sign that its efforts were working. Said Defense Minister Boonrawd Somtas, "They know that with the government's reconciliation approach more people will come to the government's side. So they must increase the degree of violence to threaten people."[150] Further, although the bilateral relationship between Malaysia and Thailand was still poor enough that there was little in the way of close security cooperation, the Thai government's overtures opened the door to greater cooperation with Malaysia. For example, following Surayud's public apology, Malaysian foreign minister Syed Hamid Albar said, "His step is a step in the right direction. It is an attitude of humility. . . . I am very glad that he has taken the first very, very constructive step. It is not easy to make a public apology for something that had happened."[151] Surayud also assured Indonesian president Bambang Susilo Yudhoyono that he would not pursue the heavy-handed strategy of the Thaksin government and that he was "inspired by the peace process in Aceh province."[152] Yet, all evidence suggests that, despite some basic public appeals, the government's policies did not change all that much. The continued violence and growing popular support for the insurgents indicated frustration with the old wine in new bottles that the locals saw being served by Bangkok. Indeed, ten "reforms" or new policies that were announced following the coup have either not been implemented or have had negative consequences.

First, while the government understands that there is a culture of impunity among the security forces, it has done nothing to address this. There is still blanket immunity for security forces and no attempt has been made at retroactive justice. Stated one palace official, "At least six heads must role, and I could think of dozens more."[153] This did not stop

150. "Hardcore Militants Still Bent on Violence," *Bangkok Post*, November 23, 2006.

151. "Malaysia Lauds Thai PM's Apology for Muslim Protesters' Deaths," *Nation*, November 3, 2006.

152. "Surayud Backs Aceh 'Model,'" *Bangkok Post*, October 22, 2006.

153. Author interview.

Gen. Panlop Pinmanee, the commander responsible for Krue Se and the poster child for impunity, from being appointed as public relations adviser to the director of the ISOC, General Sonthi.[154] Because ISOC is directly responsible for the south, his appointment was a real insult to southerners. As Human Rights Watch stated so succinctly: "The Thai Government must understand that any attempt to cover up the misconduct of its security units or to protect them from criminal responsibility could set off a cycle of killings and reprisals. The impunity of government forces has become the most common justification used by insurgents to carry out retaliatory attacks on civilians."[155]

Second, although the SBPAC was reestablished in January 2007 as a coordinating body,[156] it has been woefully understaffed and underresourced, and the government is unable to recruit employees. Indeed, fewer than 100 of the 199 designated SBPAC positions had been filled by the time it reopened. The SBPAC is now under the army's ISOC, but, as an adviser to the prime minister complained, "the ISOC still cannot control or manage interagency rivalries."[157] As a result, members of the various security services state that cooperation is as poor as it was before the coup.[158] For example, the U.S. and Australian governments have funded an explosives/IED database, but there have been vast disagreements over how to administer and manage it. For the database to be an effective tool, data from all bombings must be gathered in a uniform way no matter which agency is doing the investigating or was first to respond. From a human rights perspective, this kind of environment

---

154. The seventy-year-old general was implicated in a bombing cum assassination attempt on Prime Minister Thaksin. Ploenpote Atthakor, "Sending Panlop Back Will Worsen Violence," *Bangkok Post*, May 11, 2007.

155. Human Rights Watch, "Thailand: Government-Backed Militias Enflame Violence," April 18, 2007.

156. The SBPAC's four main goals are to reduce conflicts among local people, including threats from the insurgents; to boost the number of proficient personnel in education; to increase the benefits and welfare for officials in the area; and to solve economic problems by boosting investment with incentives. "Thai Mediation Centre in Bloody South Lacks Recruits, Says PM," *Nation*, December 26, 2006.

157. Author interview, Bangkok, December 15, 2006.

158. Author interview, Bangkok, January 8, 2007.

remains especially alarming because the ISOC is self-policing and accountable only to itself.[159]

Third, there is still a sense in the south that the security approach continues to dominate government policy. Stated one Islamist in early 2007, "There is no difference between Thaksin and Surayud. Surayud is still employing a military solution."[160] Indeed, the Emergency Decree continues to be extended every three months with no end in sight, and the government has employed curfews in some districts in Yala. In fact, the army believes that the curfews have had a positive impact and has considered extending them to a handful of districts in Narathiwat.[161]

Fourth, although Surayud claimed that the government had done away with the blacklists of suspected troublemakers in the south—stating that he had asked "the authorities to tear it up and burn them"—hit squads, which had been stopped in mid-2006, have resumed. Further, security forces, often out of uniform, have targeted suspected militants. This has obviously troubled the Muslim and human rights community. "The Thai security forces are using 'disappearances' as a way to weaken the militants and instill fear in the Malay Muslim community," noted Brad Adams, Asia director at Human Rights Watch. "These 'disappearances' appear to be a matter of policy, not simply the work of rogue elements in the security services."[162] Indeed, several top security officials revealed in March 2007 that the hit squads would resume because "the violence was lower when we used them."[163]

Fifth, the government has again turned to amnesties, but the proposed amnesty law is full of similar flaws. Further, the government scrapped the bounties for key insurgent leaders, hoping that they will turn themselves in "to give them a chance to prove their innocence."[164] In part, this was a diplomatic ploy, as the announcement came during

---

159. Author interview, Bangkok, December 20, 2007.

160. Author interview, Sungai Golok, February 12, 2007.

161. The districts are Rangae, Ruso, Sungai Padi, Joh I Rong, and Bacho, as well as Kho Pho in Pattani. "More Districts May Be Put under Curfew," *Nation*, March 17, 2007.

162. Human Rights Watch, "Thailand: Government-Backed Militias Enflame Violence," April 18, 2007.

163. Author interview, Bangkok, April 4, 2007.

164. "PM Cancels Rebel Boss Bounties," *Bangkok Post*, April 7, 2007.

the visit of the OIC secretary-general in May 2007 and right before the organization was due to issue its report on Thailand. Although amnesties were used briefly in 2005, they failed because they did not apply to anyone who had committed a crime, ergo to no insurgents. As Fourth Army commander Lt. Gen. Viroach Buacharoon acknowledged, "Many militants were forced to commit terror acts against their will. They cannot run away from the insurgent movement unless the government provides legal protection for their return."[165] Although there was thought given to broadening the new amnesty to low-level insurgents, the offer would ultimately only be for sympathizers of the insurgent groups and not for insurgents themselves. Additionally, amnesty would be given only if the supporters "showed sincerity in re-integrating themselves into society and gave full cooperation to the government."[166] According to the draft bill submitted to the National Legislative Assembly (NLA), the junta-appointed interim legislature, "An amnesty will be granted to all people who have been involved in the ongoing violence in the southern border provinces, provided they did not commit an offence under the country's Criminal Code."[167] Such language hardly inspires the confidence of insurgents who are considering defecting to the government.

Sixth, there remains an ongoing debate over the number of troops that should be deployed in the south. Clearly, twenty thousand RTA soldiers (and ten thousand police) are not enough to end the violence, but the high command is concerned that greater numbers will only feed the perception that Thai soldiers are an occupying force. Further, General Sonthi, who came out of the Special Forces, generally believes in a lighter touch. What he does not understand is that fewer numbers will not win the support of villagers, because the insurgent cells in the villages can see who is cooperating with the soldiers. There needs to be a sufficient number of troops to give people a sense of security. In late 2006, the government announced that it would dispatch three additional battalions to the south, including one from the Special

---

165. Piyanart Srivalo, "Surayud Pushes Amnesty in South," *Nation*, April 21, 2007.

166. "Prime Minister Gets Tough on Southern Rebels," *Bangkok Post*, April 21, 2007.

167. Achara Ashayagachat, "Rebels May Be Granted Amnesty," *Bangkok Post*, May 2, 2007.

Warfare Unit, but Sonthi scrapped the plans in February 2007, saying that the troops were needed more in Bangkok because of his fears of a countercoup.[168]

In mid-2007, the new RTA chief of staff, Gen. Anupong Paochinda, doubled the number of soldiers deployed in the south to forty thousand. But most remain confined to barracks or deployed in the towns and major highways. They are not deployed in the red zones or in the countryside, except in fixed static positions. Anupong's "surge" is problematic in another way. Rather than assigning troops from the First Army and Third Army (which hail from different regions of Thailand) to augment Fourth Army troops already spread across the provinces of Narathiwat, Yala, Pattani, and Songkhla, Anupong assigned each army a province, meaning the newly deployed troops have no local operating experience, network of contacts, or relevant language skills.

Although Sonthi pledged to increase the Fourth Army's ranks by fifteen thousand by 2009,[169] the Thais have also begun to rely on rangers, an army-trained and -equipped paramilitary force. The government announced in 2007 that it would recruit and deploy to the south an additional fifty-six companies of rangers, just under ten thousand men.[170] But the rangers are given less than one month's training and, for the most part, have proved to be a fairly undisciplined force. For example, on March 9, 2007, a ranger unit fired on a vehicle in Yala's Muang District, killing two teenagers and provoking mass demonstrations. Not only have the rangers and other paramilitary troops been implicated in abuses but they have also gone unpunished. While the government deserves credit for trying to recruit locals into the force—that is, individuals with the necessary language skills and cultural knowledge—no one knows how they will hold up if insurgents begin to target their family members. In a scathing editorial, the *Nation* explicitly challenged the army's competence and strategy:

---

168. Wassana Nanuam, "Sonthi Delays Troop Transfer to Deep South," *Bangkok Post*, March 9, 2007.

169. "Sonthi: More Troops Bound for Deep South," *Bangkok Post*, April 24, 2007.

170. "South to Get 3,000 More Troops after Violence Escalates," *Nation*, December 24, 2006; "More Rangers to Be Deployed in South," *Bangkok Post*, March 14, 2007; "1,700 New Rangers Sent in to Battle Insurgency," *Bangkok Post*, March 28, 2007; "20 More Companies of Paramilitary Troopers Deployed to Deep South," *Nation*, April 1, 2007.

> In order to make its own failings seem less obvious, the military set up and armed ranger units, made up of volunteers who are given only a few months of training before being deployed to areas heavily infiltrated by insurgents to fight on behalf of standing military units. Military commanders are reluctant to dispatch standing military units into the battle zones, either because their battle-readiness is very much in doubt or because they want to minimize additions to the "official" casualty list. Lowly-paid rangers are not listed as personnel of the armed forces and they are considered dispensable in the sense that the government is not required to include them in the armed forces' official casualty list or to offer substantial compensation to their families if they are killed in action.[171]

Seventh, the pledges that Malayu would become an official working language have gone largely unfulfilled, although its use in schools has increased. In fact, a new Malayu curriculum is being piloted in a dozen schools.

Eighth, although the government has pledged to improve its legal efforts against the insurgents, by the end of 2007 only two individuals had been tried and convicted as insurgents. This was largely due to the lack of cooperation among the army, police, and prosecutors. In fact, the police have done such shoddy work that the army is rarely turning over suspects to the authorities for prosecution. Indeed, the army has been so infuriated by the failure of the police to build up cases, to do the requisite interviews, and to collect evidence that it has tried to take matters into its own hands. For example, in mid-2007, the army instituted a four-month detention program for suspected insurgents under the guise of a mandatory vocational training program. The courts overturned this program because it was involuntary and all of the vocational training was conducted on army bases from which insurgents would be unable to leave. Incarceration by any other name is still incarceration, the courts ruled. The military then tried to ban those detainees who were released from returning to their home provinces, a move that was similarly rejected by the courts.[172] The country's legal code has also presented certain obstacles in the prosecution of suspected insurgents. According to the Thailand Research Fund, a new counterterrorism/

---

171. "Editorial: Military Needs Dose of Its Own Medicine," *Nation*, April 24, 2007.
172. "Angkahna: Concerned by 'Harsh' Measures," *Bangkok Post*, November 11, 2007.

counterinsurgency law is needed to close the numerous loopholes in existing law.[173]

Ninth, in the debates over the drafting of the new constitution, many Thai politicians pushed for an article that would enshrine Buddhism as the official state religion. It was hard to see how members of a government whose stated intention is to win the hearts and minds of the Muslim community could justify such a position. Indeed, opponents of the legislation stated that militants would seize upon the law as proof that (1) Buddhists are hegemonic over Muslims; (2) Muslims are second-class citizens; and (3) Thailand does not recognize people of other faiths. Although it ultimately was not included in the constitution, with the restoration of democracy in February 2008, there have been clamors to make Buddhism the state religion in a revised constitution. Such an exclusionary article would only serve to vindicate the insurgents.

Tenth, with little public participation, the NLA has drafted two laws that deal with issues related to Islam.[174] While an overhaul of existing laws may be necessary, the Muslim community remains angered that these laws are being forced on them by a predominantly Buddhist body. Adding insult to injury, the bills were drafted by the thirty-five-member security committee, giving the perception that the government equates Muslims with violence. The first piece of draft legislation, the Islamic Affairs Administration Draft Bill, would replace three existing acts—the 1997 Islamic Organization Administration Act and the Haj Affairs Promotion acts of 1981 and 1989—and change the way in which the leadership of Islamic committees and organizations at all levels are selected. The bill would establish a thirty-one-member National Islamic Council, or *shura*, chaired by Chularatchamontri, the country's highest-ranking Muslim leader, and composed of Islamic leaders and respected experts from officially registered schools. The council would not only help oversee the selection of Islamic leaders but also deliberate over and interpret controversial issues. In addition, the Prime Minister's Office

173. As referenced in Anucha Charoenpo, "National Security/Plugging the Loopholes," *Bangkok Post*, November 3, 2006.

174. Ploenpote Atthakor, "Islamic Bill/Lack of Public Participation," *Bangkok Post*, April 7, 2007.

would have its own National Islamic Affairs Administration Office.[175] The second piece of draft legislation, the Zakat Funds Bill, would establish a new government agency to regulate how charitable donations (zakat or *infaq*) are spent. Accordingly, all entities that solicit donations, such as mosques and madrassas, would have to register with the agency, which would also be chaired by Chularatchamontri, and international Muslim charities would have to channel their aid through its administrative office.[176]

Although the postcoup government's policies toward the south largely resembled the policies of the previous government, its mantra was "reconciliation." As Prime Minister Surayud Chulanont clearly stated: "We are not going to use violence to counter violence. We are not going to use the heavy-handed methods like in the past. We are going to follow the rule of law."[177] But even as his administration tried to wean itself off of the security approach and win the hearts and minds of the Muslim community, it followed the path first set by Thaksin in another important way: it was woefully naive about the nature of the insurgency. Stated the *Nation* in a caustic May 2007 editorial: "The Surayud administration and its military guardian, the Council for National Security, must be deluding themselves if they think they can restore peace in the strife-torn deep South simply by repeating the mantra of reconciliation even as Islamic militants/Malay separatists intensify their campaign of terror."[178]

The Restoration of Democracy

On December 23, 2007, parliamentary elections were held in Thailand and a new government took office in February 2008. Even with the restoration of democracy, however, there does not appear to be any forthcoming change in policy toward the south for two principal reasons. First, the new democratic system itself is in turmoil. The short-

---

175. Anucha Charoenpo and Pradit Ruangdit, "Bid to Stop Muslims Being Misled," *Bangkok Post*, March 20, 2007.

176. "Editorial: Muslim Charities in the Spotlight," *Bangkok Post*, May 4, 2007.

177. Ed Cropley, "Interview: Thai PM Sticks to Guns for Peace in Muslim South," Reuters, March 20, 2007.

178. "Peace Plan Does Not Hold Water," *Nation*, May 23, 2007.

lived administration of Samak Sunaravej was replaced with an equally unstable government led by Somchai Wongsawat, and the contestation among the political, royal, and military elites has consumed the attention of the country and the leadership. Second, the violence remains geographically contained, and the Bangkok-centric political elites care little of what happens outside of the capital. During the election, no party made the south a prominent issue or came up with any new ideas or policies for ending the insurgency. Although the election of Samak, whose People's Power Party (PPP) is the reincarnation of Thaksin's disbanded TRT Party, humiliated the military, the PPP has pledged not to punish the generals for the September 2006 coup. Indeed, Samak and his successor, Somchai, both pledged not to change the government's policies toward the south, allowing the military to run its campaign in the south without much political interference.

As a result, the government's security-dominated approach in the south continues, even though its success has been limited and, as some observers would argue, its implementation has been counterproductive. The failings of this approach have led to needed incentives and reward programs, but they, too, have been poorly implemented. The government's policies and heavy-handed actions have alienated the vast majority of the Muslims in the south. Most of them eschew the violence and goals of the separatists, but the sense of social injustice that they feel has given rise to great animus toward the government. In an NRC-commissioned poll on the Emergency Decree, 90 percent of the respondents, both Muslims and Buddhists, disagreed with the enforcement of martial law and 60 percent opposed the decree. Seventy percent of the respondents believed that local authorities discriminated against the local population, and 23 percent said that their liberty was being eroded by security checkpoints and the questioning that they face.[179] In short, the community most needed to counter the insurgents—through both religion and ideology—is not willing or able to do so. In the face of continued human rights abuses and the government's security-dominated approach, moderate Muslims have a tough sell in trying to convince fellow Muslims to cooperate with security forces, particularly because they themselves are seen by many in the community as collaborators.

---

179. "Poll Shows Public against Decree," *Bangkok Post*, November 14, 2005.

The security approach has failed mainly because of the incompetence and unwillingness of the security forces to take the initiative and go on the offensive against the insurgents. What started as an incipient insurgency gained momentum and popular support because of poor intelligence, lack of interagency coordination, and, in cases such as Krue Se and Tak Bai, disproportional—if not excessive—force against militants. As one critical editorial in the *Nation* put it,

> In the absence of effective military strategies and tactics, the bulk of the 40,000-strong security force is being kept inside their fortified barracks. Only a small number are dispatched to guard urban centres, government offices and schools. It becomes obvious that the official policy is to avoid confronting the insurgents partly through fear of causing civilian casualties but more probably because of a lack of good intelligence with which to track down insurgents who live among the civilian population.[180]

As the adviser on the south to then prime minister Surayud stated, "The Fourth Army still cannot do offensive operations. They are very static and in fixed positions; that's no way to fight an insurgency."[181] In part, this is because the RTA has had no training in urban warfare, even though so much of the violence is in urban areas. In interviews in late 2006 and mid-2007, nearly a dozen officers and many of their civilian equivalents complained that the military leadership simply does not take the issue of the south seriously. Sonthi himself has admitted that he has placed the insurgency in the south second to political matters. Frankly, few in Bangkok care about the insurgency as long as it stays in the south.

Although the government's counterinsurgency campaign has been a military failure, it has been a greater police failure. As one human rights activist explained, much of the fault lies at Thaksin's feet: "Thaksin didn't care about due process, he cared about results."[182] After the coup, the CNS insisted that police reform was on the top of its agenda. Although the police recognized the need for reform, they resented that reform was being force-fed to them by the army. As a result, the police

---

180. "Peace Plan Does Not Hold Water," *Nation*, May 23, 2007.
181. Author interview, Bangkok, December 15, 2006.
182. Author interview, Bangkok, December 20, 2007.

put up a lot of resistance. Even so, there are indications that efforts on the legal front are improving. Following the coup, for example, a strategy meeting was held for the first time that included prosecutors, police, and soldiers. It seems to have paid some results. By June 2007, the courts had passed the death sentence on nine defendants, had sentenced fourteen more to life terms, and had given another thirteen up to fifty-year terms.[183] Further, Police Lt. Gen. Jetanakorn Napeetapat, the commander of Police Region 9, has stated that the rate of prosecutions has gone up since the coup.

Despite the changes in government and all of the new overtures and policies, the insurgency has raged on. As Surayud grimly summed up while he was prime minister, "Most of the locals [in the south] still have no confidence in government authorities who travel there to listen to their opinion." Indeed, they have no reason to, because government after successive government has failed to ask the right questions. The continued failure to do so may ultimately have severe implications for Thailand, its Southeast Asian neighbors, and perhaps even the broader international community.

---

183. "Another Bomb Explodes in Hat Yai, Victim of Sunday's Attack Dies of Wounds," *Bangkok Post*, May 30, 2007.

7

The Insurgency's Impact and International Implications

As the most violent active conflict in Southeast Asia, the insurgency in southern Thailand has broad implications for both the ASEAN region and Thailand's key security and alliance partners, such as the United States and Australia. But before one can understand the insurgency's implications for the region and broader international community, one must first understand the impact of the insurgency on Thailand itself.

The Impact on Southern Thai Society

The insurgency has not only accelerated the gradual erosion of human rights, decentralized political rule and democracy in the south, and increased antipathy toward the Thai state among moderate Muslims, giving the Salafis and other militants greater room in which to operate, but it has also had a devastating effect on southern Thailand's communities, education and health-care systems, and economy.

Ethnic Cleansing

The insurgency has created a climate of fear in the south among both the Buddhist and Muslim population that will have long-term negative social consequences. Indeed, the insurgency has led to a certain amount of de facto ethnic cleansing. Thai officials believe that roughly fifty thousand Buddhists (or 15 percent of the south's Buddhist population) have fled the south. Buddhists have also fled the countryside to nearby cities and towns. As a result, villages that were once mixed no longer are. In one well-publicized case, almost a hundred Buddhists from three villages in Yala's Than To and Bannang Sata districts sought refuge at Nirotsangkha-ram Temple in Yala's Muang District after they were threatened by militants. The number quickly escalated to more than 225 people from some 53 households. The refugees garnered the attention of the Royal Family, which disbursed food and relief supplies to them. Despite the prodding of the Fourth Army, they refused to return to their villages and mobile schooling units had to be set up.[1] This prompted more than a hundred other Buddhist families from Narathiwat's Saba Yoi District to also seek refuge at a temple.[2]

Although many Buddhist farmers and rubber tappers have been forced to flee, selling their land at discounted prices for fear of attack, the crown prince has admonished them for leaving the land:

> I sympathize with you for your frustrations. The entire nation and Their Majesties the King and Queen have concern and sympathy for you. Your sufferings are serious. It's really unacceptable for a group of people who act like bandits and are a threat to society. They also fail to respect human rights. These events need to be solved urgently. [But] If you leave your houses and farms, you will need to start all over again. That way, you will allow bad people or enemies to make use of your properties. They will be able to make money from your properties and, as a result, they could do more bad acts and become bolder in doing bad things.[3]

Indeed, Muslim insurgents regularly distribute leaflets in the villages threatening those Buddhists who have remained. Interestingly, the insurgents have also distributed leaflets to Muslim villagers, warning them not to buy land from Buddhists, asserting that the land really belonged to the Muslims. One leaflet stated that, because the region was "an arena of holy war," the land would be "seized" and "distributed by the insurgents." The leaflet also threatened to take drastic action against anyone who did not comply.[4]

Because of such threats and attacks, few monks have remained at Buddhist temples in the south.[5] One temple that is under the patronage of the queen has been attacked sixteen times, while monks in all thirteen districts of Narathiwat stopped going out to collect alms in

---

1. Nakarin Shinworakomol and Charoon Thongnual, "Exodus Of Buddhists," *Nation*, November 10, 2006; "Yala Residents Take Refuge," *Bangkok Post*, November 11, 2006.

2. "Roadside Bomb Kills 3 Soldiers," *Nation*, April 22, 2007.

3. "Crown Prince Blasts 'Bandits,'" *Nation*, November 14, 2006.

4. "Insurgents Warn Yala People Not to Buy Property from Thai Buddhists," *Nation*, February 9, 2007.

5. Wassana Nanuam, "Despite Presence of Guards, Monk Prays for His Safety," *Bangkok Post*, July 25, 2005.

November 2006 for fear of bomb attacks targeting them and their military escorts.[6]

Buddhists have launched mass demonstrations on a number of occasions to protest against the government for caving in to Muslim demands, releasing terrorism suspects, and for not doing more to stem the violence. The Buddhist community has increasingly taken the law into its own hands and has engaged in retribution attacks. Indeed, Buddhists who remain in the villages are heavily armed, leading to fears that a small incident could escalate into broader sectarian conflict. Those who remain have come out vociferously against reconciliation and, in some ways, have been supportive of the heavy-handed security approach. For example, Buddhist monks criticized the NRC for being too soft on the Muslim militants and called for its dissolution.[7] It is hard to see how trust can be restored between the Buddhist and Muslim communities in the south.

Although the insurgency has increased sectarian friction and forced Buddhists to flee, it must not be forgotten that the insurgency has also had a devastating impact on the Muslim community itself. Indeed, more than half of the victims have been Muslims, with Sufis and moderate Sha'afis being primary targets. To a large extent, the insurgency has been about imposing hard-line and conservative values on society. Further, it has caused Muslim youth to be increasingly alienated and disaffected. For example, there are now more than two thousand children who have lost parents to the violence and roughly a thousand widows and widowers.[8] The government recently announced plans for a preemptive reeducation program for some sixty thousand at-risk teenagers, even though its reeducation program for alleged militants has been a failure. Roughly 10 percent of the at-risk teenagers were identified as belonging to a "critical group"—that is, vulnerable to insurgent recruitment.[9]

6. "Monks in Narathiwat to Cease Daily Alms," Deutsche Presse-Agentur, November 11, 2006.

7. Veera Prateepchaikul, "NRC Role in South Not Clearly Understood," *Bangkok Post*, October 31, 2005.

8. " Southern Violence Creates 2,000 Orphans," Thai News Agency, May 22, 2007.

9. Apinya Wipatayotin and Bhanravee Tansubhapol, "Violence in the South/Re-Education Camp Plan," *Bangkok Post*, February 18, 2006.

Education

No sector of society has been harder-hit—and nothing will have a greater long-term impact—than the militants' systematic targeting of teachers and schools. The three southernmost provinces have approximately 1,162 primary and secondary schools, 19,460 teachers, and 420,919 students, according to the Ministry of Education. As of May 2007, eighty teachers had been killed, and hundreds of schools had been the targets of arson attacks. In one educational district in Yala, twenty-five of the seventy-one schools had been set ablaze. The mood of teachers is understandably grim: no group has been more targeted than they have. They are often the only state employees in remote villages, are less risky targets than security forces, and are seen as being the agents of Thai assimilation policies.

Attacks on teachers and schools have dramatic ripple effects, causing mass strikes and the indefinite closure of schools across districts and sometimes entire provinces. For example, in the first week of February 2006, more than 300 elementary schools were shut down in Yala, Pattani, and Narathiwat, and in four districts of Songkhla, when teachers went on strike to protest the continued killing of teachers by militants and the government's inability to stop it. The one-week strike affected some fifty thousand pupils.[10] In May 2006, after an eight-week shut-down, one school in Pattani was bombed, and in a separate attack a soldier who was protecting teachers was killed by a 10 kg (22 lb.)roadside IED.[11] Following the hostage taking of two Buddhist teachers in which one was beaten into a coma, more than 200 schools were shut down, and they continue to be shut down sporadically. Following the arrest of four militant suspects, a group mainly composed of women threatened to kidnap teachers in Narathiwat's Rueso District, which led to the shutting down of schools.[12] In mid-November 2006, some fifty schools in Rueso closed for two days after a female Buddhist teacher and her vice principal were killed by a gunman riding pillion on a motorcycle. That same month, all 336 schools in Pattani closed indefinitely

10. "Yala Violence: Teachers Take a Week off after Five Colleagues Shot," *Nation*, February 7, 2006; "33 More Schools Shut in Songkhla," *Nation*, February 8, 2006.
11. "Roadside Blast Kills Two in the South," *Thai Day*, May 17, 2006.
12. "Many Schools Close after Kidnap Warnings," *Bangkok Post*, July 22, 2006.

after two teachers were killed, and 232 schools shut down in Yala.[13] More than 80 Islamic religious schools in Pattani also shut down for two days in a show of solidarity with the state schools.[14] In total, more than 944 schools were closed in November.[15]

In response to these attacks, the government has come up with a number of programs to protect teachers. Beginning in 2005, the army began providing armed convoys for teachers. The Ministry of Education also announced a plan to offer three thousand flak jackets to teachers in the most dangerous areas. Teachers are now allowed to arm themselves, and the Thai military began training teachers in the use of small arms in July 2006, setting off a bureaucratic tussle when it suggested that the Ministry of Education was obligated to buy or reimburse the teachers for their handguns.[16] Later, the cabinet approved a Bt68 million (US$1.8 million) plan to increase security at schools and teachers' living quarters.[17] Many public schools were slated to receive closed-circuit television systems and funding for guards.[18] In January 2007, caretaker prime minister Surayud agreed to have soldiers guard teachers twenty-four hours a day to guarantee their safety.[19]

Despite these measures and initiatives, teachers continued to be killed at alarming rates and little that the government did stemmed the exodus of teachers from the region. By the end of 2005, more than 1,900 teachers had applied for transfer, leaving the soldiers guarding the schools to fill in for them. In late May 2006, caretaker education minister Chaturon Chaisaeng stopped processing transfer requests from teachers in the south to arrest the hemorrhaging. Plans were even proposed to install five hundred satellite dishes at schools so teachers could provide instruction without having to be physically present at the schools.[20] By May 2007, the number of teachers who had applied for

13. "All Pattani Schools to Be Closed Down," *Nation*, November 23, 2006.

14. "Solutions Sought to Protect Teachers," *Nation*, November 29, 2006.

15. "Sixty-Five More Schools in Yala to Close," *Nation*, November 27, 2006.

16. "Southern Teachers Get Gun Lessons," *Nation*, July 11, 2006.

17. "Budget to Protect Teachers Approved," *Thai Day*, May 31, 2006.

18. "Chaturon Unveils Plan to Enhance Security at Schools," *Nation*, August 6, 2006.

19. "Teachers in South Allowed to Carry Guns," *Bangkok Post*, January 10, 2007.

20. Waedao Harai and Muhamad Ayub Pathan, "Village Gives Teachers Guarantee of Safety," *Bangkok Post*, June 1, 2006; "Distance Learning via Satellite for the Deep South,"

transfer reached more than 5,000. In Yala, Pattani, and Narathiwat, some 2,700 of the 3,450 Buddhist teachers had either stopped working or requested transfers out of the region.

The government has pursued a number of strategies to make up for the lost personnel. For example, the army announced a pilot program to recruit noncommissioned officers (NCOs) who have a bachelor's degree: "Those soldiers who prove to be good teachers will be made commissioned officers."[21] The Ministry of Education allocated Bt50 million (US$1.3 million) in April 2006 to keep some 1,600 temporary teachers in the three provinces employed through September.[22] In May 2007, nearly 2,000 temporary teachers were appointed as full-time state employees.[23]

Not surprisingly, educational standards—which have never been high in Thailand's south—have gotten worse. Since the insurgency began, students in the three border provinces have attended school only 150 days a year on average, compared with 200 days a year on average for pupils in the rest of the country. This has caused a marked drop in student performance. According to research by the Office for National Education Standards and Quality Assessment, student scores on the Ordinary National Educational Test in the south were lower than the national average in 2006—in 2004, the scores were higher. Of a total of 1,144 public and private schools assessed by the office, 857 (about 80 percent) were deemed to be of too poor quality to be accredited. Dozens of schools could not even be assessed due to the ongoing violence.[24]

Nation, July 5, 2006.

21. "Thousand Teachers and Residents Flee Deep South," *Nation*, July 5, 2005; Seth Mydans, "Schools in Thailand under Ethnic Siege," *New York Times*, July 6, 2005; "Terrified Teachers Want out of Region," *Nation*, July 12, 2005; "Guns for Teachers Move Shot down," *Nation*, July 8, 2005.

22. "Temporary Teachers to Be Re-employed," *Bangkok Post*, April 29, 2006.

23. Anucha Charoenpo and Sirikul Bunnag, "2,000 Temp Teachers to Be Full-Time," *Bangkok Post*, May 9, 2007.

24. Sirikul Bunnag, "Schools in Decline as Renewed Violence Enters Fourth Year," *Bangkok Post*, January 4, 2007.

Health Care

While it would be hyperbole to say that a public health disaster looms, the insurgency has had a decidedly negative impact on public health among both the Buddhist and Muslim populations of the south. Minister of Health Mongkol Na Songkhla admitted that of the estimated nine thousand medical workers in the region, almost half had requested transfers out of the area.[25] At one hospital in Yala, for example, which was already suffering a severe shortage of doctors and nurses because no one wants to move to the south, four doctors and ten nurses transferred out in 2005.[26] In 2007, only 29 of 46 (63 percent) doctors assigned to the south took their positions there, and a group of thirty-four newly graduated doctors refused assignments by the Ministry of Public Health in the three southern provinces, further aggravating the medical-staff shortage.[27] In April 2007, the government announced that it was offering Bt140 million (US$4.3 million) in nursing scholarships to three thousand high school students in the region if they promised to work in the troubled south for three years upon graduation.

Insurgents have principally targeted Buddhist doctors and nurses, torching many health-care clinics. Insurgents have tended to leave Muslim health-care workers alone as long as they are not seen working with or collaborating with security forces. Only one ambulance has been attacked, and at the time it was in a military convoy. Since then, ambulances have eschewed all protection, and none have been attacked.

The health-care crisis is being manifested in other ways. Insurgents are forcing Muslim women to give birth at home. In part, there is a cultural aversion to visiting state-run hospitals, because most of the doctors there are Buddhist males. This has had a dramatic impact on infant and maternal mortality. One public health official noted in 2006 that "nine out of every 100 women in Pattani, Yala, and Narathiwat

25. "Thai Govt to Train Young Nurses to Boost Medical Care in Restive South," *Nation*, April 24, 2007.
26. At the time, there were only 44 doctors (down from a peak of 105) and 547 nurses (down from 645). "Two More Shot Dead in Violence-Marred Far South," *Bangkok Post*, July 24, 2005.
27. Apiradee Treerutkuarkul, "Doctor Grads Refuse South Assignments," *Bangkok Post*, April 3, 2007.

who gave birth would die"—a rate significantly above the national average. Indeed, that rate is even higher than that of famine-plagued Ethiopia (eight of every hundred), one of the least-developed countries in the world.[28] Further, children who are not born at hospitals are not getting their immunizations, nor are they having their births registered, thus making them ineligible for the national health-care system or public schools. Infantile malnutrition rates in the south are also above the national average.

There are now concerns about the spread of polio, which had been mostly eradicated in the region. According to Dr. Thawat Suntrajarn, the head of the Ministry of Public Health's Disease Control Department, this is because both public perceptions and the general security situation have led to a dramatic drop in the south's polio immunization program.[29] As in northern Nigeria and Indonesia, where polio outbreaks have been reported, many Islamists have prevented children from receiving polio inoculations, claiming that inoculations are a part of a Western plot to sterilize Muslims. Southern Thailand is very close to the Indonesian island of Sumatra.

Generally speaking, the insurgency has directly and indirectly led to a rise in illness across the south. The number of incidences of elephantiasis in Narathiwat Province, for example, is thirty-three cases per one hundred thousand people—more than eleven times higher than the national average.[30] All of this is happening in a country that is renowned for having some of the finest public health in the entire developing world.

The Economy

The violence has led to a broad economic crisis across the south. There has been a discernable flight of capital and people, mainly Buddhists and ethnic Chinese, and little new investment is coming into the region. Every industry has been hit. More than twenty cell-phone towers have been knocked down or broken by insurgent bombs since November 2005. More than thirty car and motorcycle dealerships have been

28. "Childbirth Deaths at Crisis Level in South," *Nation*, December 20, 2006.
29. "Southern Provinces a Hotbed for Polio," *Nation*, December 7, 2006.
30. "Health Problems Rife in Narathiwat," *Nation*, February 9, 2007.

bombed, causing millions of dollars in inventory losses. ATMs have been destroyed, and more than thirty banks have been bombed—including twenty-two in one morning. Bombs are routinely planted in markets, and nightclubs, karaoke bars, and hotels have all been bombed. Because of concerns over the theft of explosives, the military even announced that it may shut down all quarries in the south, which would lead to the loss of up to ten thousand jobs.[31] Many small shopkeepers, both Muslim and Buddhist, have acceded to insurgent threats that they keep their businesses closed on Fridays. The transportation networks (trains and airports) have also been hit hard. Trains are riddled with bullets, bombed, or derailed on almost a monthly basis.

The unrest has had a particularly devastating impact on the rural economy. The average agrarian income fell by 3.4 percent in 2004–05, and it fell again in 2005–06.[32] The rubber industry, the economic mainstay of the region, has been the focus of numerous attacks by the insurgents. In one incident, insurgents cut down more than four hundred mature rubber trees. In 2006, militants set a warehouse on fire, destroying Bt30 million (US$810,000) in rubber sheet, which caused an exodus of rubber-plantation owners who are now getting government assistance to set up plantations outside of the south.[33] In February 2007, separatist rebels set fire to a large warehouse owned by the Southern Land Rubber Co., one of the largest rubber companies in Southeast Asia, causing more than Bt600 million (US$18.4 million) in damage.[34] The owner reported that 80 percent of the four hundred people who worked at the plant were local Muslims.[35] As of early April 2007, seventy-five rubber tappers had been killed (many beheaded), and nearly forty had been wounded.

31. Mydans, "Schools in Thailand under Ethnic Siege."

32. "Insurgency Pushes down Consumer Spending in the South," Thai News Agency, April 13, 2005; "Militants Launch Attacks in Thai Muslim South," Reuters, August 1, 2006.

33. Wichayant Boonchote, "Businessmen Head North to Plant Rubber," *Bangkok Post*, June 19, 2006.

34. "Suspected Rebels Set Fire to Rubber Warehouse in Yala," *Nation*, February 22, 2007.

35. Author interview, "Queen's Aide Escapes Death in South Attack," *Nation*, February 22, 2007.

The tourism industry, which accounts for 30 percent of the GDP of the south (compared with 8 percent of the national GDP), has also been severely affected. For example, the tourism industry lost an estimated Bt1.5 billion to 2 billion (US$38.5million to $51 million) in 2004 alone because of the unrest,[36] and the head of the provincial Tourism Business Association estimated that from 6,000 to 7,000 tourism-related jobs had been lost.[37] As a whole, tourism was down at least 50 percent in 2004–06, with hotel occupancy rates in Narathiwat hovering at around 10 percent. Businessmen in Hat Yai asserted in 2005 that business had fallen there by 50 percent, causing the average hotel occupancy rate to drop to 20 percent in 2006–07.[38] Anecdotally, the situation had not improved much by early 2008.

As a result of the south's faltering economy, the government has had to introduce a number of policies to assist local businesses and farmers. In 2005, the Thaksin government announced the creation of a number of funds to assist southern residents affected by the violence, including a Bt900 million (US$22.5 million) assistance program for government employees posted in the south. Later the government announced more than US$20 million in additional livelihood assistance to southerners. In late December 2006, the cabinet of caretaker prime minister Surayud approved a package of tax breaks in the four southernmost provinces and in four districts of Songkhla to try to reverse capital flight through December 2009. The package included a reduction in the corporate income tax from 30 percent to 3 percent, and a total exemption for the business revenues of individuals. Later, there were calls to reduce the tax rate further to 1.5 percent.[39] Taxes on real estate transactions also saw reductions, dropping from 3 percent to 0.1 percent.[40] In February 2007, the Government Savings Bank offered a Bt300 million (US$9.2 million) loan program for small-business owners in the

---

36. "Border Economies: Unrest Sparks Tourism Crisis," *Nation*, February 13, 2005.

37. David Fulbrook, "An Economic Battle, Too," *Asia Times*, December 14, 2004.

38. Martin Petty, "Bombarded by Alerts, Hat Yai Is Starting to Feel a Lot Less Bustling," *Thai Day*, July 11, 2006; Wichayant Boonchote, "Hat Yai Tourism in Peril," *Bangkok Post*, March 11, 2007.

39. "PM Insists on Talks for the South," *Bangkok Post*, May 22, 2007.

40. "Govt Approves Tax Breaks for South," *Bangkok Post*, December 20, 2006.

region.[41] By 2007, Hat Yai businessmen were demanding a larger-scale package from the government, including a 50 percent cut in local taxes, cuts in utility bills, greater access to low-interest loans, state contributions to the Social Security Fund on behalf of employers, and stepped-up security.[42] The government has resisted such sweeping assistance, constantly asserting that the situation is improving.

While the insurgency in the south has never been specifically about the economy, the conflict's negative impact on the economy certainly contributes to greater Muslim antipathy toward the Thai state.

International Implications

The insurgency not only continues to have a profound impact on southern Thai society, but it also continues to have growing international implications.

Malaysia and the Insurgency

There is a lot of hostility in Thailand toward the Malaysians regarding the current insurgency. While Thailand does not accuse the Malaysian government of direct complicity, it has not been lost on Thai officials that one of the reasons there have been so few arrests in the past few years is that the insurgency's leaders are all sitting in Kelantanese coffeehouses between prayers. The border is porous and there are some fifty checkpoints in Narathiwat alone. Many of the bomb components are coming from Malaysia, and it is likely that much of the funding is coming from or through Malaysia. Despite public assertions of cooperation, Thai security officials routinely confide that little of what is agreed upon is actually ever implemented and that they receive little real cooperation from the Malaysians.[43] For example, when Malaysian officials arrested GMIP leader Doromae Kuteh, they sent him to Indonesia rather than extradite him to Thailand.[44] Thai government officials

---

41. "Queen's Aide Escapes Death in South Attack," *Nation*, February 22, 2007.

42. Wichayant Boonchote, "Hat Yai Tourism in Peril," *Bangkok Post*, March 11, 2007.

43. Author interviews.

44. Although it was not reported in the press, Malaysian authorities arrested two or three others along with Doromae Kuteh. They will not say who the individuals are. Author interview, Kuala Lumpur, April 27, 2005.

point to that move as tangible proof that the Malaysians actually have a vested interest in seeing the insurgency smolder.

However, the most important arrests to date have been made by Malaysian—not Thai—officials. Indeed, Malaysians have always been very concerned about Muslim extremism within Malaysia and have been highly proactive in monitoring and dealing with the slightest hint of unrest. As a result, they have been very cooperative and are concerned about the situation in southern Thailand. If anything, they have been hampered by actions on the Thai side of the border, such as the bull-horn diplomacy practiced by the Thaksin government. As soon as the insurgency broke out in 2004, for example, Malaysian prime minister Abdullah Badawi pledged his support to the Thai government as long as it was sensitive to Badawi's political realities.[45] But the Thaksin government alienated the Malaysians through insensitive, public comments, making it much more politically difficult for Malaysian officials to work with the Thais to address what was becoming an increasingly common problem.

Part of the hostility dates back to the 1990s, when then Malaysian prime minister Mahathir Mohammed ordered his security forces to cooperate with their Thai counterparts and to arrest known militants operating in Thailand. Four top PULO members were detained and extradited to Thailand, where they are now imprisoned. However, the Malaysians felt that the sentences were too long. Malaysian authorities were also angry at perceived laxity on the Thai side of the border in 2001–02, when JI suspects were fleeing dragnets in Malaysia and Singapore. In another episode, the Malaysians turned over GMIP leader Nasae Saning to Thai officials only to learn that he had been killed in questionable circumstances before his trial could even begin. Sonthi himself has directly referenced the repercussions of such actions: "Malaysia used to help us, but we didn't behave. They had handed over people [suspected militants] but we killed them. Now they are reluctant to help."[46]

---

45. Author interview, Bangkok, January 20, 2006.
46. Wassana Nanuam and Pradit Ruangdit, "Sonthi Heads to Malaysia for Talks," *Bangkok Post*, November 27, 2006.

Despite this disharmonious relationship, the two sides ultimately agreed to step up border security in 2004.[47] Malaysia pledged more men and equipment for the security forces in their four provinces bordering Thailand. For their part, Thai security forces have tried to coordinate their operations with their Malaysian counterparts. In December 2004, joint border patrol teams were launched. Led by the Fourth Army, the teams include police, border patrol police, and immigration and customs officials. Although the border remains porous with regard to smuggling, the increased patrols and coordination have had a positive impact on counterinsurgency efforts.[48]

Both Thai and Malaysian leaders acknowledge that the sheer number of militants who hold both Thai and Malaysian citizenship at times inhibits full cooperation, especially with regard to extradition requests.[49] For example, both governments claimed Doromae Kuteh as a citizen.[50] Although the Thai government cited a bilateral extradition treaty dating to 1911 when requesting his extradition, the Malaysians stated that they did not recognize this treaty.[51] Although the two governments did not reach an agreement in this particular case, the two sides did agree on July 14, 2006, to focus on solving the problem of dual nationality for the 50,000 to 100,000 people who claim it.[52]

47. Nopporn Wong-Anan, "Thai Army Knuckles down in Troubled South," Reuters, April 29, 2004.

48. "Security Tightened at Thai-Malaysian Border," Thai News Agency, December 15, 2004.

49. "Premier's Pledge to Develop Area," *Straits Times*, April 13, 2004.

50. Malaysian officials have asserted that while they have evidence that Kuteh is a Malaysian citizen, they do not have enough evidence to conclude that he is also a Thai citizen. See "Extradition Request: Malaysia May Keep Jehku Mae," *Nation*, January 28, 2005; "Thailand to Ask Malaysia to Extradite Islamic Militant," *Nation*, February 1, 2005.

51. Prayuth Sivayaviroj, "Thai-Malaysian Spat: KL Says No Extradition after PM's Remarks." *Nation*, February 21, 2005.

52. "We will ensure that some concrete action is taken. Officials have been instructed to sit down and work it out together. It is not in the interest of either Thailand or Malaysia to allow the problem to continue," explained Malaysian deputy prime minister Najib Razak. He emphasized that Malaysia did not recognize dual nationality, saying: "They must choose either to be Thai or Malaysian citizens." Achara Ashayagachat, "Bangkok, KL Focus on Dual Nationality," *Bangkok Post*, July 15, 2006.

Despite their shared concerns and pledges of greater cooperation, there has been far less mutual operational support and cooperation on the ground than desired for three principal reasons. First, Thaksin's public statements often outraged the Malaysian government. For example, Thaksin's allegation that the militants had "recruited prospective youths and trained them in the jungles of Kelantan" was met with an angry response from Prime Minister Badawi.[53] Indeed, the Malaysians are annoyed by continued Thai assertions that insurgents train and base their operations in Malaysia. The Malaysian government has repeatedly asserted that it does not support the separatist movement in Thailand and, in fact, there is no evidence to suggest that it does.

In another example of counterproductive public statements made by the Thaksin administration, a report prepared for the prime minister and leaked to the press suggested that many of the bombs used by the militants had been assembled in Malaysia using Malaysian mobile phones. This angered the Malaysians and led to harsh denials by the Malaysian government.[54] Press leaks that claimed that the large shipment of ammonium nitrate seized in Thailand had been smuggled in from Malaysia further angered Malaysian officials. While there is significant evidence to suggest that the militants do seek sanctuary in Malaysia, public outbursts by Thai officials constrain the Malaysian government's ability and willingness to assist the Thais.

Second, there is considerable sympathy for the Thai Muslims among Malaysians, including for the militants. It is not surprising that sympathy exists in northern Malaysia for the plight of the Thai Muslims. They are, after all, ethnic Malays, with close kinship ties across the porous border. This sympathy runs very deep. In fact, evidence suggests that

---

53. Lyall, "Thailand Links Terror to Neighbors"; Nopporn Wong-Anan, "RPT-Malaysia Informed about Militant Training," Reuters, December 19, 2004.

54. There is considerable evidence that suggests that this assertion is true. In June 2006, the acting Thai interior minister Kongsak Wantana made these allegations again. Malaysian foreign minister Syed Hamid Albar angrily denied that the bombs had been assembled in Malaysia. See Davis, "Thai Militants Adopt New Bombing Tactics"; "More Than 60 Bombs Set off over Six Months," *Nation*, May 17, 2005; Kamol Sukin, "Don't Make Us Your Scapegoat: Malaysia," *Nation*, June 18, 2006.

much of the money supporting the insurgency comes from Malay donations. For example, one NGO—the Kelantan branch of the Malaysian Islamic Welfare Organization (PERKIM)—is reported to have donated RM120,000 (US$32,000) to PULO.[55] The Malaysian security forces are not immune to such feelings of sympathy. Although Royal Malaysian Police Special Branch officers are from all over the country, the local policemen along the border are predominantly Kelantanese. With Krue Se and Tak Bai fresh in their minds (and in the VCD players in their homes), it is easy for local rank-and-file security personnel to view their Thai counterparts as anti-Muslim. There is also lingering anger over the case of Nasae Saning.[56]

Third, cooperation between the two countries is limited by Malaysian political realities. Kelantan State, which abuts Yala and Narathiwat, is the stronghold of Parti Islam Se-Malaysia (PAS), the Islamic opposition party in Malaysia. PAS has always capitalized on the plight of its brethren in Thailand for political purposes. In 1992, for example, the deputy chief of PAS, Abdul Hadi Awang, publicly offered support and refuge to the Thai insurgents.[57] Such support has taken on even greater meaning in the context of Malaysia's present political landscape.

Struggling to find policies that resonated with the populace, PAS suffered an electoral defeat in March 2004, losing one of the two states that it had controlled.[58] But the Thai government's subsequent crackdown has made a strong impression on all four of Malaysia's bordering states and PAS has since made significant electoral inroads. Not only is PAS strong in Perak, Perlis, and Kedah, but another opposition party, Keadilan, is also making slow but steady gains among the Malay electorate, further eroding the United Malays National Organization's (UMNO's) lock on the majority. This situation has forced UMNO to come to the defense of popular Malay issues to avoid losing out to its political oppo-

55. "Funds Channeled to Muslim Rebels in Thailand: Report," *Malaysiakini*, December 9, 2004; "Thai Premier Links Indonesia to Southern Unrest," Channel News Asia, December 19, 2004.

56. "Battle Is on for the Hearts and Minds in the South," *Nation*, January 12, 2004.

57. "Malaysia's Opposition Party Offers Sanctuary for Thai Moslem Separatists," Agence France-Presse, August 16, 1992.

58. PAS won 1 percent more of the popular vote than in the 1999 election, but it won fewer seats and lost Terengganu because of redistricting.

sition. For example, in November 2004, UMNO readily endorsed a parliamentary motion put forward by PAS that condemned "the aggressive use of power in Narathiwat province that led to numerous deaths among Muslims."[59] Even within UMNO, Prime Minister Badawi's hold on power has not always been certain. Although he led the party to victory in the March 2004 elections, there have been a number of attacks on him from within UMNO's ranks, including those led by former prime minister Mahathir Mohammed in mid-2006. In short, Badawi is politically constrained and cannot risk any move that might be perceived as caving in to the Thais.

The UMNO-controlled government has tried to use the situation in Thailand against PAS. For example, in November 2004, the government leaked a report that suggested that PAS was instigating the violence.[60] This seemed to comport with various public statements made by PAS members. Exclaimed one PAS activist at a mass prayer rally, "It is time for Pattani to fight the Siamese *kafirs*. We will stand by our Muslim brothers and sisters in southern Thailand to fight Siam."[61] But such statements aside, PAS leaders are too smart to be drawn into anything more than fiery oratory. They are careful not to give UMNO any justification for imposing the ISA on their members. For example, a senior PAS official in Kelantan warned that young Malays could eventually be inspired to take up arms to "do jihad" with their brothers in southern Thailand, before clarifying that PAS would only give such individuals "moral support."[62]

For their part, Thai officials are aware that "PAS leaders have been very attentive to the situation" and that individual PAS members have expressed considerable support for the Muslims in the south.[63] But perhaps more surprising to the Thais than the rhetoric of PAS members

59. "M'sia Legislature Condemns Tak Bai Tragedy," *Nation*, November 25, 2004.

60. "New Report Claims PAS Linked to South's Woes," *Nation*, November 9, 2004.

61. Zainuddin Abdullah, quoted in John Burton and Amy Kazmin, "Bangkok's Handling of Thailand's Troubled Muslim South Rankles with Malay Neighbors," *Financial Times*, November 25, 2004.

62. Zulkifli Yakub, president of the PAS Youth Wing in Kelantan, quoted in Burton and Kazmin, "Bangkok's Handling of Thailand's Troubled Muslim South Rankles with Malay Neighbors."

63. Author interview, Bangkok, March 18, 2005.

was the very public statement of former Malaysian deputy prime minister Anwar Ibrahim,[64] in which he lashed out at Thaksin's handling of
the conflict in the south: "The security forces have been extremely irre-
sponsible and they must be held responsible for their crimes."[65] He
then offered a warning to the Thai government: "The situation is
extremely volatile. People are very angry and this is not just in a few
villages but the entire community across the south who are getting very
agitated. . . . This is totally legitimate and understandable."[66] Why did
Anwar speak out when he did? Clearly, he was personally outraged, but
his criticism could also be understood in the context of Malaysian politics. In short, he was plotting his political comeback. Although he was
banned from electoral politics until April 2008 and it was unlikely that
the rural-based leadership of PAS would allow him into the party,[67]
Anwar remained a potent force in Malaysian politics, and he was speaking about an issue that had direct and continuing political resonance for
him. Indeed, many of the more modern, urban-based members of PAS
supported him and believed he could be an effective leader of PAS.

   Although UMNO and its coalition, the Barisan Nasional, repeatedly
condemned Thaksin's policies, and Badawi's ability to cooperate with
the Thais was limited, Malaysian security forces did crack down on the
militants, driving many of them underground. On March 9, 2005, for
example, five Thai militants were arrested in Kuala Lumpur's central
train station. The five were in Malaysia, according to *Time* magazine,

---

64. Prime Minister Mahathir Mohammed sacked his popular deputy prime minister
and heir apparent, Anwar Ibrahim, in 1998 when it appeared that Anwar was poised to
run against Mahathir for the post of prime minister. Anwar was arrested and convicted
in highly politicized legal proceedings on two charges: corruption and sodomy. The
sodomy conviction was later overturned, and Anwar was released in late 2004, having
served six years on the corruption charge. As a result of the injustice, Amnesty
International adopted Anwar as a "prisoner of conscience." While it has never been
proved, most analysts believe Anwar was sacked and arrested for three reasons: (1)
Mahathir was politically threatened by the growing popularity of his deputy; (2) Anwar
supported the structural reforms proposed by the International Monetary Fund in the
midst of the 1997–99 Asian economic crisis, while Mahathir favored currency controls;
and (3) Anwar's anticorruption campaign was an implicit attack on Mahathir, his son,
and the corrupt factions of UMNO that kept him in power.
65. Bethany Jinkinson, "Thailand Chided over Deaths," BBC, November 10, 2004.
66. Ibid.
67. "Malaysia's Anwar Loses Court Bid," BBC, September 15, 2004.

to collect a cache of weapons hidden by JI and KMM.[68] After all, the Malaysian government had its own security concerns regarding insurgents—in particular, that a lawless southern Thailand would become a safe haven for Malaysia's own radicals and members of JI. It was also concerned that any spillover of the unrest into Malaysia would affect the entire peninsula.[69] No longer the secure rear area that it once was, Malaysia has likely drawn the militants' ire. As one Malaysian intelligence official told *Time*, "We were safe when Malaysia was seen as a place to hide. But now we are arresting militants, and they are angry."[70]

Despite these security measures taken by Malaysian officials, one case illustrated well the strained bilateral relations between Malaysia and Thailand while Thaksin was prime minister. On August 30, 2005, 131 villagers fled from Thailand to Malaysia the day after a local imam was allegedly killed by Thai security forces.[71] Requesting asylum, they were placed in a refugee center. Demanding that all 131 be returned, the Thai government alleged that PULO had encouraged the migration to "internationalize" the crisis in the south. Although Thai officials identified 34 of the 131 refugees as militants, only one, Hamzah bin Mat Saud, was the subject of an arrest warrant.[72] Former Malaysian prime minister Mahathir Mohammed infuriated the Thais by saying, "If these people are real refugees, then we need to give them some asylum."[73] Thai defense minister Thamarak Isarangura responded angrily in the press by asserting that the Thai government believed that the insurgency began after a planning meeting on the Malaysian island of Langkawi, implying that Mahathir was somehow behind the unrest.[74] The Thais were further incensed when the Malaysians allowed the Office of the United Nations High Commissioner for

---

68. Simon Elegant, "Arms at the Ready," *Time—Asian Edition*, May 9, 2005.

69. Author interview, Bangkok, March 18, 2005.

70. Simon Elegant, "Terror Visible," *Time—Asian Edition*, March 28, 2005.

71. ICG, *Thailand's Emergency Decree: No Solution*, 9–10.

72. Achara Ashayagachat, "Separatist Insurgents 'Among Those Who Fled to Malaysia,'" *Bangkok Post*, October 22, 2005.

73. "Mahathir Suggests Asylum for Thai Muslims," *Nation*, September 7, 2005.

74. "Rebels 'Plotted on Mahathir's Island,'" *Nation*, September 10, 2005; "Time to Retire the Anti-Malaysia Rhetoric," *Bangkok Post*, October 25, 2005.

Refugees (UNHCR) to screen the 131 villagers. The Malaysian government did allow Thai authorities to interview them as well, but they callously allowed the interviews to be conducted by uniformed Thai military personnel, led by Lt. Gen. Chayasit Linthong, head of the Supreme Command's Joint Intelligence Directorate.[75] This crisis lasted throughout 2005 without any resolution in sight, despite high-level meetings between Anand, Badawi, and Mahathir, and between Surin Pitsuwan and Malaysian defense minister Najib Razak. "We had a frank and open discussion about the violence in the south," Anand said. "Mahathir assured me that his country had never backed insurgents or the Pattani United Liberation Organization."[76] These assurances were not enough for Thaksin, however, who vowed that he would not meet his counterpart until the 131 people had been returned.[77]

Although Thaksin eventually met with Badawi and announced that they had reached agreement on returning the refugees, the Malaysians were obviously unconvinced by the Thai government's assurances that the refugees would not be prosecuted. Mahathir traveled to Thailand in mid-November, met with Thaksin and Anand, and had an audience with the king. He provoked anger in Bangkok by suggesting that the southern provinces be given autonomy. Thaksin commented that the suggestion was "unconstructive."[78] Denying that the Malaysian government had any contact with the separatists, Mahathir finally announced a truce in November 2005: "One thing I can tell you is that we agree there should be no megaphone diplomacy."[79] And to a certain extent, this meeting of the two most outspoken leaders in the region did bring megaphone diplomacy to an end. This meeting also arguably led to the one breakthrough in the refugee case. On December 8, 2005, Malaysia

75. Achara Ashayagachat, "Negotiations with 131, KL Get Underway," *Bangkok Post*, October 27, 2005.

76. "Anand Assured KL Is Not Backing Rebels," *Nation*, October 9, 2005.

77. "Thaksin: No Meeting Unless Malaysia Hands over Suspects," *Bangkok Post*, October 31, 2005.

78. "'Autonomy' Not a Good Word, Both Sides Agree," *Nation*, November 23, 2005.

79. Achara Ashayagchat, "Mahathir Declares Friendly Truce in Thai-Malaysian War of Words," *Bangkok Post*, November 23, 2005.

returned Hamzah Saud to Thailand. Wanted since March 2004, he was immediately charged with treason, robbery, and murder.[80]

This case has not been resolved to anyone's satisfaction. The Malaysians remain very sympathetic toward the majority of the refugees, whose plight has been made a major issue by PAS, even though the Thais maintain that other suspected militants are among the remaining 130 refugees, including Hamue Sa-u from Sungai Padi.[81] While the Malaysians may be willing to turn over certain individuals if the Thai government can present evidence that they are linked to the insurgency, the longer the impasse drags on, the harder it will be for the Malaysians to deport any of the remaining refugees. Further, the fact that they have been allowed to stay has only encouraged more people to cross the border, exacerbating the situation.

For Malaysia, the insurgency in southern Thailand has represented more than a test of the bilateral relationship. Kuala Lumpur does not support the militants and has worked assiduously since 2001 to uproot JI and KMM. It would never condone the use of its territory by Islamist militants, but the Thaksin government was never sensitive to the Malaysian government's constraints. "Whatever happens in southern Thailand has a direct effect on us," noted Malaysian foreign minister Syed Hamid Albar. "Surely we are not going to stay silent. As a friend and as a fellow ASEAN country, of course we will express our opinion without interfering in Thailand's internal affairs." Further, like other Malaysian leaders, Syed Hamid Albar denied that the insurgents were using the Malaysians to internationalize their struggle, stating "there is no such evidence."[82] In fact, a senior Thai diplomat who met with Prime Minister Badawi in 2004 said that Malaysia had promised full cooperation with Thailand at the start of the insurgency as long as the Thais kept quiet and did not bring attention to this fact. Thaksin, of course, did nothing of the sort.[83]

---

80. "Malaysia Hands Muslim Fugitive to Thailand," Reuters, December 8, 2005.

81. Supalak Ganjanakhundee, "Most of 131 Who Fled Are Willing to Return, Govt Says," *Nation*, September 14, 2005.

82. "Malaysia Says It's Responsible for Muslims after Thais Flee Violence," *Nation*, September 5, 2005.

83. Author interview, Bangkok, January 20, 2006.

Yet, there is considerable Malaysian sympathy for both their Malay brethren in Thailand and the rebels. This is particularly true in the PAS heartland of Kelantan, where personal, kinship, and economic ties to southern Thailand are strong. PAS will keep a spotlight on the conflict, which will force rank-and-file UMNO members to offer carefully worded support for the militants and criticism of Thai policies. Malaysia has to deal with external pressures as well. For example, many countries in the OIC were unhappy with Kuala Lumpur's soft line toward Thailand during its OIC presidency in 2005. According to a journalist who covered the issue closely, Malaysia was even privately rebuked by the Saudi government.[84]

Relations between Malaysia and Thailand clearly improved after the September 19, 2006, coup. Kuala Lumpur embraced every new policy of the CNS and Surayud government. During Badawi's February 2007 summit with Surayud in Thailand, the two countries agreed to exchange personal information on citizens of both countries, including photographs and fingerprints, and to start to grapple with the issue of dual citizenship.[85] Malaysia also stated its willingness to broker talks between the Thai government and the militants. Despite these improvements, however, hurdles remained. For example, in March 2007 Thai security officials complained that little had been done following the summit meeting. They feared that the Malaysian bureaucracy was resisting the political leadership's pledges.

After democracy was restored in Thailand in February 2008, bilateral relations between the two countries once again became strained. Although it was not a key issue in the March 8, 2008, Malaysian parliamentary elections, the situation in southern Thailand was one of many issues on the minds of voters, and UMNO suffered a historically unprecedented defeat at the hands of the opposition coalition. The opposition won 82 of the 220 seats in parliament (36.9 percent), while the UMNO-led coalition won only 140 seats (63.1 percent). It was the first time that the Barisan Nasional coalition had not won an impregnable two-thirds majority in parliament. Moreover, the opposition won

84. Don Pathan, in personal correspondence with author, February 14, 2006.
85. "Thai, Malaysia to Exchange Citizens' Personal Data, Aim to Resolve Insurgency," *Bangkok Post*, February 5, 2007.

control of five of Malaysia's thirteen states, including almost all the states that border Thailand.

Following UMNO's electoral loss in March 2008, Badawi came under intense pressure from opponents in his own party to resign. He ultimately agreed to step down by March 2009. In July 2008, Anwar won a by-election for parliament, becoming the formal leader of the opposition coalition. Under Anwar, it continues to make gains as the Barisan Nasional fractures. Thailand, too, has been fraught with its own political instability as the elites are engaged in their own zero-sum battle, which has played out in street protests, in the courts, and in behind-the-scenes meetings. As both countries remain transfixed on their own elite contestations, the conflict in southern Thailand has become less of a priority for them.

The OIC

At the diplomatic level, the Thai government has invested all of its resources in preventing the OIC from issuing a harsh report on its handling of the insurgency. Thailand successfully prevented such a report from being issued in 2005 primarily because the Malaysian government held the OIC presidency that year. Indeed, the OIC's October 2005 report "reaffirmed the situation in Thailand is not a religious conflict" and regarded it as a purely internal affair.[86] Not surprisingly, Thai Muslims believed that the OIC report was a whitewash.

With Malaysia no longer holding the presidency of the OIC, Malaysia was less able to set and control the agenda, increasing the likelihood that Thailand would come under greater pressure from the OIC. Indeed, Thailand's relations with the OIC began to sour slightly over Bangkok's handling of the 131 refugees. On October 18, 2005, for example, the head of the OIC issued a statement expressing "deep concern . . . about continued acts of violence in southern Thailand against Muslims, claiming the lives of innocents, and inflicting harm on properties. Some villages have been under siege and some families had to migrate."[87] Additionally, a joint communiqué issued at the end

---

86. OIC, "On Current Waves of Violence in Southern Thailand" (press release, Jidda, Saudi Arabia, October 18, 2005).
87. Ibid.

of an OIC summit in June 2006, though recognizing the territorial integrity of Thailand, warned that the south "remains a matter of serious concern."[88]

In a sign of disgust with the OIC's continued backing of the Thai government and refusal to openly condemn Thailand's policies and actions, militants targeted a motorcade of OIC ambassadors in February 2007. In May 2007, OIC secretary-general Ekmeleddin Ihsanoglu paid his first official visit to Thailand and, despite the earlier OIC statements regarding Thailand, was effusive in his praise, stating that the government had a "constructive and promising" attitude toward the insurgency and the Muslim populace. While he urged the Thai government to give the Muslim community "greater responsibilities over their own affairs," he added that it should take place "within the framework of the constitution."[89] Insulting the insurgents, Ihsanoglu added, "Muslims should be good citizens and respect the laws of their countries."[90] Unlike the 2006 communiqué, the OIC's 2007 communiqué eliminated any mention of the insurgents' secessionist aim of establishing an independent Muslim "state."[91]

ASEAN

The possibility that JI could become more deeply involved in southern Thailand and cause the conflict there to escalate represents a threat to all states of the region. Indeed, JI foments sectarian violence by creating a Manichaean worldview—that is, a sense of Muslim victimization and persecution—and by communicating the belief that the region's secular states are at best not protecting the interests of the broader Muslim community and are at worst actively complicit against it. Jihadist videos that call attention to the situation in southern Thailand are already being circulated as VCDs and on the Internet. Additionally,

---

88. Achara Ashayagachat, "OIC to Help Search for a Solution," *Nation*, June 22, 2006; Sopaporn Kurz, "Ties with OIC Are Close and 'Full of Understanding,'" *Nation*, June 22, 2006.

89. Achara Ashayagachat, "OIC Supports Government on South," *Bangkok Post*, May 16, 2007.

90. Supalak Ganjanakhundee, "Islamic Chief Here," *Nation*, May 2, 2007.

91. OIC, "OIC Secretary General Concludes Visit to Thailand" (press release, Jidda, Saudi Arabia, May 3, 2007).

Internet chat rooms are filled with rants against the Thai government and calls for jihad. As a result, JI will ultimately dispatch some operatives and young recruits to southern Thailand to give them a sense of jihad. Because the region has made progress in uprooting JI, this is particularly unfortunate.

Other groups, such as HUJI-B and the RSO, will also try to make common cause with the Thai militants. There is some indication that Cambodian Islamists, who traditionally have had close ties with their coreligionists in Thailand, are joining the insurgents.[92] For example, more than a thousand Cambodian Muslims came to Thailand in 2005, many of whom are suspected of having joined the insurgency. In late 2005, the Thai government refused to allow a group of eighty-six Cambodians into the country, although members of the group claimed that they were simply on their way to Malaysia to find work.[93] Thai authorities must also be concerned about "bleed out" from Iraq once jihadists move on to the next crisis spot. Because systematic persecution of Muslims is the light that attracts the jihadist moths, it is only a matter of time before the broader militant Islamist community focuses on Thailand's treatment of its Muslim minority.

The appointment of Surrin Pitsuwan, a Pattani Muslim and former Thai foreign minister, as the new head of ASEAN in early 2008 may help to raise the specter of international jihadism in southern Thailand and foster better interstate relations in preventing it.

The United States

The U.S. government is concerned that the insurgency is taking on a life of its own, and Washington sees it as part of a global militant Sunni insurgency. The intelligence community believes that the al-Qaeda threat is morphing into a broader network of interrelated insurgencies. As former director of national intelligence John D. Negroponte said in Senate testimony, "Thailand is searching for a formula to contain vio-

---

92. "Cambodian Muslims Flock to Thailand's Troubled South," *Thai News Agency*, May 19, 2005.
93. Cambodian Muslims Turned back," *Nation*, November 27, 2005; Wassana Nanuam, "Authorities Keep Close Eye on Cambodian Muslims," *Bangkok Post*, November 17, 2005.

lence instigated by ethnic Malay Muslim separatist groups in the far southern provinces. In 2005, the separatists showed signs of stronger organization and more lethal and brutal tactics targeting the government and Buddhist population in the south."[94] Clearly, the United States is concerned about unrest in the south and any potential for terrorism in Bangkok. Yet the U.S. government seems to have painted itself into a corner by parroting the refrain from Bangkok that there is no religious component to the insurgency. In the State Department's counterterrorism report delivered to Congress in 2006, the "roots of the southern problem" were referred to as "ethnic and not religious." The report did warn, however, that "there is concern that southern unrest has the potential to attract international terrorist groups such as JI and al-Qaida that may attempt to capitalize on the increasingly violent situation for their own purposes."[95]

Although the relationship between Thailand and the United States is multifaceted and complex, Thailand is an important treaty ally of the United States—indeed, its oldest treaty ally in the Asia-Pacific region. For example, Thailand sent 130 soldiers to Afghanistan, mainly medics and engineers who worked to restore Bagram Air Base.[96] Then, in October 2003, as a reward for Thailand's participation in the "coalition of the willing" and its commitment of 450 troops to Iraq—mainly medics and engineers deployed to the southern city of Karbala—the United States extended to Thailand the status of a major non-NATO ally, which ensures continued military-to-military cooperation between them.[97] While the deployment to Iraq was unpopular and Thai troops suffered several casualties, Thaksin did not

94. John D. Negroponte, "Annual Threat Assessment of the Director of National Intelligence for the Senate Select Committee on Intelligence," February 2, 2006, 18, www.mipt.org/GetDoc.asp?id=3203&type=d (accessed October 1, 2008).

95. The Thai counterterrorism report is available at www.state.gov/s/ct/rls/crt/2006/82731.htm (accessed October 1, 2008).

96. Emma Chanlett-Avery, *Thailand-Background and U.S. Relations*, Congressional Research Service Report for Congress (Washington, D.C.: CRS, January 13, 2005), 10.

97. Both the U.S.-led war and the Thai government's assistance in the occupation were unpopular in the south and led to demonstrations and boycotts of U.S. products. See "Thai Muslims Protest at U.S. War," BBC, March 21, 2003; U.S. Embassy, "Fact Sheet: Major Non-NATO Ally Status for Thailand" (press release, Bangkok, October 31, 2003).

withdraw troops until the committed term expired in 2004. Thailand later opened its U-Tapao naval air base to the United States following the devastating December 26, 2004, tsunami to enable relief efforts in Indonesia and Sri Lanka. The tendency of the United States was to support the Thaksin administration, although there is increasing awareness that his policies were much to blame for the rapid escalation of violence.

Although direct military ties were temporarily restricted because of the September 2006 coup, Thailand is also host to the annual Cobra Gold military exercises, which began in 1982 and are now the largest military exercises in the Asia-Pacific region.[98] The 2004 exercise included thirteen thousand U.S. troops and more than five thousand Thais, and the 2005 exercises focused on the lessons learned from tsunami relief efforts.[99] The U.S. military has suggested that Cobra Gold exercises should focus on the insurgency, but the Thais have strenuously resisted this idea for fear of fanning the insurgency. Indeed, Thailand's relationship with the United States is already a major cause of discontent in the south. Tens of thousands of Thai officers have been trained under the International Military Education and Training program, and bilateral military relations between the two countries are very close.

Thailand is also an important intelligence partner for the United States. The CIA and its Thai counterparts established the joint Counter-Terrorism Intelligence Center (CTIC) in 2002.[100] Since the capture of Hambali in August 2003, the CTIC has concentrated its efforts on the situation in the south—for example, in monitoring hundreds of pondoks.[101] It has a US$20 million budget provided by the CIA and is staffed by about twenty CIA officials, a handful of FBI agents, and

---

98. Cobra Gold now includes the full participation of Japan and Singapore, as well as observer teams from China, Australia, Indonesia, South Korea, Pakistan, and Vietnam.

99. Dalpino and Steinberg, *Southeast Asian Survey, 2004–2005*, 58.

100. For more, see "CIA, Thai Agencies United against Terrorism," *Australian Financial Review*, October 2, 2002.

101. Shawn Crispin, "Gearing up for a Fight," *Far Eastern Economic Review*, May 13, 2004; Shawn Crispin and Leslie Lopez, "U.S. and Thai Agents Collaborate in Secret— Cold War–Style Alliance Strikes Jemaah Islamiyah Where It Least Expects It," *Asian Wall Street Journal*, October 1, 2003.

members of three Thai intelligence and security organizations—the National Intelligence Agency, the Special Branch of the Royal Thai Police, and the Armed Forces Security Centre.

Thailand is also an important partner in global health monitoring and in efforts to stop human trafficking, transnational crime, and narcotics trafficking. That said, there is growing concern within the United States about Thailand's human rights record.[102] The U.S. State Department's 2003 human rights report on Thailand warned that the Thai government's human rights record had "worsened with regard to extrajudicial killings and arbitrary arrests" and that Thaksin's war on drugs had created a "climate of impunity."[103] The 2004 human rights report listed a similar litany of abuses committed by the government in the south, citing extrajudicial killings, deaths of detainees, allegations of torture, disappearances, limits on free speech and freedom of assembly, and the systematic undermining of Thailand's free press. The report was most critical of the country's extrajudicial killings:

> When the Government investigated extrajudicial killings, it prosecuted few of the accused police or military officers. Senior prosecutors and nongovernmental organization (NGO) legal associations claimed that most cases against police or military officers accused of extrajudicial killings eventually were dismissed because regulations outlined in the Criminal Code require public prosecutors to rely exclusively upon the recommendations of the police when determining whether to bring a case for criminal prosecution. The resulting routine exoneration of police officers contributed to a climate of impunity that persisted in preventing any major change in police behavior. It also discouraged relatives of victims from pressing for prosecution.[104]

The U.S. Embassy in Bangkok has stated its own concerns regarding the degrading human rights situation in Thailand:

---

102. Glenn Kessler, "Crackdown by Premier Strains Thailand's Friendship with U.S.," *Washington Post*, December 25, 2004.

103. U.S. Department of State, "Thailand: Country Reports on Human Rights Practices, 2003," February 25, 2004, www.state.gov/g/drl/rls/hrrpt/2003/27790.htm (accessed October 1, 2008). For more on the extrajudicial killings, see Human Rights Watch, "Not Enough Graves."

104. U.S. Department of State, "Thailand: Country Reports on Human Rights Practices, 2004," February 28, 2005, www.state.gov/g/drl/rls/hrrpt/2004/41661.htm (accessed October 1, 2008).

> United States officials at the highest levels expressed concern
> for the extensive loss of life in Southern Thailand and encouraged
> the Royal Thai Government (RTG) to follow up official investi-
> gations into unwarranted security force actions at the Krue Se
> Mosque in April and at Tak Bai in October with appropriate legal
> action to punish responsible officials. Deputy Assistant Secretary
> for East Asian and Pacific Affairs Marie T. Huhtala expressed con-
> cern over the Tak Bai incident to the Thai Ambassador to the
> United States, and the U.S. Ambassador in Thailand raised similar
> concerns with senior Thai officials.[105]

Despite these public reports and statements, there is little evidence to suggest that the U.S. government has pressed Thailand on human rights. Although the 2005 Emergency Decree was a major affront to human rights, it provoked little response from the U.S. government in the State Department's 2005 human rights report. In contrast, the respected independent monitoring body Freedom House downgraded Thailand from "free" to "semi-free" in its own 2006 report.[106]

While the United States was somewhat critical of the September 19, 2006, coup, it was supportive of Prime Minister Surayud's calls for reconciliation. Yet the United States does itself a disservice when it buys in to the Thai government's poor analytical framework and state of denial when discussing the situation in the south. At present, the primary focus of the U.S. Embassy in Bangkok seems to be encouraging the consolidation of democracy and monitoring the current political turmoil, as well as concluding the Free Trade Agreement (FTA) between the two countries. Although the U.S. Embassy also monitors the situation in the south, the shutdown of the U.S. Consulate in Songkhla in July 1993 removed the United States' ability to keep a finger on the pulse of the situation.

The insurgency in the south should be of concern to Washington because the terrorist threat to the United States is officially character-

---

105. U.S. Department of State, *Supporting Human Rights and Democracy: The U.S. Record, 2004–2005* (Washington, D.C.: U.S. Department of State, March 28, 2005), www.state. gov/g/drl/rls/shrd/2004/ (accessed October 1, 2008).

106. Freedom House, *Freedom in the World 2006* (Washington, D.C.: Freedom House, 2006), www.freedomhouse.org/template.cfm?page=363&year=2006 (accessed October 1, 2008).

ized as a "global Sunni insurgency." The Department of Defense's analysis—which carries the day in the United States—is that al-Qaeda has morphed into an ideology that interconnects militant Sunni organizations around the world. Whether this analysis is correct is beside the point. If it is Washington's analytical framework, then Washington should care very much about the deteriorating situation in the south and the potential for it to attract jihadists "bleeding out" from Iraq and other conflict zones.

That noted, the United States must not become directly involved in the conflict. Doing so would only risk inflaming the situation. It should, however, continue to cooperate with Thailand on intelligence matters. It should also reconfigure its military education and bilateral training programs—which for years focused on making Thai forces more professional and conventional. Specifically, the United States should focus its training and joint exercises on Thailand's key security challenges and address the fact that Thailand is currently in a low-intensity conflict. The United States has gained considerable experience from its five-year campaign in Iraq and has many valuable lessons to teach in terms of fighting an insurgency and gathering battlefield intelligence. The U.S. government must also continue to push the Thai government to implement many of the NRC's recommendations and redouble its commitment to human rights. Allowing Thailand to undermine its democracy and rule of law will not only backfire and fuel the insurgency but will also hurt the United States' long-term interests in Thailand and the Asia-Pacific region.

Appendix A

Examples of Insurgent Leaflets[1]

Insurgent leaflets, flyers, and pamphlets generally fall into one of several broad categories: threats to the Buddhist community; threats to the Muslim community; directives to village headmen; reportage of facts; statements of goals, ideology, and religion.

Threats to the Buddhist Community

Leaflets directed at the Buddhist community are generally overtly threatening in nature and call on Buddhists to leave the region—either individually or collectively.

Document 22

> Dear every Siamese Buddhist Thai who lives near the police stations. Dogs. Pigs. Shit. Garbage. Land. I'll give you three days for you to leave my land. Otherwise, I will kill, burn, destroy all Buddhist Thai property, including police stations, dogs, pigs, garbage, land. The Buddhist Thai will never live in peace. If you leave the house, travel or go to work, you will die violently. I will wait for you 24 hours, in every direction.
>
> — The Warriors of the Malay People
> — Pattani[2]

Document 17

> You kill my innocent ustadz, I kill your innocent teachers.[3]

---

1. The examples provided in this appendix are translations of insurgent leaflets that have been analyzed and catalogued by the author and that are in his possession.

2. Document 22 was left on the windshield of a Thai Buddhist's car.

3. Document 17 is a handwritten note that was left at a school.

Document 23

> The Islamic Warriors of Pattani announce the purpose that we will never stop killing the Siamese *kafir* [infidel] and will never stop destroying army weapons, the economy, politics, education and the Siamese kafir society until we regain the land of Pattani and establish the state of Pattani Darulslam. I ask for the Muslim Malays to be the witnesses.[4]
>
> — Islamic Warriors of Pattani

Threats to the Muslim Community

The most common type of leaflet is a "beware of harm" warning addressed to the Muslim community that outlines what Muslims have to do to not get killed and to avoid trouble with the militants.

Document 3

A Warning about Harm

Wishing you happy and peace.

Dear our beloved Muslimins and Muslimahs [Muslim women],

We (the Warriors of Pattani State) have declared war and are ready to use every strategy to fight the Siamese kafir who invaded the sovereign land of Pattani State. They have seized, oppressed, and threatened Muslim Malays like animals for more than 200 years. They have no humanity. We (the Warriors of Pattani State) want to serve Muslim Malays and protect Islam's honor and dignity, intelligence, property, soul, society, and off-spring according to Allah's desire. We want to return the inde-pendence of Pattani Darul Islam [Land of Islam] back to the Muslims (according to Allah's desire).

All Muslimins and Muslimahs. . . . The enemy who has invaded the sovereign land of Pattani State is the Siamese kafir. They are not only civilians but also those who work for the kafir government such as Governors, Sheriffs, Deputies, district chiefs, teachers, soldiers, police officers, doctors, nurses, perma-nent officials, permanent employees, political officials, national politicians, district politicians, state enterprise employees, trad-ers, businesspeople, and merchants. Indeed, all of them are our enemies. Undoubtedly, they are our victims and targets. There-fore, I would like to announce "warning of harm" to our beloved

---

4. This passage comes from an insurgent document titled "The Day to Announce the Purpose."

Muslimin and Muslimah Malays who work in every vocation. Please tell other people to "beware" and to not be in close contact or have relationships in work and in daily life with Siamese kafir; otherwise, you will not be safe, both physically and your property. We might not misunderstand; as a result, you might be our unintentional victim and targets of Pattani Warriors. Therefore, we announce "warning of harm" to remind our Muslimins and Muslimahs to concentrate on it seriously. (If you do, definitely you will never be hurt.)

We, the Warriors of Pattani State, have declared war and want to do everything to drive the Siamese kafir back to Siam. They are our enemies who usurped the sovereignty of Pattani State. We, the Warriors of Pattani State, are ready to sacrifice ourselves for jihad according to Allah's path to praise Islam [illegible] . . . back to the foundations of an Islamic State.

[illegible] . . . please give your blessings to all Muslimin and Muslimah Malays and to all the brave Warriors of Pattani State who are following the righteous path and succeeding in work, safety [illegible] . . . be loved by Allah. Amen.

Best wishes to you,

— The Warriors of Pattani State

Document 2

Beware: If there are some advertisements about selling real estate occupied by Siamese kafir, you must not be a middleman and do not buy any land because those are the [Muslim] nation's rightful property. We will keep them for the public and for our offspring. If someone buys it, it means that he or she is buying national property (the Islamic State of Pattani). They [Thai Buddhists] came here with empty hands, and they must return with empty hands. Please cooperate and stop buying the kafir's real estate from now on.

Document 5

Beware of Harm!

Warning to Pattani Muslims! From now on, beware and cooperate with us, the Warriors of Pattani State. Please do the following: Do not work, do not trade, do not slit [tap] rubber trees and do not do any business on Friday, Saturday, Sunday, Monday, and Tuesday. Please solemnize your praise of Islam. Do not accept any help, things, money, or gold from kafir officers because those are poisons and prohibited things for Pattani Muslims. Do not go to see doctors in kafir hospitals. It is a big sin. The Muslimins and Muslimahs cannot receive a salary from kafir officials. They have to resign and not cooperate with the kafir!

Please do the following, otherwise you will become a bad munafiq [hypocrite] and be punished by the Warriors of Pattani State. You can see many munafiqs punished by us recently.

Do the following; otherwise, you will be killed. If we kill you, we kill for Allah on high.

Document 27

Dear Head,

Dear all Muslim Malays,

We, the Warriors of Pattani, are sorry about the bombing in Sungai Golok District causing losses to our beloved Muslims. According to this event, we, the Warriors of Pattani, ask for all siblings to stay away from government officers and not communicate with them, for the safety of our offspring.

Whenever we take action, we try to minimize the loss as much as we can. We warn you many times, so please tell other people to not be close to the government officers.

We are sorry and feel sorry about this event.

Finally, we wish that Allah will protect you and he will bring the dead to rest beside him.[5]

Directives to Village Headmen

Many leaflets are directives to village headmen, most of whom are fellow Muslims. Through 2007, roughly 11 percent of the victims of the insurgents had been village headmen or deputy headmen, making them one of the largest discernable groups of victims. The insurgents have been particularly interested in using the headmen to impose their agenda in the countryside.

Document 8

To the Village Headmen in _____ Village:

Please inform all Buddhist Thais and Muslim Thais in the area of your jurisdiction as follows:

1. Buddhist Thais are strictly forbidden to hunt animals or make a living in the area regarded as Muslim land from now on, because the area belongs to the Muslim people. We would like to declare that from now on, the Buddhists there are deemed invaders and we are going to take back our land.

2. The Buddhist Thais who work for the government and receive a salary from the owners of rubber plantations, and these owners who have employees and have shops, all of them have to pay a

---

5. This leaflet was left near a mosque in Sungai Golok.

tax of Bt500 individually every month to Muslims. Payment must be paid to the mosque nearest to their house, every fifteenth of the month. Upon paying the amount, they must inform the head imam of the mosque that they want to donate money to support the Islamic religion. The people who have already paid money should tie a green cloth in front of their house to be a signal for the RKK warriors so they will not hurt you.

3. Everyone is forbidden to work on Friday. All sorts of work, whether trading, or rubber tapping, or clearing the land for planting [plantations]. And everyone is forbidden to drink alcoholic beverages on Fridays because the Prophet Muhammad designated Friday as the sacred day in commemoration of Allah. It is the duty of Muslims to produce as many children as possible. The Muslim who has four wives, must get another four wives. And everybody must take good care of their daughters, to observe their behavior so that they will get married as soon as possible so that they can produce children, who can help us take back our land.

Any household that has unmarried daughters, we the RKK warriors, regard as noncooperative and we will not guarantee their safety.

Please follow every instruction exactly.

— From the RKK Warriors of Pattani

Reportage of Facts

Many leaflets bring attention to violence toward the Muslim community by security forces and paramilitaries that has gone unreported in the Buddhist-centric national media.

Document 24

Brutal Murder at Ban Kra Thom 8

In the evening on Wednesday 22 May 2550 [2007], at 17:30 there are eight small huts close together on a plantation, four kilometers from Ban Sa Pom Tambon Pa Tae subdistrict, Yaha District, Yala. Only by walking or riding a bicycle can someone get in.

After Isa prayers, it was raining. There were armed rangers who brutally shot to death the owners [residents]. Two daughters escaped death and hid in the rubber plantation near the huts. One of the two daughters is safe, the other one, the rangers caught, raped, and killed. (The autopsy of the dead daughter revealed that her underpants were pulled down to her knees. On her neck there were green marks. On the back of her head was a gash.) Another group of rangers went to brutally shoot three people, a mother and two sons. As a result, the mother was wounded and the two sons died immediately. In this one event, there were four people killed and three wounded.

Document 26
News (Hot News, Right News, True News)
Rangers Killed the Innocents at Ta Seh

At 16:15 on Friday, 9 March 2550 [2007], there was the unbelievable event. The rangers who always protect people, angrily shot to the light green Isuzu D-Max car in which a driver and a passenger were returning from work in downtown of Yala province. Near the bridge at Ban Ta Seh, Moo 3, Ta Seh subdistrict, Muang District, Yala, the rangers ambushed and shot angrily at that car. Mr. Abukoli Ka Sor, 15 years old and Mr. Afandi Pao Mah, 22 years old were severely injured. After they were shot, they drove to pondok Ta She to ask for help from the children. They were transferred to the nearest hospital, Mae Lan Hospital. (After that, police officers transferred the injured to the Yala Hospital and charged them with being members of the United Front.) After the rangers shot them, they found the car parked in front of the pondok. They went inside the pondok and brutally shot, resulting in the destruction of the pondok buildings. Luckily, no one got injured or died. News was released that it was just fighting, but in fact, the government officers were hiding the truth that they committed those bad actions. Later, Mr. Abukoli Ka Sor, who was severely injured, died in the Yala Hospital. After the funeral, the relatives of the dead invited villages to pray in the mosque, but they were blocked by the officers. Also, the officers chased them back to their homes without any mercy and did not allow them to go inside. This is the real Siamese kafir.

— The News Office of the Warriors of Pattani DaruIslam

Document 18[6]
Same Same but Different.... Is This Justice?

Teacher
Yuling (government teacher).

---

6. Document 18 compares how the media and state treated the death of a Buddhist teacher with how they treated the death of a Muslim teacher.

The place

In Ban Kujinglupah School, Rangae District.

Good

She was a good teacher, who is praised as a heroine.

Bad

No.

Fault

No.

Religious ceremony

The state *(*kafir) totally supported and held a convenient ceremony and gathered people and students (who are unwilling) to go to the ceremony, which is not in accordance with Islam, but they still do it for the sake of appearance.

Presented by the media, which is dominated by kafir

They reported everything about teacher Yuling. Does the media have any principles?

Teacher

Aiee Sata Ibrahim (religious teacher).

The place

The officer shot at the mosque during Isa prayers in Sungai Padi District.

Good

This person was a good religious teacher, but this person has never been praised by the kafir government.

Bad

No.

Fault

[He] was blamed for being part of the separatists' United Front because he is a religious teacher.

Religious ceremony

The kafir government blocked [the ceremony] in every way: it threatened people in the area, it blocked mourners; moreover, for the seven-day period of paying respect for the dead, the officers threatened people to not to do *aruwah* [funeral rites] and closed the road in order to not allow friends and students to go pay their respects.

Presented by the media (which is dominated by kafir)

Didn't report anything about the teacher (because this person was a religious teacher). Does the media have any principles?

Do we (*Mumin*) have any hope of getting justice from the government (Siamese)?

Statements of Goals, Ideology, and Religion

In some leaflets and pamphlets, insurgents are very clear about their long-term goals and sociopolitical objectives, ideology, and religion. Almost every document mentions the explicit goal of driving the Siamese "kafir harbee" out of the region, so that the Pattani can live among themselves. A common conclusion is, "We wish Allah will protect all Muslimins and Muslimahs and all Pattani Malays will be free from the evil, Siamese Kafir." Another common sentiment is, "This land has to be free. The Islamic system has to be organized. This land is not the land of Thai, but it is the land of 'Pattani Darul Islam.'" Many documents define what that state is: "Pattani State consists of Yala, Pattani, Narathiwat, Te-Na, Sabayoi, Jana, Songkla, Kwuan Kwoon District, Satun Province."

There are two or three versions of a major strategy and goals pamphlet, each roughly three or four pages in length, that also provide religious edicts. For example, "Women have to dress up in black and men have to wear hats. *Sorkeh* has to be on a head even when we are praying. Women wear *talakong* cloth and black hijab is for being surrounded the heads." Other sections provide suggestions on how to magnify the power and presence of the Muslims. One section notes Muslim activities in Songkhla Province: "They built 145 mosques in a short period. It is good that the Buddhists will think that there are a lot of Muslims. Actually, one mosque has just twenty Muslims. Please build mosques in tourist places all around the country." Other passages explicitly call for violence: "Kill university professor Muslims who are beloved and respectful ones of students and kill old professors. Then, give all fault to the Thai government." Some sections call on the destruction of Buddhist businesses: "Make violence brutally. Attack the Buddhist Thais. We know that the Buddhist Thais do not like violence and love peace. When the Buddhist Thais cannot stand, they will surrender."

This document also encourages the inculcation of Islamic values, the conversion of Buddhists, and the mass construction of mosques: "Build small and big religious buildings all over Thailand by spending the budget from Islam bank of Thailand and build big Islam centers by spending the government budget (people's tax). . . . Build religious buildings in government places or big organizations. Prayer rooms will be in airports, bus terminals, train stations, soldier units, and government places." But perhaps the most interesting and unelaborated point in the document has to do with the nature of Islam: "Change the doctrine of religion to law and use it." It is not clear what is meant here, but it is clear that the militants have intentionally targeted the moderate Sha'afis and Sufis.

Document 19
We Are Religious Protectors Who Want to Warn

Oh Pattani Malay Islamic people, Pattani is our land, not belonging to Thailand. The lifestyle of Islamic Malays is totally different from the Thais.

About food, the Islamic people eat meat which animals are killed according to Muslim law, but the Thais do not eat meat which animals are killed in the right way. Therefore, we, the Islamic people, have to always beware that the Thais are trying to govern and instill wrong ideals to the Pattani Malays and change Islamic education [tadeeka]. They have a policy in moving tadeeka school from the mosque to Thai school. Why does it happen? This policy is accepted by the stupid Toh Imam who wanted money. He sold tadeeka which is the Islamic heritage for a very cheap price . . . is this the head of Islam?

Oh . . . Pattani Malay Islams! Remember that we are followers of Allah and the nation of Muhammad. Do not look down on our religion by being slaves of Thailand. Do not cooperate with the Thais to destroy Islam. We are Muslim people, so you have to realize that now we are in the non-Islamic country where they oppress us. Therefore, we have to fight to separate Pattani from Thailand. We must not cooperate or agree with the Thai government's policies and projects.

Our sibling Muslims, remember that! From now do not send our kids and offspring to study tadeeka in Thai school. Do teach tadeeka at mosques like in the past; otherwise, we, the religious protectors, will not guarantee your safety. We will try every way to destroy Thais' bad plans and destroy those who are against us like we used to do it clearly and secretly in the past to take our Pattani back.

— From the Islamic Protectors

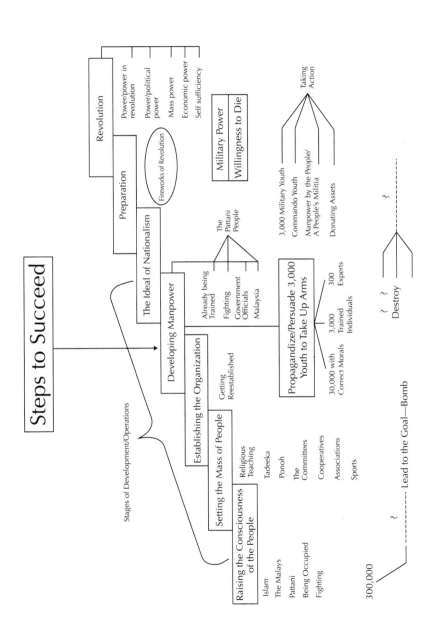

Steps to Succeed

Stages of Development/Operations

Revolution
- Power/power in revolution
- Power/political power
- Mass power
- Economic power
- Self sufficiency

Preparation

Fireworks of Revolution

The Ideal of Nationalism

Military Power
Willingness to Die

Taking Action
- 3,000 Military Youth
- Commando Youth
- Manpower by the People/ A People's Militia
- Donating Assets

Developing Manpower

The Pattani People
- Already being Trained
- Fighting
- Government Officials
- Malaysia

Establishing the Organization
- Getting Reestablished

Propagandize/Persuade 3,000 Youth to Take Up Arms
- 30,000 with Correct Morals
- 3,000 Trained Individuals
- 300 Experts

Setting the Mass of People
- Religious Teaching
- Tadeeka
- Ponoh
- The Committees
- Cooperatives
- Associations
- Sports

Raising the Consciousness of the People
- Islam
- The Malays
- Pattani
- Being Occupied
- Fighting

300,000

? ------- Lead to the Goal—Bomb

? ? Destroy ?

Appendix C

Examples of Extortion Documents

MUJAHIDIN ISLAM PATANI มูจาฮีดีนอิสลามปัตตานี

Mujahideen Islam Pattani

This document is given to Hen Bakery – Tae Shud Kong [handwritten].

Mujahideen Islam Pattani asks for a part of your income in the amount of Bt150,000 baht [handwritten].

If you do not cooperate or you contact police officers, we are not responsible for your life and family.

I hope you understand and you are willing to cooperate.

[Illegible handwriting]
(Urgently Contact)

[Islamic Script]
BRN Congress
[Islamic Script]

Patani Malay National
Revolutionary Front
[Symbol]

Buddhist Era 2543/25/199
   Letter No. 619

Dear Sir, Madam:

Goodwill.
I would like to inform you as follows:

1. As you have assets and income, I would like you to contact us (BRN) urgently to pay a per person tax and an income tax in the amount of Bt600,000.

2. If you ignore or refuse, we will send the commandos to destroy you, your family, and your property everlasting.

I hope you understand it.
Goodwill and nonviolence.

From —
ABRIP

Warning —
If this document has been changed, I am not responsible.
Representative —
   1. Pohmah Suhaibatu   ([signature]   )
   2.   (   )

باريسن ريبولوسي ناشيونال ملايو فتاني

B.R.N. CONGRESS

الجبهة الثورية الوطنية لتحرير فطاني

PATANI MALAY NATIONAL
REVOLUTIONARY FRONT

พ.ศ. 2543 125/199

ฉบับ 619

เรียนท่าน   ที่หวังดี

<u>ขอแจ้งให้ท่านทราบตามข้อความดังต่อไปนี้</u>

1 - อนึ่งจากทรัพย์สิน และ รายได้ ที่ท่านมีได้อยู่นั้น ขอให้ท่านมาติดต่อ   และ
จ่ายค่าภาษีรายหัว และ รายได้ ต่อกองทัพ ของขบวนการปลดปล่อยแห่งชาติ
ปาตานี โดยควร เป็นจำนวนเงิน   600000   บาท

2 - หากท่านละเลย และ ไม่ปฏิบัติตามดังที่ได้กล่าวแล้ว กองสงหน่วยฆ่าสังหาร -
หน่วยกล้าตาย เพื่อจู่โจม หวังลายต่อชีวิต ครอบครัว และ ทรัพย์สินที่ท่านมี -
อยู่ตลอกสิบไป และ ไม่มีวันสิ้นสุด

ท้ายนี้หวังว่าท่านคงเข้าใจดี

หวังดี และ สันติวิธี

จาก -

ABRIP

คำเตือน -

หากมีการปลอมแปลง เอกสารใบนี้ ข้าไม่รับผิดชอบ
ตัวแทน -

1 . เปาะ ยะ สูไหงบาตู   (   )

2   (   )

Appendix D

Key Points of the Emergency Decree

Section 9

The prime minister is authorized to limit

- freedom of movement in the country.
- freedom of public assembly.
- freedom of the press.
- use of routes and vehicles.
- use of buildings and places.

Section 11

The prime minister may declare that the emergency situation is a "serious" situation. Once a situation is declared serious, the prime minister is authorized to

- empower the competent official to arrest and detain a suspect.
- empower the competent official to seize any suspicious items, including arms, goods, consumer products, and chemical products.
- empower the competent official to issue a warrant to search, remove, withdraw, or demolish buildings, structures, etc.
- empower the competent official to inspect, cancel, or suspend any communications.
- prohibit any action.
- empower the competent official to ban anyone from leaving the country.
- empower the competent official to deport an alien.
- prohibit trade of any goods.
- order the use of military force.

Section 12

With leave of the court, a competent official is authorized to arrest or detain a suspect no longer than seven days. If necessary, the detention may be extended seven days at a time, but not more than thirty days.

If it is necessary to extent the detention beyond thirty days, the official must proceed according to the Criminal Procedure Code.

Section 13

The prime minister is authorized to prohibit the trade of certain electrical devices in the entire country if they are being used for terrorist operations.

Section 17

The competent official or anyone equivalent to this rank is NOT subject to civil, criminal, or disciplinary liabilities.

Index

About the Author

Zachary Abuza is professor and chairman of the department of political science at Simmons College in Boston, Mass. A specialist in Southeast Asian politics and security issues, he is a graduate of Trinity College and received his MALD and PhD from the Fletcher School of Law and Diplomacy. His past books include *Muslims, Politics, and Violence in Indonesia*; *Militant Islam in Southeast Asia*; and *Renovating Politics in Contemporary Vietnam*. He also authored two studies for the National Bureau of Asian Research titled *Funding Terrorism in Southeast Asia: The Financial Network of Al Qaeda and Jemaah Islamiyah* and *Muslims, Politics, and Violence in Indonesia*. His monograph, *Balik Terrorism: The Return of the Abu Sayyaf Group*, was published by the U.S. Army War College's Security Studies Institute. He is currently working on a study of Jemaah Islamiyah and is undertaking a major study of the Moro Islamic Liberation Front with support from the United States Institute of Peace, where he was a senior fellow in 2004-05, and the Smith Richardson Foundation. A former Vietnam country adviser for Amnesty International (USA), he is a frequent commentator on Southeast Asian politics and security issues in the press. He is also a visiting guest lecturer at the Foreign Service Institute, the U.S. Department of State, and the U.S. Department of Defense's Joint Special Operations University.

Jennings Randolph Program
for International Peace

This book is a fine example of the work produced by Senior Fellows in the Jennings Randolph fellowship program of the United States Institute of Peace. As part of the statute establishing the Institute, Congress envisioned a program that would appoint "scholars and leaders of peace from the United States and abroad to pursue scholarly inquiry and other appropriate forms of communication on international peace and conflict resolution." The program was named after Senator Jennings-Randolph of West Virginia, whose efforts over four decades helped to establish the Institute.

Since 1987, the Jennings Randolph Program has played a key role in the Institute's effort to build a national center of research, dialogue, and education on critical problems of conflict and peace. Fellows come from a wide variety of academic and other professional backgrounds. They conduct research at the Institute and participate in the Institute's outreach activities to policy makers, the academic community, and the American public.

Each year approximately twelve senior fellows are in residence at the Institute. Fellowship recipients are selected by the Institute's board of directors in a competitive process. For further information on the program, please contact the program staff at (202) 457-1700, or visit our Web site at www.usip.org.

United States Institute of Peace Press

Since 1991, the United States Institute of Peace Press has published over 125 books on the prevention, management, and peaceful resolution of international conflicts—among them such venerable titles as Raymond Cohen's *Negotiating Across Cultures*; *Herding Cats*, and *Leashing the Dogs of War* by Chester A. Crocker, Fen Osler Hampson, and Pamela Aall; and William I. Zartman's *Peacemaking and International Conflict*. All our books arise from research and fieldwork sponsored by the Institute's many programs. In keeping with the best traditions of scholarly publishing, each volume undergoes both thorough internal review and blind peer review by external subject experts to ensure that the research, scholarship, and conclusions are balanced, relevant, and sound. As the Institute prepares to move to its new headquarters on the National Mall in Washington, D.C., the Press is committed to extending the reach of the Institute's work by continuing to publish significant and sustainable works for practitioners, scholars, diplomats, and students.

VALERIE NORVILLE
DIRECTOR

Conspiracy of Silence

Text: Janson Text LT Std
Display Text: Bauer Bodoni
Cover Design: Kim Hasten/Cynthia Jordan
Page Layout: Cynthia Jordan
Developmental Editor: Kurt Volkan
Proofreading: Amanda Watson-Boles
Indexing: Potomac Indexing